COMPANIONS
ON THE INNER WAY

Morton T. Kelsey

COMPANIONS ON THE INNER WAY

The Art of Spiritual Guidance

CROSSROAD · NEW YORK

1983

The Crossroad Publishing Company
575 Lexington Avenue, New York, NY 10022

Printed in the United States of America

Library of Congress Cataloging in Publication Data

Kelsey, Morton T.
Companions on the inner way.

Bibliography: p. 211
Includes index.
1. Spiritual life—Anglican authors.   2. Spiritual
direction. 3. Experience (Religion)   I. Title.
BV4501.2.K4267   1983   248.2   82-23541
   ISBN 0-8245-0585-9   0560-3 pbk

To Betty and Robert Buffum,
friends and companions on the inner journey
and benefactors for those who
would become companions on the way

CONTENTS

PREFACE

This book has been incubating for a long time. When I entered training for the Christian ministry I began to realize that unless I found some experience of God, it was very nearly useless to talk about religious reality to modern men and women (and to myself). My quest continued for over thirty years with many ups and downs, but gradually I found a pathway that kept me from being inflated by the highs or defeated by the lows. It contained elements of three quite different maps; the first was the writings of the masters of the devotional life, the second, the understanding of the psyche presented by depth psychology, and the third, my own fumbling but persistent religious practice.

About ten years ago I met Richard Payne, who became my friend, editor and publisher. He shared an interest in some of the same maps and he urged me to write down what I had discovered. The result was *The Other Side of Silence: A Guide to Christian Meditation.*

For many years people had come to me and asked me to walk with them on their own spiritual journeys. After the publication of *The Other Side of Silence* I received many more requests, not only for spiritual guidance, but also for some guidelines for training people who could serve as spiritual companions. During my years of teaching in the Department of Graduate Studies in Education at the University of Notre Dame I had formulated much of this material. I came to believe that religious educators with little or no understanding of the process of spiritual growth into mature religion were indeed blind guides for the blind.

When the Department of Graduate Education was liquidated I found myself a tenured professor without a department, and I looked around for what I might do. I drew up a proposal for the education of spiritual directors, which seemed to be the area in which I had most competence. The basic outline of this book was contained in that proposal. I sent out some eighty copies of the proposal to various institutions of higher learning and found a great deal of interest, but no actual offers to implement this proposal from my own university or any other educational institution. I went through the tenure process again, this time in the Department of Theology at Notre Dame, but there was little interest in a program such as I proposed.

Over the past several years three groups have attempted to put into effect some of the ideas of my proposal. First my friend Abbot David Geraets and the community of Benedictines at Pecos, New Mexico inaugurated a program for spiritual directors and have continued this program in an attempt to raise the level of spiritual direction within the Catholic Church, and particularly within the charismatic movement. The abbot once said to me that when we open people through the charismata to the realm of the spirit we need to either put on the lid with an authoritarian framework or to offer people spiritual direction and train some of them to give this kind of guidance. At about the same time the director of Wainwright House in Rye, New York became interested, and through his efforts the Guild for Spiritual Guides was launched there and has continued.

Several years ago I came into contact with the San Francisco Theological Seminary in San Anselmo, California. After lengthy discussions they became interested in implementing a program of psychology and spiritual disciplines. Dr. and Mrs. Robert Buffum were interested in supporting this program in order to get it underway. Roy Fairchild was installed as professor in charge of this program. In February of 1982 I had the privilege of giving the inaugural lectures. These lectures form the basis of this book. I am happy to serve in a continuing relationship with this important venture.

On my own spiritual journey I have been graced with a group of guides and friends, companions and fellow travelers. On the whole I find it far easier to be objective about the condition of another's spiritual life than my own. I can usually be more optimistic about the love of God for others than for myself. These guides and friends have offered me that objectivity when I have needed it in my own doubts and questions and darkness.

Three of these people were of great help in some of the earlier years of my pilgrimage. All three of them were professional psychologists or psychiatrists—I did not find the lack of understanding among professional psychologists of which Gerald May complains in *Care of Mind Care of Spirit*. Indeed, these three gave me a world view that enabled me to take my Christian heritage seriously. All three were Jews who had escaped from Nazi Germany, and they knew human evil at its blackest and worst. They also knew anxiety in a way few of us ever experience it. Max Zeller provided an atmosphere of understanding and concern and started me on the religious path with a new understanding. Hilde Kirsch continued with me and helped me work through many of my inner fears and deepen my religious practice. James Kirsch provided a depth of wisdom concerning the contents and working of the personal and collective psyche. All three were intent on their own inner journeys. They had all known C. G. Jung and had found that his understanding and methods had enabled them to survive and grow.

Through these people, I was introduced to Jung, first in his writings, then by studying at the Jung Institute in Zurich, Switzerland, and finally by meeting Jung himself. Integrating the insights of Jung and his followers with my own Christian heritage, I came to a formulation of Christian psychology that was recently published with the title of *Christo-Psychology*. In Zurich I had the unique experience of working analytically with Franz Riklin and Barabara Hannah at the same time, and I perceived how objective this process of inner discovery was. Jung wrote in *Memories, Dreams, Reflections* that some of those who came to him for analysis or help became his closest friends, and I have found his experience true to my own.

Throughout this time I had a colleague who was on the same inner journey. John Sanford and I both thought that we alone had found this strange way to the divine. Providence brought us together to work in the same parish and has kept us close friends through the years as we have shared our conflicts, difficulties, insights, ideas and moments of light.

Some twelve years ago a student at Notre Dame came to see me. He was caught in the dark night of the soul, which secular psychologists interpreted as mere psychological conflict. We worked through it and became close friends. He continued studying and became a practicing therapist. Few people have been more helpful as companion on the spiritual journey than this former student, Andrew Canale. And then, during a recent period of outer crisis (which nearly always produces inner crisis), two other people whom I had accompanied on their journeys supported me in mine: one is a psychologist, George Lough, and the other a priest of the Church, James Maronde. The bread cast upon the waters was more than returned. It would be impossible to say how much I have gained from these guide-friends, as well as from others too numerous to mention.

Certain writers have given me much help in learning about the inner way and how we can be trained as guides upon it. Baron Friedrich von Hügel was the first to show me something of the quality of mature religious life and mature Christianity, and I shall speak of him often. The writings of Jung have been invaluable as the most comprehensive discussion of psycho-religious phenomena that exists. However, I would not have understood them had I not been guided through them by reflecting on and comparing my own religion and religious experience.

Jung, however, never provides a systematic exposition of his conclusions about religious experience. What Jung lacks in organization William James supplies in his monumental Gifford Lectures, *The Varieties of Religious Experience*. There he anticipates much of what Jung verifies and elaborates.

Von Hügel's spiritual director was Abbé Huvelin, and recently a fine biography of this remarkable man came into my hands: *Un précurseur, L'abbé Huvelin*, by Lucienne Portier. Few books have touched me more or given me more confirmation of what I present in the pages that follow. A person attending one of my lectures sent me a copy of the *Letters of Direction* of Abbé de Tourville, which also gave me more confidence in sharing these reflections.

One of the most interesting and important attempts to provide a well-founded program of spiritual direction was begun a few years ago through the efforts of a priest of the Episcopal Church, Tilden Edwards, and a psychiatrist, Gerald May. Both of them have written important books on their experiences in developing The Shalem Institute of Spiritual Formation. *Spiritual Friend*, by Edwards, and *Care of Mind Care of Spirit*, by May, offer invaluable help to anyone who is interested in training in the art of spiritual guidance. Many subjects are covered so well by them that they need not be treated here. Kenneth Leech's *Soul Friend* provides an excellent history of spiritual direction.

For nearly forty years my wife, Barbara, and I have both been on our separate spiritual journeys. We have quite different needs and practices. Over the years we have found a way in which two very different people can share their journeys. My own understanding of one important and common pathway of spiritual growth would have been ever so much poorer had she not shared her practice with me. In addition, she has been a constant source of encouragement, ideas, insights and research. She has also aided me in editing and proofreading and in all the other tasks required to bring a manuscript to publication.

Cindy Wesley has put my incomparably bad typing and worse handwriting into readable typescript, and John Whalen has offered helpful editorial suggestions and advice. Paisley Roach secured permissions and Joan Lane did proofreading.

The major portion of this manuscript was put into final shape on a freighter traveling from Seattle along a large part of the coast of Asia.

Gualala, California

Chapter 1

THE SPIRITUAL JOURNEY

A large part of me would much rather not write this book. For many reasons it has been one of the most difficult tasks I have undertaken. The subject of guiding or accompanying other people on their spiritual journeys poses many problems. And yet something speaking within me insists that I must go through with it and do the best that I can.

First of all, I am confronted with how little I know about God and how to bring people to the God of love who touches and transforms us so that we can become agents, ambassadors, beacon lights and examples of the Kingdom—so that the Kingdom may come on earth as it is in heaven. We do see through a glass darkly. God is so full of surprises, as Gerald May points out. I never know where and how the Inscrutable One will be manifested the next time. I am in the shadow or in darkness much of the time, yet I have been given a glimpse of the light in the darkness. For a moment the dark night is illumined with a flash of lightning, which turns night into day. When the light has vanished I have felt beside me the hand and person of the forgiving, compassionate and loving One and known that the light and the love were the same.

When I reflect on accompanying anyone on the inner way I am confronted with the inadequacy of my own spiritual life. For over forty years I have been struggling on this way, and still I find within me cowardice and fear, anger and lack of compassion, lust and greed, selfishness and pride, stupidity and lostness. And then at times I am again in the great desert of doubt and dryness and of lostness. At still other times I am confronted with the real presence of evil, which belittles, mocks, tortures and would destroy me. Sometimes these very experiences of inadequacy, dryness and attack are the occasion of knowing that I am helpless of myself and by myself. They force me to turn again to the One who has conquered the Evil One and Death itself and will rescue me still from their depredations. But who am I to tell others how to be guides for those venturing forth on the spiritual journey?

When I first shared these struggles in *The Other Side of Silence*, I revealed some of my own depths and feared what readers would think. To my complete surprise, I have received more appreciative notes for sharing these inner turmoils and their resolutions than for anything else I have ever written. I find that far more people pass into these depths than we ordinarily realize. In *The Varieties of Religious Experience*, William James showed nearly a century ago how common these inner religious conflicts are. Only a few years ago Alan Jones wrote, "The pilgrim, if he is honest, will have to take the mystery of evil, and more important, will have to encounter the awful possibilities of evil with himself. The journey will involve a kind of crucifixion, an entering into the heart of darkness before the pilgrim can be bathed in light."[1] Alan Jones directs one of the major programs in spiritual growth in the United States.

Lecturing in many places in the world, I have found the same turmoil. After listening to a lecture on the inner journey, a young man in a seminary in Australia said that he had confronted such evil while using drugs and feared that he might not survive. Since then he had been afraid of the spiritual journey for fear that he might have to confront that reality again.

This inner evil is an inner encounter with the reality of evil that surrounds us throughout the world. If we would make this inner journey we may well have to confront this inner evil, and then we must deal with the outer manifestations of evil, which so often we try to forget.

I am writing these words on a freighter in the harbor of Chittagong, in Bangladesh. We have been in and around the harbor for over a week. We have made several trips out into the city. This is one of the poorest nations on earth. It has just emerged from a bloody war of independence. Most people struggle just to stay alive, and many do not make it. Children are abandoned because their mothers cannot feed both their infants and themselves. My wife and I visited St. Scholastica's orphanage, run by some native Catholic nuns, where such children were accepted from infancy and cared for with love. Between eighty and ninety million (or more) people live in an area no larger than Illinois. Deformed children, youth and adults are on the docks and streets begging. Less than twenty-five percent of the people can read and write. The population continues to explode since the only insurance for old age is one's children.

There is martial law in the country since the assassination President Zia, the leader who many believed did more than anyone else to bring some improvement of living conditions for the people. One friend with whom we spent some time said, "It is better for the common people that there is martial law, for now we can walk about on the streets without fear of being mugged and beaten."

And on top of these difficulties, the people face colossal natural disasters. Cyclones and flooding occur every few years. In 1970 a tidal bore and a hurricane struck at the same time, and many hundreds of thousands were drowned in the low-lying delta of the Ganges and Brahmaputra rivers. How many more died of exposure and hunger would be difficult to calculate. This says nothing of the loss of homes and livelihood and property. Only the devastating flood of the Yellow River some decades ago was more disastrous in our recorded human history.

If I would accompany people on their inner journeys, not only do I have to go with them into their own private hells (and one never makes such a trip unscathed), but I must be willing to face the problem of this kind of evil all over the world. Most of us in the West are quite outwardly comfortable and remain blithely unaware of the pain and agony in the world. When we listen deeply to Jesus and consider who is indeed our neighbor, we are confronted with the pain and agony of the global community. The journals of Abbé Huvelin, one of the most accomplished spiritual directors of all times, show the agony of his suffering as he shared the struggles of those he directed, the superficiality of the people he confessed, and the hurt of the world.

It is one thing to be able to help someone through his or her own personal hell, but it is another to help people to see the Love that has rescued them personally reaching out into the world and to take part in sharing that Love. If the love of God that we have experienced could be shared throughout the world, how much more of the Kingdom of love and plenty and peace might abound among us, how much better things could be for us all.

And why all this suffering and pain and agony? The very evil that I find incipient within me is out there in the world plundering it unchecked. This is the very evil that Jesus confronted with love, the evil that brought him to the cross. I don't like to contemplate all this in depth, and again I wonder how I dare speak about accompanying people on the spiritual journey.

As I look back over forty years of ministry and my attempts to share my own inner journey, I see that often I have failed and in some cases even done damage. I remember my brother saying as I was accompanying him on his rounds in the hospital where he was professor of pediatrics, "At least we should try not to damage the patient." How easy it is to see only our failures and to forget those times when we have been channels for the Divine Lover. But so often I have given too little or too much.

I am reminded of the story of the social worker who believed that the other person must ask for help before any could be offered effectively. She watched an old lady rocking in a chair on a pier on a lake. Her chair backed closer and closer to the edge. Finally chair and woman tumbled into the water, and she cried out for help. The social worker gave a sigh of relief and exclaimed, "Oh thank heavens, now I can help." How difficult it is to discern when we should accompany people on the inner journey, and how far.

There are also times when we do too much. We give too much of ourselves, or too many ideas, or our love is unwisely given and we turn people away not only from us but from the source of life as well. Sometimes we guide people lost in the forest by leading them in circles. It is not pleasant to reflect on the failures and mistakes we have made. Yet paradoxically, if we are on the journey and trying to learn, it is by these very mistakes that we become better equipped as instruments of the Divine Lover. Those of us who will not try to minister (and Jesus called us all to minister as well as to be ministered unto) to those around us often find that we are cutting ourselves off from that Love that alone gives ultimate meaning to life. There are many different ways of ministering and carrying one another's burdens.

Going on the Journey with Others

Over forty years ago I began my own attempt to be open to God and allow the Holy One to take part in my life. Over thirty years ago I came in touch with some guides on this journey and found some ways of opening myself to God's incredible love. These people, whom I have already mentioned by name, also provided me with a view of the universe in which the spiritual domain is as real as the physical one. Since most churchgoers think that ministers are not supposed to be in darkness—I made no declarations that I had been in darkness and had found some light—I hung out no shingle. However, people began to come and share their spiritual journeys with me—searching teenagers, college students, business men and women, housewives, the sick and the elderly, the bereaved, the dying.

Most of these people professed that they could not find anyone with whom to share their spiritual quests. It seemed to me that if a minister had one legitimate task, it was to try to accompany these people on their journeys. Perhaps, I felt, my own inner journey was bearing fruit. It was flattering to think that I might truly be useful to people, but I realized that it was no particular holiness or maturity in me that brought them knocking on my door. It was simply the lack of available resources! We people of the Western world live in an age as ignorant of spiritual things as medieval cities were of sanitation and hygiene, not only ignorant, but even contemptuous. The naive materialistic optimism about human progress widespread in the first part of our century has been pretty well smashed to bits by two major world wars, a depression, and the loss of Western power. The hope for and need of a positive spiritual dimension becomes more and more important to more people, as we shall show in the next chapter.

I had been given a view of reality that made sense to people and made Christianity, real and vital Christian experience, a viable option. I had also been given a method that could undergird Christian practice. These I could share even if I was an inadequate example of what one could become on the inner way. I came to see that we never provide the light. We can, however, point out some of the pitfalls into which we have fallen and some of the traps that have been sprung on us. We can urge patience and the following of certain faint lights that have not turned out to be will-o-the-wisps.

On the black night when terror seizes us, any human being to cling to is better than none; even a dog is better fellowship than being alone. Not to offer fellowship to those alone in the storm is a more wretched pride than being a friend, however inadequate. We convert no one, but our openness and fellowship sometimes allow others to become their best selves. Abbé Huvelin writes that it is a mysterious stroke that brings a tree down on the side of God. "Conversion is something divine, impossible to explain."[2]

What I have to share comes from others who have been caught alone in darkness and who have found some light. They gave me the courage to fight on and avoid some of the snares into which they had fallen. I have also learned much from those who came seeking fellowship and direction. In every good hour of spiritual companionship I have often gained more than the person seeking fellowship.

It takes courage to set out on this journey, but it takes even more courage to accept the responsibility of walking along with another once we have really known the dangers ourselves. I usually suggest that people avoid the journey if they can help it. One of the wisest pieces of advice ever given me came from my childhood minister, George McKinley. When I was seriously considering preparing for the ministry he said, "Don't do it if you can help it." This is a journey in which turning back never brings us to the same place from which we started. But when people are flung out into the darkness and come to us asking for some light and companionship, how can we fail to go along with them? We have no recourse but to accompany them, in spite of our inadequacy. When men and women seek us out because they want fellowship on the inner way and profess that they can find no one else, are we living in the spirit of Jesus of Nazareth to turn them down?

I once asked Jung why people came to talk to me. He replied that people are subconsciously able to discern when we are on our journey. Then he told how a complete stranger once spoke to him on a train, seeking guidance.

If we find ourselves being called upon to listen to others tell of their religious experiences or being asked to be companions for those who are caught in spiritual darkness or who find it necessary to go the inner way, we need to prepare ourselves as well as we can. If we find a calling in the very depth of us that we cannot avoid, suggesting that this is our destiny, then we need to prepare for it. How do we prepare? The following chapters offer some suggestions from one who has found himself cast in this role for a number of years. These ideas have grown over the years and are certainly not final, but they are the best I can offer at the present.

Before we go any further I need to clarify what I mean by spiritual guidance and companionship. It can be distinguished from spiritual formation, pastoral care and care of souls. Spiritual formation includes all that we do to lay the foundation for religious belief and practice. It ranges from the education we give small children to the preparation that is *not* given to students preparing for the ministry. However, having taught those who would be in charge of the spiritual formation of other people, it is my measured conclusion that *it is most unwise for people to be charged with spiritual formation who are not on their own spiritual journeys and who are unable to be spiritual companions.* Pastoral care is still another aspect of ministry in which we try to bring consolation, healing, and compassion to those who suffer *without prodding them further into their own journeys.* Cure of souls is often very similar in meaning to the care of people. Spiritual guidance is the conscious and deliberate attempt to accompany other people on their journeys to and in God. The term *spiritual direction* is misunderstood in many circles and associated with an authoritarian attitude, but direction, as May points out, can mean offering some direction, but not forcing it. Spiritual guidance is the deliberate attempt to accompany other people on their journeys into God and, in the process, to share what we have learned as we have made our own journeys. We shall discuss these distinctions further in a later chapter.

Only in the rarest situations can we grow as spiritual companions and guides when we have not felt the necessity for fellowship and guidance ourselves and, what is more, sought it out and found it. There is very little solid spiritual companionship that is not rooted in the fellowship and learning of others who have been on the way. There is very little impersonal spiritual help and fellowship within the context of the Christian world view.

There is another distinction that it is necessary to make as we start out. There are two quite different ways of leading people on the spiritual pilgrimage, which have often been seen as opposed to each other. The first way is the sacramental method, in which we try to mediate the divine through images, pictures, symbols and rituals. Often this results in confusing the image or symbol with the reality and can lead to idolatry. This is known as the *kataphatic* way, from the Greek word meaning "with images." This has been the way of much Christian practice.

The second way is based on the idea that we can best find the divine through emptying ourselves of all images and contents. This point of view stresses the fact that all descriptions and pictures of the holy are inadequate. As we come to total silence, emptiness, and loss of self, and even of ego, we recognize our oneness with the divine and allow ourselves just to experience it, to abide in it or lose ourselves in it. This is known as the *apophatic* way from the Greek word meaning "without images." This point of view often gives few methods of handling direct confrontation with the evil within us and in the world around us. Sometimes the detachment it requires leads to a lack of reaching out to others. This has been the way of much of Hinduism and Buddhism in the East and of Plotinus and some movements within the Christian Church in the West.

My basic point of view, which I shall examine later on in detail, is that we need to reject the *naive* kataphatic approach and realize that no symbol, image, or description *ever* contains all of an experience. On the other hand, we need to go beyond the *naive* apophatic approach, which fails to give our religion enough content and also does not offer adequate methods by which to deal with inner and outer evil. It is my conviction that these two approaches cannot be separated from one another, but are both necessary parts of a sophisticated and informed spirituality.

A Plan for Spiritual Guidance

Walking with others on their spiritual pilgrimages is an art like painting or sculpture or poetry. In painting there are many things we need to learn. One learns some simple things about drawing, about perspective, about pigments and how colors balance with one another, the use and care of brushes, the preparation and use of canvases and other materials, and even the best ways of framing and hanging what we have created. Great artists usually learn from others, and through sharing their discoveries, magnificent new advances often occur. In only a few generations the sculptors of Greece developed a perfection of art that has been seldom duplicated since.

In order to discuss the art of spiritual guidance we shall first of all examine the growing need and desire for spiritual fellowship. Then we shall provide some explanation of how this vacuum of spiritual companionship developed in the West. We shall then look at three quite different visions of the world. They give us very different ways of approaching the art of spiritual guidance. Our world view, our vision of the ultimate nature of things, determines the kind of fellowship that we will offer.

This will bring us to the six different strands that form the basic thread of the art of inner guidance. These are as different as knowing how to stretch a canvas is from the use of perspective, and each of the six is necessary. After describing in chapter 3 how all these are essential to the development of mature Christianity we shall look at each of these six strands in more detail.

In chapter 4 we shall then look at the nature of our Christian tradition, so that we know the context within which this fellowship is taking place. It is difficult for people who are traveling on different paths to give each other significant and specific help. The fifth chapter will deal in some depth with the proper use of reason and thinking in the religious journey and how this can be used to help people caught in atheism and agnosticism to return to the religious way.

In chapter 6 we shall examine the rich and varied tapestry of religious experience, of the many ways in which we are opened to the holy, the divine and the whole world of spirit. Chapter 7 presents some suggestions for a specific devotional practice using the journal as the means of bringing ourselves to a transforming and mature relationship with God.

At this point we shall describe the different ways in which we can accompany others on their spiritual pilgrimages. Chapter 8 shows how psychology and spiritual direction and religious practice overlap. This will involve looking at some aspects of the nature and structure and growth pattern of the human psyche and how we can best be helped toward the destiny and fruition of our spiritual lives. We shall conclude by looking at the mystery of love, the essential fruit of the spiritual life from the point of view of Christianity. We shall sketch out some of the ways by which we can facilitate our growth in love. According to Abbé Huvelin, after everything is said and done, "only love explains everything."[3]

NOTES

1. Alan Jones, *Journey into Christ* (New York: The Seabury Press, 1977), p. 6.
2. Lucienne Portier, *Un précurseur, L'abbé Huvelin* (Paris: Les Editions du Cerf, 1979), p. 239.
3. Ibid., p. 250.

Chapter 2

SPIRITUAL GUIDANCE
AND THE WESTERN WORLD

At the present time the spiritual journey is an increasing hunger for many in our American culture. Millions are seeking instruction in some form of meditative practice. Meditation, as I use the word, is the direct, conscious experience of spiritual reality. There is an increasingly widespread interest in the inner journey among many modern Americans from Seattle to Jacksonville, from San Diego to Boston. Most of those who have begun to practice some form of meditation have turned to the East, or at least away from the commonly understood traditions of the Western, Christian world. It is difficult to jump from one culture to another, as any returned Peace Corps worker can verify. The following questions then arise: Is there a viable Western form of meditation to which these hungry people can turn? And a method of instruction and initiation into it? Has the West made significant contributions to the practice of the inner life?

In order to answer these questions I shall first of all look at the interest in the spiritual life that has developed over the last few decades in our own culture. I shall then take a critical look at the most popular world view in America and the West and see what implications this view has for the inner life. I shall contrast with this the popular understanding of the world and the human psyche that is the foundation of most traditions of Hinduism and Buddhism. I shall then offer a third option, the classical view of the Judaic, Christian and Islamic traditions. I shall conclude by indicating some important contributions that this tradition has made to the understanding and practice of the spiritual life. It is my conviction that any mature spirituality will integrate these values into its overall religious practice.

The Meditation Boom

If spirituality has not become respectable, it has at least become popular. A visit to any large bookstore is clear evidence of this interest. A few years ago the religion section of the bookstore was dwindling. Now there are shelves of books on meditation, alpha-genics, the coming end of the world, astrology, demonology and hundreds of related topics. The statistics confirm this visual demonstration. In 1976 a Gallup poll surveyed the interest in the spiritual life. It was discovered that six million Americans had tried Transcendental Meditation, five million had tried some form of yoga, three million had become involved in the charismatic movement in the Christian churches, three million more were involved in some kind of undefined "mysticism" and two million more in other forms of Eastern religion. This amounts to nineteen million Americans, or nearly ten percent of the total population.

In addition, there is the widespread use of hallucinogenic drugs: marijuana, mescalin, hashish, LSD and others with similar properties. It is important to distinguish these drugs from those which merely reduce pain and tension, tranquilizing and giving a sense of well-being or euphoria. Alcohol, barbiturates, cocaine, and opium products produce this effect and are addictive psychologically as well as chemically. Among many of the college students in the drug boom of the 1960s and 70s there was frequent use of hallucinogenic drugs and little of the latter. In his excellent book *The Natural Mind*, Andrew Weil analyzes this interest in these drugs among the young and not-so-young of our country. He concludes that most of the use of the mind-expanding drugs is an attempt to touch another dimension of reality, to reach an altered state of consciousness. Drugs are "pop" meditation.

On the whole, the students I taught at the University of Notre Dame were quite conservative, but the use of these drugs was common among them. They agreed almost entirely with Dr. Weil's thesis. A recent survey by our National Department of Health and Human Services reported in the June 30, 1980 issue of *Newsweek* that between sixty and seventy percent of our young people have tried one or more of the hallucinogenic drugs. I found the same percentage of use among students at Notre Dame. (As an aside I would suggest that anyone who deals with young people from high school age on and does not know Weil's study has his or her head deeply buried in the sand.) Those who have tried drugs are likely to have tried astrology, been interested in holistic medicine, meditation, the American Indian culture, natural food, Dr. Moody's study of near-death experience, and certain other esoteric practices.

The most significant data on the American interest in things spiritual comes from Dr. Andrew Greeley. With the help of a grant from the Luce Foundation, Dr. Greeley added several questions on mysticism and the experience of communication with the deceased after their deaths to a national random sociological survey. He could hardly believe his eyes as the computer began to spit out the results. Thirty-nine percent of his sample indicated that they had had a mystical experience as Greeley had carefully defined it in his questionnaire. He followed William James's fourfold criteria of mystical experience. Half of this thirty-nine percent had never mentioned this experience to any other human being before the survey. They had been browbeaten into silence by our materialistic culture. The post-test recheck revealed that the last person to whom most of these people would describe this experience would be the clergy or professional religious of the standard-brand churches. They felt that these people did not believe in such things any more. Twenty-five percent of those questioned replied that they had also had an experience of the deceased.

Dr. Greeley had a psychological maturity scale built into the survey. The mystics, as a group, were among the most mature who had ever been tested by this scale. They were not regressing and returning to the womb. This study has been replicated in Great Britain by the Religious Experience Unit at Manchester College, Oxford, as well as in Germany. A priest friend in an Episcopal parish in suburban Washington, D.C. recently told me that he found the same results in an adult class he held there. He would never have suspected these results from either his ordinary contacts or his pastoral care of the same people.[1]

The Failure of the Churches

One of the strangest and most interesting aspects of this resurgence of interest in meditation and the spiritual world is that it has hardly touched the traditional Christian churches. Few are the churches where one can ask when the next meditation group is going to meet or when one can come for spiritual direction without being greeted with a blank stare or actual hostility. Because of this apparent lack of interest in the spiritual world, it seldom occurs to non-Christian researchers to suspect that Christianity has a practice of meditation, a method of dealing creatively with the spiritual world. Neither Dolores Krieger, a professor of nursing at New York University, who is interested in the relation of healing and the human touch, nor Charles Panati, who is investigating the connection between ESP and meditation, makes any reference to the history of Christian practice in these areas. It was evidently unknown to them. The idea that clergy and lay experts should guide people in their explorations of this domain is obviously not considered a central task of the Church, and very few seminaries think it important to give instruction or training in this area.

Paulist Press has begun publishing sixty volumes of the classics of Western spirituality. Many of these important works had simply become unavailable. Many of them had never been adequately translated into English. Equally interesting are the brisk sales of this series. People do seem to be hungry.

Why is the spiritual tradition of the West, and of Western Christianity in particular, so little known? The answer is a complex one, which I have examined in detail in my book *Encounter with God*. Simply stated, the story is this: The classical Christian view of reality (which has never been lost in the Greek Orthodox tradition) was supplanted in Europe during late medieval times by the philosophy of Aristotle. Within that philosophical system human beings have no direct contact with a spiritual world. We are limited to experiences of the five senses, with which to explore the knowable world, and reason, with which to make logical deductions and inferences about the world we do not experience through the senses. Aristotle cast grave doubts upon the existence of any world not discovered by reason and sense experience.

The beliefs of Aristotle came to be the foundation for both Protestant and Catholic scholasticism. In the eighteenth century the Enlightenment, following the lead of Thomas Hobbes, went even further, denying the existence of any spiritual world. Then, in the nineteenth century, chemistry, physics, medicine and the other sciences produced dramatic successes without taking any spiritual dimension into consideration. Many thinkers concluded that science had final truth and the spiritual world was illusion. William James refers to this pervasive point of view as rationalism and points to its inadequacy in *The Varieties of Religious Experience*.

This point of view could be diagramed in the following way:

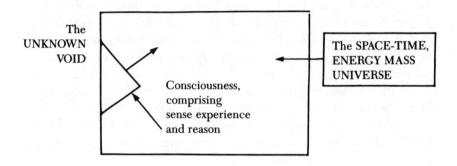

If we truly believe that reality and knowledge about it are confined to the space-time world, then spirituality, meditation and spiritual guidance, which may give access to another aspect of reality, are indeed nonsense.

Some writers on spirituality attempt to rescue mysticism and direct spiritual experience by describing spirituality as an ecstatic experience of the physical world. Matthew Fox's writings exemplify this point of view.

We can understand why so many Protestant theologians, caught in this framework, have an aversion to mysticism, to those practices that might lead to a direct experience of God. Barth, Bultmann and Bruner all view practices that lead to such an encounter as a blind alley, as a "work" (as opposed to faith), or as simply wrong. Harvey Egan has pointed out this hostility to mystical experience in his article "Christian Apophatic and Kataphatic Mysticism."[2]

Remember also that what we do is a better indication of what we believe than what we think we think. If we have no meditative practice and seek to have none, this tells what we most likely actually believe. The world view of rationalistic materialism has largely taken over the intellectual world in the West. In the process it took over academic Christianity and most of the nonfundamentalist seminaries. Even the practice of Christians who take scripture literally is often not too different from their more liberal brothers and sisters. In neither tradition is it often suggested that one can find a spiritual realm through experience. One relies on inference from the physical world in one tradition and upon the authority of the infallible book, the Bible, and deductions from it, in the other.

This lack of practice and theory in relating to the spiritual world is strange in a tradition in which authoritative scripture is constantly referring to the immediate divine-human encounter. Let me illustrate the effect of this rationalistic and materialistic tradition upon most recent biblical criticism. In the New Testament the gifts of the spirit, the charismata, are considered the observable evidence in the space-time world of spiritual activity. If we are totally immersed in the materialistic view of the world, the idea of such gifts is obviously meaningless. Rudolph Bultmann has clearly demonstrated this thesis in his article on demythologizing the New Testament. He maintains that any statement is mythological in which a reality other than physical is said to be operating in the space-time world. He believes that only by demythologizing, by eliminating all such statements, can modern Westerners make sense of the gospel narrative.

The nine gifts of the spirit described by Paul in I Corinthians 12:6 ff. can be summarized in five categories. There are gifts of healing and miracles, gifts of revelation (dreams, visions, intuitions) and gifts of discernment, in which one is able to distinguish between the powers of evil and good as they operate in all dimensions of reality, including human lives. There are also gifts of wisdom and knowledge, through which we obtain information that is inaccessible to reason and sense experience. Last of all, there are the gifts of proclamation: prophecy, tongue-speaking and interpretation of tongues. Any genuine practice of spiritual companionship or guidance will require a knowledge of these gifts and a generous infusion of the gifts of discernment and wisdom, as well as knowledge of historical religious practices and a practical understanding of human processes of learning.

A friend of mine and I carefully read through the New Testament, looking for these things rather than trying to avoid them. We colored all the verses contaminated with one or more of these experiences in different colors. We discovered that 3,874 verses of the 7,957 of the New Testament were contaminated with these gifts.[3] To make this more dramatic we took a razor and cut out these passages in order to provide a "Gospel of Jesus Christ according to rationalism." With the Christian narrative as full of holes as this, it is no wonder that many hungry people turn for nourishment to fundamentalism and many others turn to Eastern religions. Far from being critical of Bultmann, I am deeply grateful that he had the courage to point out the implications of this world view. Most of his contributions to biblical criticism are quite independent of this theological framework.

The Rich Tradition of the East

There is no question that Hinduism and Buddhism provide a rich tradition for understanding the depth of the human psyche and for dealing with the spiritual world of which human beings are a part. Dr. C. G. Jung, the renowned Swiss psychiatrist, was a student of Eastern thought and had patients who came to him out of the Eastern religious traditions. He comments again and again on the Eastern wisdom in regard to the human soul. Jung's discussions of Eastern classics reveal a profound admiration for *The Tibetan Book of the Dead*, *The Tibetan Book of the Great Liberation*, the *I Ching* and *The Secret of the Golden Flower*.[4]

There is a problem, however, for those spiritually undernourished Westerners who plunge into these Eastern traditions with only the materialistic Western understanding of the world, which we have outlined above. Eastern religions provide many very helpful devotional practices, but these practices are usually based upon a view of reality quite different from the one current in modern America. Dr. Jung points out the religious nonsense that is often offered by many people who take over Eastern spiritual practices without understanding the differences between the world views of the East and the West. It is obviously ridiculous to describe all variations of Eastern religion in a few paragraphs. And so I was pleased when a native of India, who knew Christian thought in depth, told me that the description that follows reflects the point of view of the vast majority of worshippers in both great traditions in India and to a lesser extent in the rest of the East.

Rudyard Kipling may have been more correct than he knew when he wrote, "East is East and West is West and never the twain shall meet." At least it may be impossible for the two to meet and fertilize each other creatively unless the differences between Buddhism and Hinduism and the great Western religions are clearly understood. These two Eastern religions have been a major force in determining the outlooks of the people of India, China, Southeast Asia and Japan, nearly two-thirds of the earth's population. In these religions the outer, physical world is usually viewed as *maya*, or illusion. Our emotions, which are the evidence of our conscious participation in that world, are on the whole to be suppressed, overcome and eliminated. The goal of life is to become passionless, emotionless. Love, pity, anxiety, anger, desire and self-concern are to be rooted out relentlessly. The distinction between subject and object is also illusion, as all reality is psychic in nature.

The world view that is the foundation of this thinking and practice can be diagramed in the following manner:

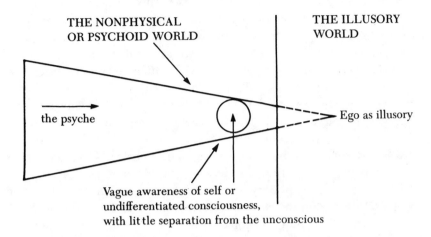

Most Eastern spiritual practice is quite consistent and springs from this base. Joseph Campbell describes this well in his book *Myths to Live By*. Let me point out nine characteristics of this view of spirituality:

1. This understanding of reality expresses a point of view at the opposite pole from Western materialism; here the physical world is illusion, and the nonphysical or spiritual world is real. In some forms of Buddhism even the spiritual images are seen as illusory. Only the total imagelessness of nirvana, the ultimate in apophatic (imageless) prayer, is real.

2. The specific human personality is an expression of the spiritual within the context of the material world. Human individuality shares in the illusory quality of the world in which it is expressed. The eternal is alone real; the individual personality is *maya* and to be transcended.

3. In the outer, physical world the clear distinction between the perceiving subject and the object that is perceived is illusion. This distinction between subject and object is a creation of the ego, and when one is enlightened it blurs or disappears.

4. The goal of life is detachment from *maya* and the recognition that we are one with the absolute or the eternal principle, which alone is real.

5. The critical scientific attitude that emerges from the serious study of the physical world is almost unknown. Thinking and logic are not linked to concrete, specific physical experiences as in Western scientific

practice. Matter-as-illusion is seldom worth attention, and the study of it will provide little significant data.

6. The life process is understood as essentially cyclical, everything inevitably returning again and again to the static perfection of spiritual reality. Reincarnation is the way the soul grows and matures as it passes through cycle after cycle of illusion until at last it is free.

7. Concern for specific human beings in their sickness or tragedy or grief is also illusion. A Hare Krishna leader once told me that by principle they were not supposed to go out to help other human beings because it might interfere with the karmic value of their suffering; the person helped might have to come through this existence once again because we had interfered. Thus there is little emphasis on acts of kindness or charity. All people are getting exactly what they deserve. Our task is to accept this, realize the illusory nature of existence, and in this detachment to be released from the chain of reincarnations. In this tradition charity consists in helping others become aware of this process and achieve this bliss.

8. Spiritual direction or guidance is a virtual necessity since the goal requires the true knowledge of the nature of things. Serious seekers reach out and attach themselves to some holy one, a *guru*, to whom they give unquestioning obedience, adulation and respect. It is the task of the teacher to provide the conditions that result in the state of bliss. The neophyte is totally submissive to the master.

9. There are some traditions of Buddhism that emphasize the importance of compassion and "love." However, it is difficult to give these qualities centrality if other human beings are only illusion and if compassion for the soul is all that matters. There is no concern for the physical condition of people. In Mahayana Buddhism it is acknowledged that there is no logical reason for the action of the bodhisattva, who refrains from entering nirvana in order to help save others and bring them to salvation.

The Classical Western View of Reality

Few people realize that there is any reasonable alternative to these two understandings of the universe in which we live. Either the physical world is seen as real and the human soul as an illusion—in which case all spiritual striving is madness or stupidity—or else the physical world is illusion and concern with it leads us away from salvation. Konrad Lorenz, in his book *Aggression*, has argued with disarming clarity that the essential human problem is that human beings simply will not submit to the truth that they are only material animals, and so they try to be more than they truly are. According to him this is the root cause for aggression. On the other hand, if one has ever been in India during the summer among the teeming millions, one can understand why Buddha saw no hope in redeeming the world and suggested that the only way of salvation was getting off the world by seeing through its illusory character and becoming detached and free.

There is, however, another view of the world. It is widespread and has been accepted in many times and places. This view proposes that both the physical world and the spiritual world are real. Human beings need to participate in both of these worlds if they are to be fully alive. It took me ten years of work with some of the friends and followers of Dr. Jung to realize that Jung was suggesting this very point of view.

Once the hold that materialism had on me was shaken loose, I realized that this third view of reality was the point of view of primitive medicine men or shamans the world over. Mircea Eliade has ably described this phenomenon in his book *Shamanism*. Then I realized that this was also the understanding of Plato. Indeed, he used his enormous powers to put this very world view into philosophical language. This was also the essential understanding of many of the Hebrew prophets and the way that Jesus of Nazareth talked about the universe. This point of view undergirded the theology of the early Church, which combined the insights of Plato and the teachings and practices of Jesus. The great fathers of the Church—figures like Origen, Athanasius, Gregory of Nyssa, Gregory of Nazianzen, Basil the Great, Chrysostom, Jerome, Ambrose and Augustine—hammered out Christian dogma using the same base.

This point of view gave rise to a rich and lively devotional practice, which animated the early Church and continued through Medieval times. There are few more magnificent spiritual writings than those of Bernard of Clairvaux, Mother Julian, Catherine of Siena, Catherine of Genoa, Bonaventure, and Jacob Boehme, to mention but a few. (It is just these magnificent writings that Paulist Press is bringing back into publication.) The actual religious practice of the Middle Ages, as it took place within the monastic communities, was gathered together and systematized in classic form by Ignatius of Loyola in his *Spiritual Exercises*. This is what is known as the kataphatic tradition of prayer, prayer that uses images in devotional practice to mediate the divine.

In the eighteenth and nineteenth centuries this point of view was largely lost or debased within the Church for a variety of reasons. During the same period the secular world became increasingly satisified with rational materialism. It looked as though scientific inquiry had solved most problems and had only a few untidy ends to tie together to complete its perfect understanding.

And then came the science of the twentieth century, which has become increasingly dissatisfied with rational materialism as a comprehensive answer to the question of the nature of things. Physicists, mathematicians, medical doctors, sociologists and psychiatrists became less sure than they once were about the satisfactory nature of the materialistic hypothesis. There appear to be all sorts of things about the world that cannot be explained by this world view. Werner Heisenberg has stated that scientists have become so skeptical that they have become skeptical of their own skepticism. Bob Toben, in his cartoon book of modern physics, *Space-Time and Beyond*, entered into conversation with two theoretical physicists. They suggest that only a biogravitational field of consciousness can explain how all the various particles of matter fit together to make up our world. The religious tradition describes God as something very like a biogravitational field of consciousness.

Freud and Jung both offered new hypotheses about the nature of reality that had much in common with the classical view of Plato and the Church fathers. Jung, in particular, opened my eyes to a "new-old" understanding of the world that had been lost to most Westerners for several hundred years. Baron von Hügel, the Catholic modernist, did the same sort of service for me, showing the relevance of this point of view for vital Christianity in his incomparable study of St. Catherine of Genoa, *The Mystical Element of Religion*.

Aldous Huxley at one point in his life ingested a considerable amount of mescalin. He reflected upon his experience in a little book, *Doors of Perception*. In it he offers an understanding of human knowing that expresses the most adequate understanding in recent Western thinking about the world and how we know it. He agreed with Dr. C. D. Broad of Cambridge

> ... that we should do well to consider much more carefully than we have hitherto been inclined to do the type of theory which Bergson put forward in connection with memory and sense perception. The suggestion is that the function of the brain and nervous system and sense organs is in the main *eliminative* and not

productive. Each person is at each moment capable of remembering all that has ever happened to him and of perceiving everything that is happening everywhere in the universe. The function of the brain and nervous system is to protect us from being overwhelmed and confused by this mass of largely useless and irrelevant knowledge, by shutting out most of what we should otherwise perceive or remember at any moment, and leaving only that very small and special selection which is likely to be practically useful.

Huxley goes on to suggest that the vast amount of data that humans can receive is funneled through the brain and nervous system. "What comes out at the other end is a measly trickle of the kind of consciousness which will help us to stay alive on the surface of this particular planet."[5] The many divergent practices of spirituality are ways in which we can open up our capacities of knowing and come into contact with the other realms of experience that impinge upon us. I have found some thirty different ways by which we are given knowledge beyond ordinary sense experience, ways that we shall discuss at length in a later chapter.

What are the characteristics of Western Christian spirituality, which is based upon this view of the world? It is good to remember that a very similar point of view is found among the Sufis of Islam and in much of mystical Judaism. Love mysticism is not unique to Christianity, but is probably more organically central to classical Christian theory and devotional practice than to any other religious tradition.

This point of view can be simplistically represented in the following diagram:

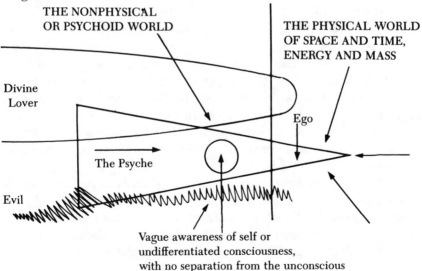

THE NONPHYSICAL
OR PSYCHOID WORLD

THE PHYSICAL WORLD
OF SPACE AND TIME,
ENERGY AND MASS

Divine
Lover

Ego

The Psyche

Evil

Vague awareness of self or
undifferentiated consciousness,
with no separation from the unconscious

The spirituality of the West arises out of the nature of its world view:

1. Both the physical and spiritual realms are real and valuable. They are interrelated. Human beings are caught in the tension between these two.

2. Unless human beings are in touch with both realms, they are likely to fall into neurosis or psychosis.

3. Inner images can relate to and refer to a real, nonphysical or spiritual realm, just as sense experience and sense images bring us into touch with a real physical world. We need to develop a capacity for critical thinking in order to deal with each realm. Then we will not be so easily deceived by appearances. When we accept sense experience uncritically we fall into all sorts of ridiculous notions like the flatness of the earth and the earth as the center of the universe. If we see images from dreams or visions or outer religious symbols as ultimate and final representations of reality we fall into equal absurdity. The apophatic tradition in prayer is a reaction against and correction of this kind of religious literalism found in some fundamentalist and charismatic traditions, as Tilden Edwards points out so clearly in *Spiritual Friend*.

4. To facilitate integration of the total psyche, ego consciousness is necessary. It interacts with the depth of the psyche (often called the unconscious) to unify the personality and create a new being. This integration requires scorching self honesty in self-examination, love relationships, and spiritual struggle. Ultimately it is achieved only through the action of divine grace. In this integration the ego is expanded and transformed, not eliminated.

5. Individual existence does not necessarily cease with death. Physical existence and history may provide a basis for the uniqueness of the ongoing development of the individual, but physical existence does not exhaust the reality of the human being. This belief in an afterlife for the individual is not wishful thinking; it follows logically from the idea that the ego is needed in order to learn to deal with both the spiritual and physical realms. Individuality is not to be discarded, but rather to be transformed and brought to its unique destiny, to its fullness and fruition.

6. Emotions like love and desire, anger and fear can push us towards the center of meaning if they are properly understood, if they are used and not misused. Charles Williams has written a masterful paper describing this understanding entitled "The Theology of Romantic Love."

7. The motivating and creative core of the universe is often seen as

Divine Love or the Divine Lover. This is true of mystical Christianity, Sufism and Hasidism. There is a vast difference between being absorbed into the cosmic One (which is the goal of Plotinus, much of Christian apophatic prayer and much of the Eastern traditions) and encountering Divine Love, which is the goal of Plato and most of Christian kataphatic prayer. Friedlander makes this point well in his study of Plato. How we view the center of spiritual reality will determine our religious practice. For example, worship of Wotan can produce Hitler and Naziism; worship of the loving Christ, a Francis of Assisi.

8. One cannot become worthy of love. Love by its very nature is a free gift and grace. Within the Western tradition of which we are speaking the final consummation or resolution of the individual quest is never achieved by self-help alone, but is given by God. But this experience of love is seldom given unless we are trying to shape ourselves according to Divine Love.

9. Both East and West offer the same disciplines for the beginning of the spiritual life. Both emphasize detachment, quiet, stilling the emotions, withdrawal, receptivity, listening, and ceasing ego activity and striving. The soul needs to be detached from an exclusive preoccupation with the physical realm if we are to find the spiritual realm and its central meaning.

At this point the spiritual understanding of the West diverges from that of most of the East. The Eastern way plunges into the depths of detachment and imagelessness seeking extinction of the subject-object duality and individual consciousness. The hero of the Hindu classic, the Ramayana, must leave his beloved wife in order to attain his spiritual goal. (Following the Eastern point of view, Joseph Campbell fails to offer much understanding of the mythology of love in his book *Myths to Live By*.) Once detachment has been achieved in the Western view we have been describing, the individual is redirected back to attachment, but attachment to human love and compassion that are part of attachment to the Divine Lover. There is a continued use of images that leads deeper into a real spiritual realm and that enables individuals to achieve more and more wholeness and integration of their complex inner selves. According to the most profound of the Western masters of spirituality this leads the individual into a relationship with the Divine Lover, which results in the individual's being transformed into the likeness of that which he or she beholds and relates to. In any such relationship the images describing it are always inadequate.

We cannot remain in relation to that love, however, unless we begin to express the same kind of love to others. St. Catherine of Siena clearly points out in one of her letters the importance of outward actions of concern and love. Then we must withdraw again in detachment, sometimes having moments of ecstatic imageless bliss, and again return to the image and the world. Both are necessary aspects of the mature Christian way.

Von Hügel describes this alternation between detachment and attachment in this way:

> ... the movement of the specifically Christian life and conviction is not a circle round a single centre,—detachment; but an ellipse round two centres,—detachment and attachment. And precisely in this difficult, but immensely fruitful oscillation and rhythm between, as it were, the two poles of the spiritual life; in this fleeing and seeking, in the recollection back and away from the visible (so as to allay the dust and fever of growing distraction, and to reharmonize the soul and its new gains according to the intrinsic requirements and ideals of the spirit), and in the subsequent, renewed immersion in the visible (in view both of gaining fresh concrete stimulation and content for the spiritual life, and of gradually shaping and permeating the visible according to and with spiritual ends and forces): in this combination, and not in either of these two movements taken alone, consists the completeness and culmination of Christianity.[6]

It is very difficult for us human beings to be satisfied with a goal of life that contains two elements, a goal that is not simple and straightforward. The same thirst for one ultimate reality leads many people to reject our experience that data comes to us from both a physical and a nonphysical dimension of reality. Modern physics is above reproach intellectually, and it tells us quite calmly that light is both a particle and a wave, a paradox quite incomprehensible and devastating to the human mind. According to Werner Heisenberg, these two descriptions of light are complementary to one another. In the same way, detachment and attachment are two aspects of the spiritual journey and the spiritual goal. Both are necessary if we would understand the nature of the spiritual journey.

In my book *The Other Side of Silence*, I have outlined several methods that can be used on this inner voyage of discovery after our initial period of inner silence and detachment. In a later chapter I shall describe these at greater length. Spiritual guides need to know all of these methods, even though some of them are not particularly helpful in their own personal practices. All of them can be of great help to some of the people whom they would accompany on the inner journey.

10. It is nearly impossible to come to full development on the inner way alone. We need others to keep us honest; we need them as teachers, guides and companions. We need the experience of history and tradition. Since it is so easy to deceive ourselves, we need companions who can view us with objective love. We need training in critical thinking, in spiritual practices and disciplines, the nature of the human psyche and in the art of loving. We need help and training in both content and process. We shall look at each of these areas of growth in more detail in the next chapter.

The Contribution of Western Spirituality

The classical Western tradition of spirituality offers a unique meditative practice that has important implications for all devotional practice. It results in a unique life-style. I personally believe that it is more inclusive than either of the other points of view I have discussed and is worth serious consideration by anyone embarking on the inner way. It is particularly important for Westerners. It is a practice that has to be learned. It requires spiritual guides and friends and teachers and companions. Let us look at some of the implications of this point of view for those who are interested in the spiritual journey within the Christian tradition. These apply to leaders as well as to those who are led.

1. The physical realm is valuable in itself. For those of us living in this world, our meditation is never completed until it results in our attempt to make the influence of divine love felt in that world. To be specific, my meditative contact with the Divine Lover is never complete until some other human being feels more loved by me because of that contact. And conversely, no study of the secular physical realm is complete until it is related to the center of meaning and value of love. There is no sharp division between secular and the religious, the physical and the spiritual. All are part of God's world.

2. Each individual human being is unique. Each and every individual has value. No individual is expendable. Each person has a destiny and unique value to the Divine Lover. Realizing this destiny is no easy task. Helping another to do so is no easier. What I do unto the least of these my brothers and sisters, I do unto the Divine. In a real sense I need to be

a mediator of Love to all I meet. For some I may be a specific companion and guide. Those of us who have children become spiritual guides whether we intend it or not. This is an awesome responsibility.

3. As I learn truly to love another human being, I often find the Divine Lover revealed within the other human being. This kind of love can be one of the most creative forms of Christian meditation and one of the most tricky and dangerous. Dante and Charles Williams speak of this reality. We shall deal with this reality in chapters 6, 8 and 9.

4. Physical science is a study of one part of the divine creation. It can lead to the One who made that creation. The seeker need fear no truth. The objectivity that genuine scientific study gives can be a great help in overcoming superstition, prejudice, and uncritical sentimentality. It can also help us to deal maturely with the spiritual realm, as we shall see later. Baron von Hügel makes the point that highly developed religious practice requires this kind of objectivity. The spiritual guide needs some knowledge of one of the hard sciences.

5. The life beyond death is neither a matter of successive reincarnations nor absorption into the absolute. It is rather the continuing development and growth of one's own individuality through the companionship of others under the guidance of the Divine Lover. A kingdom or a banquet is a better symbol of this kind of life than a void. Worship, love, learning and growth continue. The hope of such an extension of life beyond the grave removes some of the bitter evil of this life.

6. In this tradition it is almost always necessary to have guidance and companionship, but the relation between the teacher and the student or guide and follower is not one of inequality, but rather of mutual interchange and increasing trust and love and openness. The guru in this tradition tries to be a genuinely humble example and instrument of the kind of unmerited love he or she has experienced in encountering the Divine Lover. The minister is the servant rather than the lord. Abbé Huvelin is a magnificent example of this tradition.

7. The growth potential of the human being is infinite. Coming into the fullness of being the sons and daughters of God is open to all. Growth goes on in the next world as well as in this one, and we may even be able to change the direction of our lives in the next life. To achieve my full growth I must continuously work towards this goal, using all the methods at my disposal, including finding a soul friend to help me on my journey.

8. Since growth and transformation are ultimately given, not earned,

and a simple childlike trust is often as important as wisdom and strict spiritual practice, the simple peasant with no education can come through sacramental means to the same growth and wisdom as the most adept at spiritual practice. If, however, we are capable of some inner spiritual journey and do not set out upon it, we are likely to be left far behind by the peasant.

9. A Christian meditative practice that does not result in horizontal outreach to suffering and lost human beings has gone astray. No Christian meditator can have total peace while there is sickness, bloodshed, war, racial tension, discrimination, exploitation, prejudice, poverty, human agony, or a foul prison system. Evil exists in both the outer and inner worlds, but it can be overcome by Christ's way of conquering it with love.

There is usually a tension between the sense of joy in the presence of Love and living in a world so often devoid of it. Thomas Merton is a good example of this aspect of authentic prayer, as are John Woolman, William Wilberforce, Martin Luther King Jr. and most Christian saints. The more deeply we encounter the Divine Lover, the more sensitive we become to the agony of the world. The cross becomes all too real.

10. Time is linear as well as cyclical. We look forward to growth within ourselves, in the world around us and in the world to come. History is significant, and yet we can at times step into the timeless, eternal now.

11. Desire need not and should not be totally eliminated. It needs to be purified and redirected, but not indulged. Followed relentlessly with competent direction, it can lead the individual to Divine Love. The spiritual way is active as well as passive.

12. The cross stands at the center of the Christian faith and points to the reality of evil. Evil cannot be dismissed as an illusion created by our egocentric point of view, nor can it be seen as only the accidental lack of perfection of the universe. In addition to the Divine Lover there appears to be a reality that would drag us away from our final meaning in life: communion and relationship with God. It is a part of God's world that has revolted against God. Human beings need salvation, and they cannot obtain it by their efforts alone. We may not understand the nature of evil, but Christianity offers a way of being lifted up out of its power and being saved again and again.

13. Our knowledge of this physical world is real, but imperfect. As we seek to know more of this world, our knowledge improves. In the same

way, our knowledge of God in Christ is imperfect. We can use the best traditions that we can find, and we can test them by our own experience in prayer, meditation and contemplation. We can use all our intellectual powers to reflect upon these traditions and experiences. Our knowledge of God will still be limited and fragmentary. Our knowledge and understanding of God can continue to grow as long as we live. Our limited and inadequate language can never express our experience as we would wish. However, the fact that our knowledge is partial and unsatisfactory is no reason to conclude that we have *no* knowledge or experience of God. This is another reason we need spiritual companionship: to check and verify our insights and knowledge. This learning to know and love God continues in the life beyond death.

14. This kind of religious practice should result in psychological as well as spiritual maturity and will in many instances result in improved physical functioning. Spiritual and psychological well-being are not at odds with one another. They cannot be totally separated.

This classical Western spirituality is not an easy way, but it is a great way. It leads to transformation of individuals and requires effort and the bearing of tension. It is the essence of the Western contribution to the understanding of all spirituality. It is not entirely different from other ways, but it offers different emphases. It deserves serious consideration by all who are interested in the spiritual way, and especially by Westerners who undertake the spiritual journey. The purpose of this book is to provide some concrete suggestions for those who wish to lead others in this kind of spiritual adventure. Those who set out upon such a journey need guides upon the way, guides who understand the world of spirit and the ordinary world in which we live, guides who know how these different worlds interact and interpenetrate. There are few more important tasks in the Church today than equipping men and women to serve as guides to the multitudes who wish to embark upon this journey.

NOTES

1. Andrew Greeley, *The Sociology of the Paranormal: A Reconnaissance* (Beverly Hills, CA: Sage Publications, 1975).

2. Harvey Egan, S.J., "Christian Apophatic and Kataphatic Mysticism," *Theological Studies*, Fall, 1978, pp. 399 ff.

3. The detailed list of these passages is found in the appendix of my book *Encounter With God*.

4. These are largely found in Vol. XI of Jung's *Collected Works, Psychology and Religion: West and East,* and his comments on *The Secret of the Golden Flower.*

5. Aldous Huxley, *The Doors of Perception* (New York: Harper and Row, 1970), pp. 22 ff.

6. Baron Friedrich von Hügel, *The Mystical Element of Religion* (London: J. M. Dent and Sons Ltd., 1927), Vol. II, p. 127.

Chapter **3**

WHAT IS MATURE CHRISTIANITY?

I t has been said that theology consists of three things: from what, to what and how. The *to what* is quite clear in what we have already written. Christianity offers personal fellowship with the Divine Lover, a communion so well described in the poem of St. John of the Cross, "The Dark Night."

> *Oh, night that guided me, Oh, night more lovely than the dawn,*
> *Oh, night that joined Beloved with lover, Lover transformed*
>   *in the Beloved!*
> *Upon my flowery breast, Kept wholly for himself alone,*
> *There he stayed sleeping, And I caressed him, and the fanning*
>   *of the cedars made a breeze.*
> *The breeze blew from the turret As I parted his locks;*
> *With his gentle hand he wounded my neck And caused all my*
>   *senses to be suspended.*
> *I remained, lost in oblivion; My face I reclined on the Beloved.*
> *All ceased and I abandoned myself, Leaving my cares forgotten*
>   *among the lilies.*[1]

Christianity offers this kind of consummating experience to those who desire it and seek it, in spite of evil and death. We can experience this kind of love now and have an eternity to grow into it. We will then seek to be instruments of this love toward other human beings.

The *from what* is a little more difficult to describe. Most of us conscious human beings who have found no religious way are at sixes and sevens with ourselves and with the world around us. We are lost, alienated, confused, in a wasteland. We are not comfortable with ourselves, with other people or with the universe around us. We are subject to pain, frustration, anger, fear, stress, egotism, inflation, hopelessness and depression. Many of the existentialists, Camus and Sartre for example, describe this sense of lostness magnificently, but they offer no solution. Celia, the strange heroine of T. S. Eliot's *The Cocktail Party* describes the alienation that so many of my students at Notre Dame felt, what the critics who first saw the play had experienced. Eliot, however, provides a solution. William James gives a classic description of these states of alienation in *The Varieties of Religious Experience.* Carl Jung discovered this lostness at the basis of much neurosis.

There is much written on the *from what* and the *to what,* but not so much is found in Christian theology or instruction on the *how.* The task of spiritual guidance, spiritual formation or spiritual direction (as well as that of genuine Christian education) is to provide ways, methods and practices that will help us move from our alienation to our consummation. It is not easy to travel from one to the other, and since each of us is unique, each of us will have a unique way of coming to the right path and staying on it. General prescriptions can be helpful, but each of us has his or her particular pit to escape and his or her specific journey to achieve the goal.

Baron Friedrich von Hügel was rescued from his abyss through the guidance, care and concern of Abbé Huvelin. He never ceased to be grateful and spent most of his adult life as a Catholic layman endeavoring to share his experience of transformation, of being saved, with other seekers in the Christian world. He became one of the most profound and original religious thinkers and writers of modern times. He was certain that regeneration such as he had experienced was only possible as we are enabled to bypass the many roadblocks in our way and come to an *experience* of God. He was interested in finding the conditions that made possible such experience. He was convinced that the only way of studying mysticism was to make an empirical, scientific, in-depth study of a great mystic. He selected Caterinetta Fieschi Adorna, St. Catherine of Genoa, because she was married (and he believed that mysticism was not confined to celibates), because she lived in pre-Reformation times, before the Church was split physically and spiritually, and also because few studies had been made of her astonishing experiences and her life devoted to the sick and the poor.

At the end of many years of study and research he was convinced of the genuine nature of her direct experience of God. He realized that the philosophical point of view in which he had been reared, German Idealism, did not provide an adequate framework for understanding her experience of communion with the Divine Lover. He reformulated his entire philosophical stance and came to a world view very much like that we have described in the last chapter. He also came to the conclusion that mature religion of this depth and reality required three elements. First of all, it was necessary to have a religious tradition that had been revealed in history and been refined through institutional practice. Secondly, it required openness to and cultivation of direct experience of God; this was the mystical element. And thirdly, mature religion required the refinement and development of our rationality, our capacity for critical, analytical thought as it has been developed in the scientific method.

In his *magnum opus, The Mystical Element of Religion,* von Hügel outlines his conclusion that vital religion consists of the interaction of these three elements. In a later book, *Eternal Life,* he suggested that the new science of psychology had much to offer in aiding people to find mature religious experience, but he considered this subject beyond his competence. I would add this fourth element as necesary if we are to help others on the spiritual journey: the knowledge of the nature of the human psyche and how it operates within itself and in interaction with both physical and spiritual worlds, and also how it responds to other human beings in a one-to-one setting and in groups. Closely related to this understanding of human beings in their fullness is the realization that we do not know instinctively how to care for one another, and since love is central to the religion that Christians profess, we need to learn how to care, how to love. Let us look further at these five elements and also at the consequences when any one of these elements of mature religion is missing from our religious practice.

The Institution and the Tradition

If indeed, as we are suggesting, the spiritual world is as real as the physical one, we learn about it as we accumulate knowledge; we build upon the foundations laid by others. Knowledge of the spiritual world is the result of the addition of one understanding on another; it is the product of accretion and development. Without the tradition of Judaism the life and teaching of Jesus would have been incomprehensible. Some religious writers, like Ira Progoff in his recent book on meditation, suggest that all we have to do is turn inward and all necessary truth will be revealed to us. According to this point of view, we could burn all the religious documents and suffer no great loss because we would simply turn inward and discover the truths they contain once again. If this is so we really have no need of the religious institution. This kind of thinking can lead to all kinds of superstition and nonsense and arrogance. It can even result in the tragedy at Jonestown in Guyana.

People who offer new religions should be watched with great care. There is no greater or more dangerous inflation than thinking that one of us is the final, innovative mouthpiece of God. Gunther Bornkamm pointed out in his book *Jesus of Nazareth* that Jesus added only two basic new elements to Judaism. The belief that we can enter the spiritual world and discover a totally new way to relate to it can lead not only to hubris and egomania, but to psychosis as well. Likewise, the idea that each person's religious opinion is of the same value is pure nonsense. There is truth value in religious traditions and religious statements, and some of them describe the reality of the spiritual world much more adequately than others. I have dealt with this subject at length in my book *Myth, History and Faith.*

All of the great religions have been the result of growth and development. Later on we shall describe in greater length the religious development of Judaism, which began among the ancient Hebrews and still continues. The same process can be seen in Islam, in Buddhism, and in the various sects of Hinduism, as well as in Christianity. It is far better to be part of an historical religion that has been tested and refined by time than some new sect that pretends to have a new revelation of final truth. Let us beware of spiritual guides who would take us on a totally new path. It is good for those of us who are directing others to be careful about thinking we have a totally new way and leading people upon it, for we might well lead them astray.

There is an equally great and grave danger when the totality of religion is limited to the dictates and prescriptions of a religious tradition and law. Religious beliefs that are not tested in experience and are not subject to criticism and change can degenerate into bigotry and brainwashing. Those with this purely institutional frame of mind have a tendency to reject, ostracize or shun those who do not follow the one accepted tradition. Rabbi Zalman Schachter once told me that brainwashing occurs whenever we are made to feel guilt for doubt.

When ready-made dogma with a set of hand-me-down practices is accepted without question or reflection, then we are not far from superstition. No code of laws can deal with all the varieties of human beings. Since Jesus revealed God as the Lord of love, as well as of law and order, reducing Christianity to tradition denies God's intention to relate to each of us personally and individually. Paul made this point with great force in his letter to the Galatians. Jesus pointed beyond the law in many of his actions and teachings, while at the same time affirming its value. According to Jesus, each of us has our own *individual* value and our own unique journey to God.

When the institutional element dominates religion, to the exclusion of other aspects, there is often an obsession with the organization and the details of its regulations. Blind obedience is required. This often results in rigidity, sterility and deadness in the institution. The church or religious institution then becomes a museum rather than a vital, living force. When religion has become only a matter of outer rules and rituals then those who deviate from the accepted practice and beliefs are not tolerated. Such religious prejudice drives thoughtful people away from the religious institution, and then the church is further entrenched within this kind of sterility. There is no new life or fermentation of the spirit, and the institution itself loses its mystery; the symbols and rituals of the church lose their power. The religious institution becomes as exciting as *Robert's Rules of Order*. There are few people except scholars who find much stimulation in reading the books of Leviticus or Deuteronomy. However, most oppressive Christian religious institutions have fallen into this mind-set.

Perfectly obvious implications of our tradition can be ignored when we do not use our rational capacities. It took eighteen hundred years before Jesus' teaching of the equal value of all human beings resulted in the abolition of slavery. It took nineteen hundred years before women were accorded the place that Jesus gave them. Cultural accretions quite at variance to a religion can creep into religious tradition and corrupt and dilute it. Tradition needs continued reaffirming experiences of God, reflection, a knowledge of what makes us human, and love, or it can become destructive and oppressive.

Mystical Experience

The word *mysticism* has had a bad religious press, as I have already indicated. To many people, the attempt to be open to the direct experience of God and the spiritual world is either a flight into illusion or a flight away from reality and responsibility. We have already seen how many modern theologians view mysticism in this way. They would agree with the statement of Joseph Fletcher, author of *Situation Ethics*, that mysticism begins in mist and ends in schism. Some years ago in a meeting of theologians we were discussing the difficulties of training people for ministry. As part of the discussion I introduced Andrew Greeley's data on the frequency of mystical experience. I asked the rector of a seminary who was present what use should be made of this data, and he replied, "And what does mysticism have to do with training seminarians?"

A direct and energizing encounter with the spiritual world and with God can occur in many different ways. If indeed there is a nonphysical, psychoid world, then we must make quite an effort to avoid it. An experiment in the cognitive learning laboratory at Harvard shows how difficult it is for us to deal with experiences of reality that are contrary to what we believe about the world. Postman and Bruner devised an experiment to test cognitive dissonance, experiences that do not fit into our accepted mode of belief. They took the six of spades in an ordinary deck of playing cards and had it painted red. The card was then reinserted in the deck, and the deck was shown to a group of subjects. Practically none of them saw the red six of spades. It was seen either as a regular black six of spades or as the six of diamonds or hearts. They actually did not "see" what was there because it did not fit their conception of a deck of cards. A trial attorney friend was struck by this experiment because it confirmed his experience that many drivers of automobiles run down motorcycles and maintain that they have not "seen" them. They were looking for a car at the corner and never "saw" the motorcycle. If it is this easy to fail to see what is presented visually before us, how much easier to deny a whole realm of being that comes to us in nonsensory ways. Once in a group of Mennonites I told this account of the red six of spades and evoked no response because most of them had never seen a deck of playing cards. They might have detected the red six of spades. They were still open to what cards looked like and their perceptions were not based on what they thought cards *should* look like.

There are many different ways through which we can come into contact with this spiritual world. We shall discuss these at greater length in a later chapter. There are, however, several ways that have been used and accepted in the Church throughout history. First of all is the autonomous experience of God that is described by Andrew Greeley. Although these experiences can come to people who have not actively been seeking them, they are more likely to be experienced by people who have sought them.

One of the main reasons for the rituals and sacraments of religion is to open people to these experiences of the beyond. The spiritual can be conveyed through the material, the inner through the outer. Immersion in the water of baptism can convey the sense of dying and rising again. The more collective the culture or the group that participates in the sacrament, the less differentiation is made between the outer and the inner reality. Bread and wine, peyote, confession, absolution, rosary beads, the stations of the cross—can mediate a reality beyond them. Dr. Weil suggests that marijuana is more sacramental than chemical in its effect. It is an activated placebo. The expectation and the social setting have as much influence in producing the high as the chemicals involved. Some students of the peyote cult maintain that the social situation is the decisive factor in the experience of this cult, as the peyote consumed is minimal. The drug environment provides the occasion and the sanction to enter an altered state of consciousness. Likewise, many people find it easier to enter into silence in a prayer group. For the early Christians the Eucharist undoubtedly opened the possibility of an experience with the risen Christ because of group expectation, not because of the wine consumed. The wine was the occasion, not the cause.

There are also certain mental practices that have been used by nearly all developed religious groups to aid people in becoming detached from total immersion in the physical world around them and to open them to an experience of another dimension of reality. These methods have much in common, whether they are the practices of Eastern religions or they are Christian in background. In both traditions the practices usually begin with the intention of becoming still and centered within ourselves. It is like turning from the person sitting next to us in the theater and concentrating on the stage. In the Eastern religious traditions the silence and imagelessness is often a goal in itself. We come to a union; we lose our ego consciousness and are absorbed into cosmic consciousness. As von Hügel pointed out, this is one valid focus of meditation.

Some Christian practice emphasizes this kind of meditational pursuit. The goal is to be lost in the unknowable center of reality, the dazzling darkness, about which we can say little or nothing. The Pseudo-Dionysius and *The Cloud of Unknowing* emphasize this aspect of meditative practice. It is important to remember that in any experience there is an ineffable or unexpressible element, whether the experience is of blue cheese or of the Divine Center of reality. *Words or concepts never ex-*

haust or convey all of any experience. Words are usually abstractions from the experience.

We can maintain that this ultimate reality is essentially unknowable and that the experience of detachment is an end in itself, or we can follow the lead of many Christian traditions and seek to become attached and related to the Divine Lover, trying to allow this reality to change and transform us more and more deeply. Here the use of images, human relationships and the imagination can aid us in growing into deeper fellowship with God in Christ. The growth that the mystical journey provides as we experience God's energizing love does not come to an end, even though we may find moments of rest along the way. At times these seem like the goal of the journey, but the goal is continuing transformation, not bliss.

We should note here that we can only be in earnest about mystical experience if we truly believe in the existence of spiritual reality. Because Western society, including most theologians and many clergy, is caught up in a materialistic world view, we need to make sure that our allegiance is to a world view that includes both physical *and* psychic (spiritual) reality. Certainly the Incarnation embodies this viewpoint, for God, who is spirit, was revealed in a specific flesh-and-body person, Jesus of Nazareth.

The *Spiritual Exercises* of Ignatius of Loyola gathered up and systematized with genius the religious practices that had been normative for several centuries in Christian.devotional practice. His exercises use images and imagination to give access to the Jesus of history, both divine and human. We can imagine ourselves with Jesus at Gethsemane or watch with him on the cross or meet him on the mountaintop where he has gone to pray. In this way we can have imaginative fellowship with Jesus that can lead to a genuine spiritual encounter. We can step into any part of the gospel story and participate in the events, as Walter Wink shows in his book *Transforming Bible Study.* We can live out the meaning of Jesus' parables. C. S. Lewis and Charles Williams remind us that "myth is a pattern of reality which can be revealed either in imagination or in history." Reflecting upon and stepping into the biblical narrative can bring us into a present-day encounter with the pattern of reality that is revealed there.

In most cultures and religions the dream has been viewed as the natural altered state of consciousness and the revealer of the spiritual dimension. As I have shown in *God, Dreams and Revelation,* this was the view of the Old Testament, the New Testament and most of the Church fathers and doctors until the influence of Aristotle became central in the scholasticism of the Middle Ages. Paying attention to the dream as a possible message from God is another way of direct experience that has been common practice in the history of the Church.

Just as the institution and the tradition can go dead without the enlivening touch of a direct experience of that of which the Church speaks, so mysticism without a grounding in tradition can fall into the wildest excesses. The moment that personal experience is given exclusive priority over tradition, we are likely to get into deep trouble. In her novel *The Abyss*, Marguerite Yourcenar describes the wild excesses of the early German Anabaptists. In *Civilization in Transition*, Jung describes the horrors of Hitler and National Socialism centered around the Germanic god Wotan. There are many elements and aspects of nonphysical reality, and we need a sound tradition to guide us to the creative center of spiritual reality, which is the Divine Lover. Mystical experience needs to be subjected to the same kind of analysis, comparison and understanding as any other experience if we are to grow religiously. When we leave behind our rationality and critical judgment, mysticism can become superstitious nonsense or silly exuberance. We need to keep our feet on the ground and decide which aspects of our experience come from within the human psyche, which elements come from ambivalent or negative psychoid elements, and which come from God and the Holy Spirit. I have discussed this matter at length in *Discernment*.

In order to guide ourselves or others on the mature spiritual journey we also need to be prepared psychologically in three ways. First of all, we need to know something of the depth and complexity of the human psyche and of what experiences it is capable. Of modern psychologists, only William James and Carl Jung and his followers have provided a framework and understanding that enable us to give guidance and understanding to those thirty-nine percent of the people who have reported having mystical experiences. Many modern psychologies simply have no criteria for assessing these powerful experiences, as the psychiatrist Gerald May shows so clearly. Even in sixteenth-century Spain, St. Teresa complained that she could not find a confessor who could listen to her experiences and help her understand them and integrate them into her life.

We need to know something of the history of Christian spirituality. Roy Fairchild described prayer as "paying full and fervent attention to all of God you know—in Jesus Christ—with all of yourself that you know." Knowing the depth of the human psyche gives an opportunity to know more of ourselves and to bring more of us to the encounter; the history of the many variations of Christian spiritual practice help us know more of that God. Urban Holmes has provided a good starting point in his book *A History of Christian Spirituality: An Analytical Introduction.*

And everything that we have already said is pure theory until we take the time to develop our own practice and to discover that we can find these levels of experience within and through ourselves. We can certainly guide another person no further than where we have gone ourselves. Each of us is unique, and each of us needs to find his or her own way if we are to discover our own fulfillment and accompany others to their fullest religious experience and practice.

The Proper Use of Reason

Von Hügel was deeply impressed by the growing scientific knowledge of the late nineteenth and early twentieth centuries. He believed that the scientific method, which had discovered so much about the natural world, was valid for the accumulation of any knowlege. He was convinced that mature Christianity is seldom mindless or superstitious. We need to reflect upon how we know and how we think. Like many modern philosphers of science, he believed that growth in knowing occurs when we deal with all the data at our disposal and then through imagination form an hypothesis. Then we infer the implications of our theory and test it again in experience. When new data comes to us that does not fit our hypothesis we must find another, as von Hügel did when he realized that his own world view had no place for the *experiences* that actually occurred to St. Catherine of Genoa.

The Christian need not fear any honest scientific study. It is God's world, and it will reveal the divine hand at work everywhere. Painstaking and careful assessment of data and critical evaluation and inferences concerning this data provide the best frame of reference for dealing with spiritual reality as well as physical reality. When we deal with *all the facts* we will be led to the reality of the spiritual world, as was Bergson in his study *The Two Sources of Morality and Religion*, or as Jung was when his data forced him out of the materialism of nineteenth-century German medicine. Materialistic science does not have final truth, as T. S. Kuhn points out in *The Structure of Scientific Revolutions*; indeed, modern science is not as certain as many believe. In his carefully reasoned article in the June 1980 issue of the *American Journal of Psychiatry*, Roger Walsh shows that the behavioral sciences must take the data of the disciplines of consciousness into consideration, i.e., they must take account of human spirituality, if they are to be *scientific*.

One reason that the early Church proved so powerful as it stood against and conquered the ancient pagan world was that it not only outlived and outdied that world; it also outthought it. If the Church is to have the same effect upon our contemporary world it must know the deepest currents of the scientific world and outthink that world in the way the early Church did.

And yet nothing is more sterile than religion that is pure thought, without the flesh and blood of religious experience and psychological understanding, of caring concern and of tradition. When human beings make religious faith a matter of logical deduction and try to attain certitude it becomes as dry as moon dust. Theologians of this ilk talk about religion and spirituality, but they avoid an encounter with God. So many modern theologians write intellectually about God and the divine-human encounter and lead few people toward it. Aristotle's *Metaphysics* is a perfect example of this kind of rational religion, and the Protestant and Catholic scholasticism based on it are not much better. After all, it is much easier to think about and discuss evil and God than to be enmeshed in one' and seeking deliverance through the other. When thought and reason are the only elements of religious life, God is dead as far as providing transformation is concerned. A god who is only inferred seldom changes life. Purely rational theology often has little place for love and spurs few people towards it. This kind of rational, theological Christianity is a travesty of the real thing.

Psychology and the Spiritual Way

The great directors of conscience, the great spiritual guides, have had an instinctive knowledge of what makes human beings tick, and so they were able to reach other human beings and to facilitate miracles of transformation. However, few of them could pass on their intuitive understanding. The science of psychology is not yet one hundred years old. It has provided an accumulated body of data about how human beings operate. If we would lead others or ourselves upon the spiritual journey it is foolhardy to ignore the findings of the best of modern psychology. It is like going to a hungry third-world country with no knowledge of modern agriculture.

The findings of right-brain and left-brain research tie in closely with the findings of depth psychology. Both of these fields of study show that the human psyche is more mysterious than we thought at one time. It is more than conscious mind. The study of parapsychology supports these observations. Ironically, it was not the Church that showed me how to begin a meditative practice and how to engage in real prayer. Rather, it was several of the followers of C. G. Jung with whom I worked who opened me to the riches of spiritual reality. They believed that I could not be healed psychologically until I dealt with spiritual reality. I found that much the same methods had been used by Ignatius Loyola and had been known and taught in the Church by his followers.

In later chapters I shall discuss at greater length what we need to know about the growth and development of the human psyche. We shall also examine the many different ways in which we can be open to this spiritual dimension, and how careful we need to be in dealing with this depth. Going or sending someone into the spiritual world without caution is like turning a ten-year-old loose onto a freeway in a Porsche. In addition, we cannot give spiritual direction without knowing the depth of another person, and people are very careful about revealing all of themselves. People will only reveal the depths of themselves if we are trustworthy, open, caring, and aware of our own shadow and darkness. Providing an atmosphere in which others will disclose themselves requires real skill. Another difficulty is that in most one-to-one encounters there is the danger of emotional involvement or transference. Even the most mature find it difficult to handle transference creatively. There is a new and important body of knowledge concerning group dynamics. Psychological and religious growth can be fostered in well-led groups. In my experience, most of us are best able to grow toward our spiritual potential when our religious experience includes both a group of peers with a director and the more personal individual counseling and direction.

When this kind of important psychological knowledge is not used in religious practice, or when that practice is not based on a commitment to genuine caring for others, religious leaders can become distant, unrelated or ineffective. On the other hand, when psychology has no base in *some* profound religious tradition, the religious questions are not likely to be ministered to, and these can be our greatest need. Often psychologists are abysmally ignorant about religious traditions and their value. A recent survey of mental health professionals undertaken by Timothy Kochems for his doctoral dissertation at Georgetown University, shows how seldom they will initiate questions pertaining to religion and how uncomfortable they often feel when these issues arise. Our religious strivings, practices and attitudes are often all mixed up with authority and sexual problems, as well as with anxiety neuroses and other psychological problems. I doubt if either the religious or psychological dimensions of life can be dealt with adequately without a knowledge of the other.

Few psychologists show the insight into the interrelatedness of spirituality and psychology demonstrated by C. G. Jung. In 1945 he wrote a letter to P. W. Martin, an early religious interpreter of Jung. There he stated that "the main interest of my work is not concerned with the treatment of neuroses but rather with the approach to the numinous. But the fact is that the approach to the numinous is the real therapy and inasmuch as you attain to numinous experiences you are released from the curse of pathology."[2] And yet even Jung was sometimes naive and uninformed in religious matters. Psychology without knowledge of some religious tradition, an experience of the divine, critical thinking and genuine caring will not resolve some of our most urgent problems. Psychology alone is not enough for salvation or spiritual direction. If I had not had a knowledge of the Christian tradition, theology, and philosophy, I would not have been able to integrate the experiences of analysis into the fabric of my religious life.

The Centrality of Caring

In the last two decades there has been a rebirth of Christian concern for those in need: the poor, the psychologically disabled, those in depressed urban areas, those subject to racial and sexual discrimination. The Church had ignored its call to social action for a long time. As we have already stated, a spiritual life that ignores this practical dimension of religious life can hardly be called Christian. It is not easy to learn to care intelligently for those who love us and for whom we wish to care. Most of us do not care truly for ourselves, and when this is the case we are most likely to project our darkness on others, even those closest to us. If this is true of our personal relationships, how much more true it is of our attitudes toward those who are ignored and rejected by the society of which we are a part. Christian spirituality is not complete until we have learned how to care for ourselves, for friends and family, for our enemies, and even for strangers. As any social worker will tell us, it is no easy task to learn to treat other people as equals so that they feel genuinely cared for. Yet this is essential to the following of Jesus of Nazareth. I have sometimes found more healing in psychologists' offices than in churches.

One of the qualities of all the great directors of conscience has been a sense of compassion and love that springs from their own poverty of spirit. Being truly cared for and loved draws us out of ourselves in a mysterious way and makes us vulnerable to the presence and love of God. Huvelin writes, "Only love explains everything." Those who knew him as a spiritual guide witnessed to his incredible love. One central purpose of spiritual direction is to share with others in their individual need the love and compassion that God has poured out upon us in our brokenness, darkness, depression, sin and hopelessness. Those who know the depth of their unworthiness, and God's love in spite of it, can best accompany others to the love that transforms.

Huvelin wrote that the greatest human problem is our deep sadness, and that our greatest need is to be consoled. The Church is not a museum for saints, but a hospital for sinners. When the Church does not provide caring, love and healing for those who are sick of heart, it is not functioning as the body of Christ. An unloving Christianity is a contradiction in terms. And loving action means that others experience our love, not just that we intend love towards them.

And yet love alone is not enough. Without tradition and theology it can dwindle off into sentimentality, turn into lust or encourage dependency. Without solid reflection it can minister in the wrong way to people, even encouraging them in destructive attitudes. Without a firm foundation in religious experience and religious practice we can believe that we are the final source of love, and this can lead to inflation of the worst kind. And without psychological knowledge we can minimize the dangers of transference and cause untold damage, or we can avoid the discipline that real love requires.

Unfortunately, when the whole substance of ministry and spirituality is caring and social action, with little experiential or traditional knowledge of God, we often observe the phenomon of religious burn-out. Caring not based in being cared for in some cosmic way often degenerates into frantic ego activity, which dries up and is blown away. I have met many social-action ministers on the lecturing circuit who have realized that unless they found a spiritual dimension to their lives, a contact with a Divine Lover, they simply could not go on trying to care. Often they had left the ministry and become secular counselors. Caring and loving are not enough. They are but one element of the mature religious life.

NOTES

1. St. John of the Cross, *Dark Night of the Soul*, trans. E. Allison Peers (Garden City, NY: Doubleday & Company, Inc., 1959), p. 33.

2. *C. G. Jung Letters*, selected and edited by Gerhard Adler, in collaboration with Aniela Jaffé, translated from German by R. F. C. Hull, Vol. I (Princeton, NJ: Princeton University Press, 1973), p. 377.

Chapter **4**

THE CHRISTIAN TRADITION

T he Christian tradition is a complex and difficult tradition to master and understand. It is almost ludicrous to try to summarize that tradition in a few pages. It consists of many strands, and any simplistic reading of the Bible will lead us into difficulty, if not absurdity. Both the fundamentalist and liberal interpretations of the text are attempts to cut the Gordian knot rather than unravel and understand it. There is, first of all, the Old Testament, a library of books that the Hebrews brought together as the essence of their religious life and culture. Second, there is the Apocrypha, those books found in the Greek version of the Old Testament that was used by the Christian Church but not found in the authorized Hebrew Bible. And then there are those writings that were finally accepted as canonical by the nascent Christian Church, writings relating to the ministry of Jesus of Nazareth and to that of his followers, with some reflections on both. In addition to these were other writings in Hebrew and Greek that were never accepted by the Church as canonical or inspired.

There have been occasional attempts to simplify this confusing and complicated interlocking of traditions and writings by neglecting or rejecting the Old Testament narrative. It is simply impossible, however, to understand Jesus of Nazareth and Christianity without knowing this tradition in depth. Jesus was born a Jew, was raised as a Jew and died as one. He was part of a very distinct religion and culture, which were different from and often at odds with the syncretistic Graeco-Roman world in which he lived. Jesus spoke from this tradition. He assumed that his hearers would know it and understand it. One of the real problems Christianity faced in its first years was explaining itself to the pagan world. Paul wrestled with this problem, and so did many of the early Church leaders.

One of the reasons for the years of education required of catechumens in the early Church was the mass of strange Judaic traditions that early Christians had to learn. Günther Bornkamm has pointed out in his book *Jesus of Nazareth* that Jesus made only two significant changes in the Hebrew tradition of his time. We shall look in depth at these two departures from the mainstream of Hebrew tradition a little later.

Judaism is far more than a liberal interpretation of the Old Testament text. In the time of Jesus there were many different parties among the Jews, each with its own practices and understanding of this text. There were Pharisees, Sadducees, Essenes, Samaritans, and Zealots. This was brought home to me quite dramatically several years ago when I was lecturing on holistic healing to a group of doctors and ministers. I made the statement that Judaism placed little value on the physician and even saw healing as interfering with God's will. A rabbi in the group rose during the question period and objected to my statement. He said that I was entirely correct in my statement in regard to the Old Testament text, but that no Jew lived literally by that text. Rather, they interpreted it through the Mishna, the Talmud, or some other tradition. He suggested that only fundamentalistic Christians tried to live by the Old Testament text literally. The early Christian Church made another interpretation of this text and was actually viewed as a sect of Judaism by the Roman government during the first century A.D.

In addition, we can discern quite clearly a process of growth and development from the earliest levels of the Old Testament narrative down through sacred texts that were written after the Jews returned from their exile in Babylon; we discover a continuing and a progressive revelation. God revealed more aspects and facets of the divine reality as people were able to absorb and understand more. Much of this revelation was given in the context of the events of Hebrew history, and this understanding of God can only be comprehended in terms of a history that is real and meaningful, a point of view quite different from that of most Hinduism and Buddhism. God's self-revealing was a gradual unfolding, which from the Christian point of view came to its culmination in the Incarnation in Jesus of Nazareth.

The Judaism of Jesus' time was highly legalized. Many of the Jewish peasants were unable to live up to the law and were considered nearly outside the pale. The religious law prescribed the direction and details of the individual's life. These laws were an attempt to put into concrete action the basic moral convictions of the great prophets within the distinctive ritual of the Jewish people. The unique revelation of the great prophets was that God was more interested in morality than in ritual, more concerned with how we treated one another than in our ritualistic observances. The tragedies of Jewish history were understood as a failure to get this message and live by it. God is lovingly just and expects human beings to treat one another in the same way.

In addition, the Old Testament traces the gradual emergence of the first personal monotheism in history. Gradually the Hebrews moved from seeing Yahweh as the god of the nation (henotheism) to perceiving the Lord as the one and only God. Within this development there was little place for the reality of metaphysical evil in any way separate from God. The one God was the source of good and evil, the one who met Moses and nearly killed him shortly after his experience at the burning bush, the one who brought upon the disobedient the incredible catalogue of illnesses described in Deuteronomy 28: 27 and the verses that follow.

The Hebrews were very much interested in this world. Undoubtedly this was in reaction to the emphasis on an amoral life beyond death among the Egyptians and other peoples surrounding them. However, to understand them as perceiving only the physical aspect of reality and valuing physical reality as alone significant is to misunderstand them. The Hebrews were not rational materialists like the scientists of the late nineteenth century, any more than classical Greeks were totally rational beings, as men and women of the Enlightenment wished to believe. Both of these peoples lived in a world in which the physcial and the spiritual were not clearly distinguished, but both were very real and important.

Dreams and visions were both viewed as significant messengers of a spiritual dimension, beyond the confines of the physical world. The prophet was indeed seized by a spirit that operated from beyond space and time. There were gifts of knowledge and wisdom that did not come through the five senses. If we read the Books of Samuel without putting our blinders on, without the mentality that closes its eyes to the possibility of a red six of spades, we will realize how deeply and frequently the nonphysical world impinged upon the world of time and space and history. How often we need to remind ourselves that Saul first met Samuel as he sought him out for Samuel's clairvoyant powers. After all, Samuel was a seer, a see-er through the veil of ordinary reality. Also, Saul's experience of Samuel's ghost is central to the story of his death. If we read the

Old Testament only through the eyes of Western materialism we will not see much of what is there. Also, we will not understand those who come to us in our time with visions of burning bushes and ghosts, of angels and prophecy, with ecstatic dreams and conversion experiences. Obviously these experiences must be subjected to careful scrutiny and analysis, but they cannot be denied on the basis of theory without falling into absurdity. Theory must always yield to experience.

The New Testament and the Kingdom

When we come to the New Testament we find an even clearer emphasis on the reality of the spiritual world, both good and evil, which is available and experienceable now. The Kingdom of Heaven is at hand, and the kingdom of evil is being defeated. One of the unique messages of Jesus is his declaration that the Kingdom of God is *within us;* "the kingdom of God is within you" (Luke 17:21). The Greek for this phrase is *entós humōn estín.* We do not know what the Aramaic rendering of these words was, but as John Sanford pointed out in an introduction to his book *The Kingdom Within,* at least twelve of the early Church fathers translated these words as "within you," and never "among you." The word can be translated "among you," and many modern translators, because of their materialistic prejudice, prefer this rendition. There is all the difference in the world between the Kingdom being present *among* the people in the presence of Jesus Christ and the Kingdom being *within* in the sense of being available and accessible to us now in the depth of ourselves.

It is also interesting to note that Mr. Sanford's introduction to his book was not included in any edition of *The Kingdom Within,* though it is essential to the understanding of his presentation. However, I have printed it as an appendix to my book *Afterlife: The Other Side of Dying.* Obviously, if one does not have a world view that provides for the intercommunication of spiritual and physical dimensions of reality it is much easier to translate *entós* as "among."

The message of Jesus appears to be that the Kingdom, the reign, the reality of God's presence are now available. Heaven has come close to earth. God is not far away in a far-off heaven and unconcerned with human affairs. God is within us, among us, around us. The Kingdom is neither far away in the future nor far removed in space. It is near at hand. It can be experienced through one dimension of our total humanity.

Jesus proclaimed that God's victory over evil and death are near at hand. There is to be a decisive change in the closeness of God to humankind. Jesus' incarnation and birth, his life, with its healing and teaching, his death and resurrection, are a sign of the closeness of the spiritual reality of the Kingdom of Heaven. This Kingdom is a present reality insofar as it is a reality that already exists within the reach of men and women—all can participate in the Kingdom who are aware of it and who will come forward with childlike simplicity and love and enter it. The Kingdom is still to come in the future in another sense, for it cannot be said to be completely established until all human beings on earth come into it. I was not prepared to find some 638 references to the Kingdom in the pages of the New Testament as I looked up the various names used to describe this reality there. I have detailed these findings in *Afterlife*.

The people living in the world at the time of Jesus believed that there was a spiritual world that was close to human beings and that interacted with them. It was, however, a dangerous world, which only the experts should enter, or those belonging to some mystery cult. Some modern depth psychologists say much the same thing about the reality of the unconscious. Jesus confirms the closeness of this spiritual reality, but also proclaims that at the heart of that world is a loving reality, an incredibly caring *Abba*, who is reaching out to us from the spiritual dimension so that we can know and share in this love. Those who follow Jesus and try to love one another as he has loved them need not fear, but can turn inward and enter the spiritual dimension with confidence and relate to this God. We can talk and listen to this loving one. The spiritual world is near and contains incalculable treasure.

The Gifts of the Spirit

The gifts of the spirit, which are described in several places in the New Testament Epistles, are the evidence that this world is indeed close at hand and is constantly pouring forth into human life. For the last twenty-five years I have been studying these gifts, which occupy such a large portion of the New Testament narrative. Earlier I pointed out that the nine gifts of I Corinthians 12:6–31 can be compressed into five categories.

I first became interested in healing, particularly since this was so frequently described in the ministry of Jesus and the early Church. I was also interested in the fact that practically nothing was said about this major section of the Gospel in modern theological writing. I was introduced to the importance of healing through the writings of Agnes Sanford. I found that the healing ministry of Jesus was continued by the early Church and was one of the unique characteristics of that fellowship. The apologists, the first defenders of the faith, all spoke of this aspect of the Church's life. The doctors of the Church,. East and West, wrote about the healing power of the Church, which embodied the spirit of Christ. Gregory of Nyssa wrote that the healing ministry was the first fruit of the resurrection, a sign of the efficacy of the atonement. I found services for exorcism and healing in nearly all of the early service books of the Church. These services continue right down to the present in the *Euchologion*, the official service book of Greek Orthodoxy. Vatican II reinstituted the sacrament of healing in the Roman communion.

This is not the place to give in detail the evidence that healing has indeed occurred from time to time as a sign of God's love, from the days of the Book of Acts to the modern Pentecostal revival, as men and women were open to that love and allowed it to break in upon their lives. During the Middle Ages the same healing power was often effective through the men and women called saints. The fact of healing was considered evidence that the life of the Kingdom does indeed break through, as I have shown in my book *Healing and Christianity*. This is a significant and vital aspect of Church tradition, one which has been obscured or forgotten in Western Christianity for several centuries. The fact that healings do occur is not invalidated by the fact that, for reasons we do not understand, they do not always occur. A church that ignores or rejects this aspect of ministry and tradition will not be bringing its people to the full measure of God's healing love and will not be facilitating all that is possible in spiritual direction.

When I was ten years old I had an attack of religious fervor and read the Book of Acts. It touched me to the core. It was better than *The Wizard of Oz*. I brought the matter up with my mother, who was the daughter of a minister as well as the granddaughter of one, and asked her why things like this did not occur in the Church anymore. She replied with a straight dispensationalist answer: God permitted these things to occur to convert people to the Church, but once they were converted God returned to "things as normal." In other words, once they took the hook, the bait was removed. My reaction to this was to put down the Bible, and I did not pick it up until, in desperation, I went to the seminary to see if there were any hope of meaning in Christianity. I was not interested in a God who manipulated human beings into belief. I was looking for a God who gave such gifts as a sign of love.

As I came to my dead-end street, I learned from a psychologist friend that God still spoke to us humans if we learned how to listen. I learned, first of all, that he spoke in dreams and that he was trying to reach me even when I did not understand what the dreams meant. These dreams were trying to show me a way out of my lostness that my highly developed rational side had not even considered. I thought that I was an odd-ball in the Church to believe that God still spoke to us poor mortals, and not liking to be strange I searched scripture and the Church fathers. Again, I could hardly believe my eyes. I found dreams, visions, visitations of God and angels, revelations and ecstasies from the Book of Genesis to the Book of Revelation (which is one continuous vision). I wondered where this tradition of divine/human intimacy and communion had ceased. I read the ante-Nicean fathers and the doctors of the Church. I discovered that this divine desire to communicate lasted in Eastern Christianity up to the present and lasted in Western Christianity until the time of scholasticism, when the thinking of Aristotle took over the thinking of the Church. Even in the West, saints claimed to continue to have such experiences. I described these findings in *God, Dreams and Revelation* and *Dreams, A Way to Listen to God*. I discovered that Freud and Jung and their followers had rediscovered truths that the Western Church had known, but had forgotten, truths that the Orthodox Church still knew and continued to use.

Prayer, Evil and Discernment

I also learned that I could dialogue with dream figures and images, and they would reveal more of their identity. I also discovered that I could dialogue with spiritual reality as well. I found that as I got up in the silence of the night and listened attentively something did speak to me, that I could have a dialogue with one who cared, who helped me bear the tension of those difficulties that could not be resolved. Here I found a fellowship, a guidance, a wisdom, and a love that I had read of in the Bible and in the history of the Church, and it was reaching out to me and to all human beings who would be quiet and respond in their individual ways. Out of these night encounters have come most of the understandings and ideas that I have used in my writing. I found that the Kingdom of Heaven was indeed available *through the "within."* The Divine Lover was real and present and available.

Anyone who has struggled with inner confusion and darkness and anxiety knows the reality of evil. The liberal Christianity in which I had been reared and educated considered the idea of autonomous spiritual evil—the demonic—an absurdity. Again, it was Jung and my Jungian friends who suggested that I reconsider Jesus' view of evil, that perhaps he was not misguided, taken in by a faulty world view, or silly when he talked of the Evil One and his minions. As I studied the New Testament I found that the earliest and most authentic tradition contained references to this demonic, down-pulling reality. Here the New Testament moves on to a slightly different position than the Old Testament. A loving father does not send a little leukemia or emphysema when we have disobeyed him; these things are rather the action of a spiritual element that has turned against the Divine Lover.

Most of the New Testament writers and the early Church fathers believed that God became a human being and lived among us, died under the attack of the Evil One and rose again in order to *deliver* us from the power of evil. Evil was for them a reality, which they often called *death*, that goads human beings on to sin in their daily lives and produces physical and mental illness. This point of view is not too different from Freud's idea of the death wish or Jung's description of the negative or destructive aspect of the collective unconscious. If we are to guide people toward their fulfillment and fruition, psychologically and religiously, we must be able to discern those aspects of their lives that are merely shadowy and repressed parts that are reacting to our refusal to let them live, and those aspects that are downright evil, from which they need to be delivered. Jung once said that our shadow, that part of us that seems to torment us from inside, is ninety percent pure gold, and the other ten percent unrelenting evil. We integrate one aspect and seek to be delivered and protected from the other.

Christianity offers no satisfactory philosophical theory of evil, but it provides a way of integrating the natural parts of ourselves that we have forgotten and delivering us from those irredeemable aspects of darkness that bedevil our social and personal lives. Once we have recognized that we need deliverance, we can turn to the one who confronted the Evil One upon the cross, submitted to this reality, and conquered him/her by rising from the dead. Those who invoke the presence of the Risen Christ find that they are usually lifted out of the inner despair that evil has created, and they often find that their lives are outwardly saved as well. Invoking this reality is more than just having ideas about this deliverance; it means actually experiencing this conquering, loving power through imagination and meditation.

Our Christian tradition provides us with a theory of evil, with a means of distinguishing radical evil from psychological repression, and a practice of meditation and action by which deliverance can be experienced. Atonement was the name given to the experience of being given victory over the radical evil that oppresses us. Spiritual guides are those who know something of the reality of evil and who also know how to discern evil from repression and psychological fragmentation. But most important, they have experienced the creative love of the Risen Christ and can offer others methods of coming into contact with this redeeming presence. And this experience of redemption is not once for all, but something we must come back to again and again, for evil is, if anything, persistent.

At the beginning of our century William James wrote these words: "If one has ever taken the fact of the prevalence of tragic death in this world's history fairly into mind—freezing, drowning, entombment alive, wild beasts, worse men, and hideous diseases—he can with difficulty, it seems to me, continue his own career of worldly prosperity without suspecting that he may all the while not be really inside the game, that he may lack the great initiation."[1] Most writers of the spiritual journey speak of it as a way upon which we *will* discover perils and pitfalls, but still a path that leads to a goal of indescribable worth. I have written about this process of discerning and overcoming evil with Christ's help at some length in my previous books, but in particular in *Discernment, A Study in Ecstasy and Evil, Myth, History and Faith, The Other Side of Silence*, and *Christo-Psychology*.

Still Other Gifts

We have been brought up in a materialistic culture and society and have been brainwashed to believe that we can obtain knowledge only through our five senses and the integration that reason works upon these. Most of us simply assume that there is no other way to obtain knowledge. When we assume something we have ceased to think about it. People within this mind-set simply do not hear the story of Saul coming to Samuel for his clairvoyant powers. My premedical students read

Jung's autobiography and did not perceive that one whole chapter was devoted to a near-death experience of the beyond. These experiences are red sixes of spades for the materialistic prejudice in which most of us have been nurtured.

There is no doubt that throughout the Old Testament and the New it was believed that certain people were gifted with extraordinary abilities to see through space and time. Some of these gifts described in I Corinthians 12 are heightened natural abilities, and some seem to be gifts of totally new and fresh insight. We shall discuss later on the many ways in which the spiritual world impinges upon us and communicates its reality and content to us. This communication was found in certain monumental figures in the Old Testament, but now that the Kingdom of God is at hand and within, these gifts of relating and communicating are available to ordinary individuals and churches that share in that Kingdom.

This brings us to the controversial gifts of prophecy and tongue speaking. Prophets appear to be possessed by some spirit other than their own and to speak forth and foretell in their own language what that spirit wishes to say. Anything that comes through an individual, whether in dream or prophecy, needs to be discerned carefully before it is taken seriously. In tongue speaking people speak a flow of nonsense syllables that sound like a language. These words are sometimes interpreted by another as if the speaker were given the message from the same source and was speaking prophetically.

The Pentecostal movement, which has been a fast-growing sect and is also a movement within some of the major churches, has laid great importance on these particular gifts. Whatever else this movement has done, it has brought people once again to the awareness that the Holy Spirit is working now, is available now, that the Kingdom of Heaven is indeed at hand. It has brought to many people a renewed sense of urgency in their Christian profession and practice. It has also at times produced an anti-intellectualism and superstitious enthusiasm. Here again we need the gift of discernment.

If indeed Jesus came to announce and inaugurate a new openness to spiritual reality, then those who are members of Christ and a part of his body, the Church, have an opportunity and an urgent need to deal with this reality. This contact is mediated both through the sacraments and through an inner immediacy. The leaders in the Church thus need to combine the qualities of priest and shaman as well as teacher and preacher. There is no strict division here between priest and minister and laity. Many Church members will have the ability to go the inner way and share in the shamanistic gifts of mediating this realm for one another. This emphasis by Jesus does usher in a new kind of religious attitude. It gave urgency and vitality to the life of the early Church. When we perceive the meaning and reality of Jesus' message, it can do the same for us today.

God as Daddy

The second major departure of Jesus from his Judaic tradition was in calling God *Abba*. We have heard this word so often that we have become immune to the radical effect of truly calling God *Abba*. *Abba* does not mean "father" in the sense of mere paternity. It is rather the word that small Jewish children would have used to call out for loving parents when they were in need. A friend told me of hearing a lost Jewish child in a big city crying out, *"abba, abba."* The word contains something of the quality that we associate with mothering. There is the sense of tender concern, loving care and protection. "Daddy," "mommy," or "papa" would be better translations of this word than "father." Günther Bornkamm stated so clearly in *Jesus of Nazareth* what I had come to grasp intuitively. He wrote: "This is also shown in the expression by which Jesus chooses to address God in prayer, an expression which would have appeared to any Jew too unceremonious and lacking in respect. Abba—Father, this is the word Jesus uses (Mark XIV:36), and which the Hellenistic Church has taken over in its original Aramaic from the oldest records about Jesus (Rom. VIII:15; Gal. IV:6). It is a child's familiar address to his father here on earth, completely uncommon in religious language."[2]

Certainly one finds echoes of this kind of spirit in Hosea and in some of the psalms, such as 103, 131 or 23, but it was uncommon in the time of Jesus and in much of earlier or later Judaism. A friend who is a Christian monk was talking with a Jewish mystic and was asked, "But don't you have a sense of terrible fear as you approach God?" My friend pointed out that this was just what Jesus' name for God helped him overcome. One of the most difficult tasks for Christians is to treat God as if this one were *Abba* and then live within the quality of life that this can produce.

It is very different as a small child to approach a loving father than it is to approach a stern or demanding one, let alone an angry or unfair one. And this is very different from coming before a judge, no matter how righteous, or before a powerful, capricious, oriental monarch. And this is very different from merging with the Cosmic One. Jesus is trying to convey to us through instructions on prayer, in parable and in teaching, that God, the very creative power at the center of the universe, is loving and caring like a *truly devoted parent.* This love is not one aspect of God, or one god among many who has this quality, but the very organizing reality at the heart of things. God is love. Jesus' message could only achieve its radical imperative within the context of Hebraic monotheism. There may be parts of the universe that have rebelled against that love, but they are temporary and insignificant in the long run.

One can understand why people would avoid God if he were like a strict parent, a demanding judge or a despot, and unfortunately my experience is that most of the nominal Christians with whom I talk in depth regard God in one of these lights. At least they show this by their actions, if not by their professions of belief. If the spiritual domain is open to us and if there is a loving one like this reaching out to us and we do not respond, we are either not very bright or else we really don't believe that such a one is there. Our actions tell more about our beliefs than what we say we think and believe.

It is nearly impossible to give love to those who will not receive it. Love cannot be forced upon anyone. Love is a gift that has to be received. If my children think I am a monster, there is no way in which I can get close to them and give them love. Our very attitude toward God determines how much love and caring can be poured out upon us.

Some Christians emphasize the justice and judgment of God, and certainly there is justice behind the love of which Jesus speaks. My own experience over many years of listening to people is that most of them are already judging themselves too harshly and that further emphasis on judgment only drives people away from God rather than drawing them to Abba. Most of us do not believe that anyone could accept us as we are, and we do not even try to turn toward God and receive the incredible gift of his love. It is so difficult to believe in God's love when so few of us have received unconditional love from any human being. One purpose of the Church and those who would be spiritual friends is to provide a human atmosphere in which the love of God may seem more plausible, and to give people the courage to have fellowship with the Holy One. When we are truly loved, we are drawn by that love to its life and goals, and judgment is seldom necessary for us. Research shows that children raised in a loving environment develop the most sensitive sense of conscience.

When we get a vision of the God of whom Jesus speaks we will want fellowship with this one who combines the best qualities of a good father and good mother. We are children. There is no question about Abba's receiving us. All we need to do is acknowledge our childishness and come. This is the reason why the broken and simple, the poor in spirit, the anxiety-ridden, the mourning, the meek, the unsatisfied and unfulfilled, the hungry and thirsty, the persecuted and ridiculed find it so easy to turn to the God Jesus reveals. Those who are doing quite well on their own and think that they have life securely within their grasp don't like to admit their ultimate helplessness and come as children before Abba. They don't feel the need of it. It also may be beneath their dignity.

This message comes through again and again in the parables of Jesus. The last laborer receives as much as the hard-working one who has labored all day. The lost sheep is sought out and found. And the prodigal son is received back by his even more prodigal father. Kenneth Bailey has pointed out in his book *The Cross and the Prodigal* that this story would have been even more ludicrous to Jesus' hearers than to us. And how many of us have ever been treated as prodigals when we have returned home from the swine swill? I have never been terribly impressed by the son's conversion. He was hungry. He was not going home for mercy, but to survive, and arriving there he had poured out upon him grace upon grace, new shoes, the best brocade robe, and that strange and useless gift of the ring, maybe a signet ring giving him once again legal status in the family. And then the feast . . . And the father even goes out to seek the elder brother, who has probably broken Semitic custom more grievously by his scornful refusal to come into the feast than the other son has done by his profligacy.

This emphasis of Jesus on God's caring does not mean that we do not have to do anything to get it. The importunate widow continues to call out, and the neighbor knocks at his friend's door at night for a long time before he is answered. People who do nothing usually get nowhere. It is better to keep striving, even in the wrong direction, than to go and bury one's talent in the ground. Faust is hardly the model of conventional Christian virtue, but as Mephistopheles comes to collect Faust's soul, which he had willingly sold to the Devil, he is rescued and carried off to Heaven by the Blessed Virgin and a troupe of angels. Their song as they lift him up and hover in the high atmosphere is this: "For he whose strivings never cease is ours for his redeeming."[3]

The love that Jesus spoke about he also lived. In the chapel at Notre

Dame, on one side of the altar, is a statue of the prodigal with his head buried in his father's bosom, and on the other is a monumental marble of the pieta, Mary holding her dead son in her arms. One is the story Jesus told, the other the one that he lived. Paul says it so well and so clearly: "It is a difficult thing for someone to die for a righteous person. It might be that someone might dare to die for a good person. But God has shown us how much he loves us; it was while we were still sinners that Christ died for us. . . . We were God's enemies, but he made us his friends through the death of his Son. Now that we are God's friends, how much more will we be saved by Christ's life."[4]

This is a difficult tradition to convey to human beings. It is about as obvious as differential and integral calculus are to high school students before they receive any instruction. People need a lot of guidance if they are to cast off primitive ideas about God and begin seeking this one of whom I write. They need a lot of fellowship and encouragement if they are to continue being open to Abba's love and find the healing, transforming power of that love in the midst of their discouragement and affliction by inner and outer evil. Few people are able to come to this victory unless they find someone who has met evil and survived and who brings them the love that enabled that individual to make it through.

There seems to be only one demand that this God of love lays upon those who have received forgiveness, mercy, love and redemption from evil. It then becomes their task to treat other men and women around them as they have been treated by God. And this takes some doing. We have to unlearn most of the ways that we have been taught about dealing with other human beings, ways learned from infancy on. To continue to love consistently requires objectivity, insight, help and guidance from someone. Spiritual guides can learn a great deal from depth psychology and pastoral counseling. Both of these fields are attempts to care for people with unconditional love. Nothing else seems to bring human beings to the place where transformation is possible.

Conclusion

The Christian tradition begins with the acknowledgement of our human helplessness before the onslaught of evil within and among us. Christianity is the only major religion of the world that faces the full horror of evil and still remains essentially optimistic. The Kingdom of God is within us, and we can reach it and be reached by it in the here and now. The King is well aware of our evil and ugliness, but instead of judging us reaches forth with the self-giving, self-sacrificing love of the cross. Through the Spirit we are given ways of discerning the nature of evil and ways of coming into an effective relationship with the Divine Lover who can save us as brands from the burning.

I find that my task as a minister of Jesus Christ, a minister of reconciliation and unconditional love, is essentially threefold: first, to be aware of my own spiritual poverty, evil, and unconsciousness, and of the futility of any attempts on my part alone to achieve spiritual wholeness; second, to *know* the love that is in God in Christ through my tradition, through sacramental experience, and through my own prayer and meditative experience, as well as through the loving guidance of those who have been my spiritual friends; third, to share the love and salvation that I have received with God and with others by every means at my disposal.

The basic meaning of spiritual guidance is to stand by people in their seeking and searching, in their lostness and despair, in their ugliness and evil (even when they are not aware of their condition). The spiritual guide needs to be open to the darkness, and sometimes to enter it with those whom they guide. And then the guide must produce an environment in which others are open to and transformed by a conquering love greater than most of us have ever imagined. The reality of the transformation is tested as we try to help people to live in the Kingdom now by living in accordance with and empowered by the love that we have experienced.

NOTES

1. William James, *The Varieties of Religious Experience* (New York: Longmans, Green and Co., 1920), p. 360.

2. Günther Bornkamm, *Jesus of Nazareth* (New York: Harper and Row, 1960), p. 128.

3. Goethe, *Faust*, Part 2, Translated by Philip Wayne (New York: Penguin Books, 1977), p. 282.

4. Romans 5:7,8,10, *Good News for Modern Man: The New Testament in Today's English Version.*

Chapter 5

ATHEISM, AGNOSTICISM, AND SPIRITUAL GUIDANCE*

Ⓞne of the most critical issues facing the Church and spiritual directors today is the pervasive agnosticism and atheism in our Western culture. Toynbee pointed out that Europe and the West used to be synonymous with the Christian world, and yet now much of that world professes no belief in God, let alone in Christ, the church or in religious practice. In most Protestant churches there has been a gradual dwindling of numbers. The *1982 Yearbook of American and Canadian Churches* reports a half-million decline in church membership over against an increase in population, and most of this decrease is among the major Protestant churches.[1] In addition, many of those within the church structure are members more out of convention than out of deep and genuine conviction concerning the Christian faith. I wish I had hard sociological data to support this conclusion, which has come from observation of churches and church groups as I have lectured all over the world during the last twenty years.

The principle of the wounded healer applies to those who would reach out to unbelievers and offer them the solace that meaning can provide. Jung pointed out that many churches, ministers and laypeople treat non-believers as though they had the plague, rather than as people who have an inadequate point of view that needs to be broadened and developed. Those who have never been troubled by doubt or who have never let

* The subject of agnosticism and atheism is a very difficult one. There is no way of dealing with this pervasive problem without becoming involved in some technical and specialized material. The person who finds this material hard going should skip it at present, finish this book, and then return to this chapter. It is important to have some grasp of this material if we would deal with the spiritual problems of our age.

themselves become aware of their doubt (conscious or unconscious) are likely to react angrily and defensively to disbelief rather than to support doubters through their questioning. The hostile treatment that unbelievers often get from church members and leaders is in many instances a result of their inability to face their own questioning. To help the questioning, the agnostic and the atheist, we need to be people who have struggled with doubt ourselves and come out on the other side with a meaningful faith. This does not mean that those who have been through this struggle no longer have any doubts or questions. Abbé Huvelin puts it well in a letter to one he was guiding: "In faith we have just enough light to follow the right way, but on either side there is the abyss."

I was brought up in a conventional Christian church and was fairly active. When I was twenty-one my mother died; she was the only person who I felt truly accepted and cared for me. I then went off to graduate school to study philosophy. There I read Immanuel Kant's *Critique of Pure Reason,* which swept away any structure of intellectual belief I had and plunged me into an abyss of almost total agnosticism. The trouble with most people is that they are not agnostic enough; they are not consistent in their agnosticism and do not go into it far enough to see its darkness and agony. They disbelieve what is inconvenient and believe what they want to believe. Total rootlessness can cause unbelievable pain and suffering and so I went to seminary to see if Christianity could provide meaning for me.

Reading von Hügel and A. E. Taylor showed me that my agnosticism might be based on bad thinking. I emerged from a liberal seminary in 1943 with the blazing conviction that there were as many good reasons to believe in God as not to believe. With this conviction I set out to convert the world.

Intellectual belief was not enough though, and I soon fell into the abyss again. It was through the writings of Jung and personal contact with some who had known him that I came to realize that the spiritual world was real and the Divine Lover could be known and shared. Since then, only the experience of Love *plus* intellectual belief have kept me from permanent residence in the pit.

Later I met Jung, who told how he was jolted out of the rational, materialistic agnosticism of his medical training. He learned that there was a nonphysical dimension of reality, which was observable to anyone who would take the trouble to experience it. It was, as he said, as experienceable as were the two moons of Jupiter to those in Galileo's time who would take the trouble to look through his telescope. He believed that one of his most important therapeutic tasks was to free people caught in the constricting materialism of our time and open them up to a more adequate view of reality. He viewed the person wholly caught up in materialism as more sick than amoral or immoral. We need to outthink our modern materialistic world, just as the early Christians outthought the ancient world.

Emerging from Paradise

Emerging from an unconsciously held collective world view is as rude a shock for most of us as being expelled from Eden was for Adam and Eve. There is something quite paradisiacal in being totally enveloped within a social framework with an unquestioning frame of mind. We can still find this kind of belief in some places like Bali and some Islamic cultures. But once we have begun to question there is no returning to Eden or unconsciousness without disaster. "Humpty-Dumpty had a great fall, and all the king's horses and all the king's men can't put Humpty-Dumpty together again." Superficial compulsory education has provided just enough consciousness to drive a great percentage of the people in the Western world out of Eden and leave them in the wastelands.

Telling people with this background to buck up and take the dogmas and dictates of an authoritarian church or book on faith simply doesn't work. Their problem is that they do not have "faith." Most of us have lost our confidence in authority. The Documents of the Second Vatican Council are revolutionary. In that Council a church that had relied on absolute authority gave that final authority back to individual conscience and left people to choose by their own best light. For many people in the United States the events surrounding Watergate destroyed the last vestiges of the idea that any authority can be relied upon uncritically.

A belief system can be a way to help us find our way in reality, or it can be a defense mechanism in which we hide from life. Unfortunately, many people want the security that a rigid and unwavering belief system provides and will sacrifice freedom, rationality and independence to be given absolute certainty. Many of those drawn to fundamentalistic religious cults and absolute "isms" exhibit this need for security. Jim Jones gave such "security" and removed the mind. People caught in this mind-set need very careful shepherding, direction, and pastoral care.

We human beings can only tolerate so much anxiety. In his important book *The Structure of Scientific Revolutions*, T. S. Kuhn notes that scientists who have their basic convictions shaken by a new theory often become very anxious. Very few people can live in the limbo of uncertainty, having no solid view of reality. For some people it seems better to live in an acknowledged meaningless materialism than to be without any basic theory of reality.

During World War II I was a pastor in a small church. I found that the only people who could not adjust to the deaths of their loved ones in battle were those who had no body to bury and so could not accept the certainty of the deaths of their loved ones. Even a hopeless world view is better than none at all. Most liberal Protestant churches and many of the priests of the postconciliar Catholic Church are caught between belief and unbelief. They have no clear picture of how Christianity fits into the modern secular world. The Church has not addressed the matter of agnosticism in an adequate manner, either theologically or pastorally. Before we go further, let us look at the disastrous consequences of living in a meaningless world.

The Consequences of Alienation and Meaninglessness

Feeling alone in the midst of a meaningless world often results in a lot more than existential despair. It has emotional and physical consequences as well. It is far more than a theoretical or purely theological matter. One of Jung's important contributions to modern psychology and theology was his recognition that the inability to believe in anything, or the belief in a meaningless world, can be classified as *disease* or *sickness* and can cause as much damage as childhood trauma, acute tension or a dose of poison. Believing that one has no meaningful place in the universe can result in emotional and physical illness. The very fact that health is linked to meaning and purpose supports the idea that the universe has meaning.

Six devastating emotions may result from the sense of being an alien in a hostile or indifferent universe: fear, anger, stress, depression, loneliness and psychic infection. The first three of these are related. They engage the sympathetic nervous system, so their effects can be traced and monitored quite clearly. First of all there is fear: fear of meaninglessness, fear of extinction at death, fear that we are faced with more than we can handle, fear that no one loves us, fear of sickness, etc. Then there is anger, which is the aggressive reaction to the same threatening feelings. Sometimes it is violent, sometimes smouldering like a slow, unquenchable fire. In anger we turn upon this meaningless world that has betrayed us. We strike back at it in hatred and revenge. And then there is stress, which is the quite understandable result of our belief that we alone have the power to protect ourselves from threat and that we can do this only by our own relentless alertness and energy. In a meaningless world we are faced with an impossible task, and stress is inevitable.

Depression, on the other hand, is giving up in the face of meaninglessness and hopelessness. When there is no friendliness in the universe, there is less reason to expect if from other human beings, and less reason to reach out to others. So we can be overcome with loneliness, being separated from and unrelated to other human beings or any meaning in the universe. Our separation from social meaning can lead to isolation and to loneliness, and when we are lonely, fearful and depressed we are susceptible to psychic infection, to contamination by the fear, anger, depression, stress and hopelessness of others. Thus the problem is compounded. The drugs that have earned the greatest financial reward for their manufacturers are the three leading tranquilizers, which help to dull our fear, stress and even anger by chemical means.

In fear, anger, and stress, and even in guilt (which is related to fear of censure and wrongdoing) we can struggle to hide or destroy or fight on. In depression our inner stance collapses, and we fall into the cesspool in the cellar of our inner being. Rebuilding seems hopeless; we just give up inwardly and outwardly. Loneliness carries something of the quality of depression and may easily lead to depression and suicide. Psychic infection usually strikes below the conscious level and is difficult to deal with consciously.

We can trace the effect of threat from its first registration in the hypothalamus, which is the oldest section of the brain and under little conscious control. Within the last twenty years it has been discovered that when the hypothalmus is stimulated by threat it secretes a measurable chemical into the pituitary gland. The pituitary sets off the entire ductless gland system, and the adrenals in particular, to start the chain of command. Immediately the blood vessels to the stomach and intestinal areas shut down; there is no point digesting our food if our lives are threatened and the blood is needed elsewhere. The heartbeat and the breathing rate increase. The blood pressure rises in order to hurry the blood to the furthest extremities of the body. The bronchial tubes open up, forcing more oxygen into the blood; blood sugar pours out of the liver and other storage depots in the body. These combine to give a burst of energy, so that we can climb a cliff we never could have scaled before or we pick up a rock we couldn't have budged before and bring it down on the head of the charging tiger. The blood-clotting time also goes down, preparing for a possible wound.

What an admirable system this is for the caveperson faced with a tiger. Without conscious intervention, the entire system is mobilized. And if the animal tears the person's arm in its death throes, the cavewoman simply sits down, wrapping her animal skin tunic around the wound, and she does not bleed to death, for the blood-clotting time has diminished.

This is excellent protection for cavepeople, but it is out of place in our modern world. Unfortunately, we have exactly the same physical responses when the fear, anger or stress is directed at a boss who ridicules us, an in-law in the house, a child we can't control, or the threat of living in a meaningless world under the shadow of a nuclear bomb, with only the grave as a goal. And fears and stresses we do not know we have produce more response than those of which we are aware, simply because we can do nothing to counteract them.

If we are constantly afraid, angry or under stress, the entire sympathetic nervous system is constantly stimulated. If the heart continues to pound, it gets tired and can give up. Blood sugar poured out continuously upsets the chemical balance of the blood. A constantly elevated blood pressure does damage to the blood vessels. When the blood-clotting time is maintained at a very low level, blood clots can form within the blood vessels and get lodged in the lower limbs, and we come down with phlebitis; in the coronary vessel around the heart, and we have a coronary thrombosis; in the brain, and we have a cerebral accident. What has been a purely functional reaction has now become an organic disease. Studies have shown that sixty percent of those who have been under continuous stress suffer some serious physical illness within twelve to eighteen months. One of the best simple descriptions of the effects of stress is found in the first chapter of the Simontons' book *Getting Well Again.*

How can we help but be afraid in a world in which there is poverty, violence, war, sickness, no life after death, and no meaning to guide us through to something? We do not quite have all of our wits about us if we are not afraid in such a meaningless world.

We can react to the same conditions with anger or hostility or violence. How can we overcome our burning inner rage unless there is some satisfaction in this life and the hope of some meaning beyond this one? This anger is usually turned upon other human beings, since a meaningless world cannot be attacked. The results of this blind rage let loose in war and pillage, in gossip and nastiness, cannot be calculated.

If we are trying to lay a solid foundation in such a meaningless world with no one to help us but ourselves, stress is an inevitable result, ruining our bodies and driving ourselves and others to distraction.

This brings us to depression, the common cold of modern psychiatry. Antidepressant drugs are not as effective for depression as tranquilizers are for stress, and most other secular therapy has fallen short. But why shouldn't I be depressed if my world view is confined to a materialistic world, if I have received little genuine love and care in this world and have nothing to look forward to in the next. It is no wonder suicide is on the increase all over the Western world. Anyone with any imagination will be depressed within this mind-set. Depression is normal in it. The only final healing for this emotion, which causes a slowdown or shutdown of many bodily processes, is being touched by a center of meaning and concern that is transcendental. Jung put it well when he wrote, "the approach to the numinous is the real therapy."

James Lynch's brilliant book *The Broken Heart* demonstrates the murderous effect of loneliness on the human body, and particularly on the functioning of the heart. Lynch, a professor of psychiatry at the University of Maryland Medical School, takes the Church to task for abandoning its people to a materialistic world view. First the Church capitulated to the idea that science alone heals, and then the churches adopted the stance of objectively assessing faith systems, which robbed people of their confidence in religion. People need to feel part of the caring universe if they are to risk being close to one another.

And lonely, alienated people with no place to turn for meaning or help are subject to psychic infection. They are open to the fears, angers, tensions and despairs of others, as the Simontons have shown over and over again. One of the functions of the Church is to provide a decompression chamber into which we can step out of the negativity and hopelessness so rampant in our society. When the Christian Church is alive and vital it offers a place where we can step into an environment of love, meaning and concern, both human and transhuman. If the salt has lost its savor, of what value is it?

The Nature of Unbelief

How can we avoid these six destructive emotions and their insidious effects and remain within the framework of a meaningless, materialistic world? The answer is simple: we can't. And the tragedy is that most intelligent, educated Western men and women see no way out of the materialistic maze. (It should be noted, however, that studies of the right-brain/left-brain have shown that women are more balanced and less onesided than men and often not as defeated in finding meaning as men.) However, a clear understanding of the process of how we know (known philosophically as epistemology) can lift us out of the flatland of disbelief.

When so many of our contemporaries suffer from the sickness of disbelief there are few more important dimensions of spiritual guidance than having the thread that can lead us out of our materialistic maze. This aspect of spiritual companionship is a specialized ministry, but one of which all spiritual guides need to be aware, even if it is not their particular expertise. Those of us who take up the heavy task of spiritual companionship need the ability to discern this materialistic spiritual malaise and be able to make referrals when they are not competent to deal with this problem themselves. The children of light need to be as intelligent and clear-thinking as the children of this world.

Many years ago, in his Gifford lectures, William James noted that the inability of many people to believe and be converted to religious faith "may in some cases be intellectual in origin. Their religious faculties may be checked in their natural tendency to expand, by beliefs about the world that are inhibitive, the pessimistic and materialistic beliefs, for example, within which so many good souls, who in former times would have freely indulged their religious propensities, find themselves nowadays, as it were, frozen; or the agnostic vetoes upon faith as something weak and shameful, under which so many of us today lie cowering, afraid to use our instincts."[2]

A personal example may make this problem clearer. My brother and I were brought up in the same household. He became a medical doctor and professor of medicine and was trained in the materialistic medicine of the 1930s. He said to me one day, "You know, Morton, I would be very religious if I were to take my frequent religious experiences seriously, but I know from my view of the universe that they can have no meaning."

In the pages that follow I will sketch out a point of view that gives a basis for belief while remaining within the canons of critical understanding and valid thinking. There is an alternative to blind belief and total disbelief. We can have as much confidence in spiritual reality and in the loving God who made both the physical and spiritual dimensions of reality as we have in the material world that is so much with those of us who have been brought up in the materialism of the Western world. Von Hügel provided a sophisticated view of the universe for the Modernist movement in the Roman Catholic Church. Jung has done the same thing for the people who came to him with little or no belief and realized that it was their agnosticism which was making them *sick*. Many of Jung's patients were brilliant scientists who suddenly found that life had lost all meaning; they had lost their ability to cope with life. Obviously, within the scope of this book we can only provide a brief sketch of this understanding of how we know the universe. In other books I have dealt with the subject in greater detail.*

The Inadequacy of Reason Alone

Few people are convinced by purely rational arguments or "proofs" of God and the spiritual world. People have lost faith in both reason and authority as ways to conviction about God and spiritual reality. Why? Because by using reason alone we can prove nearly anything we wish to prove. Hegel "proves" that the final peak unfolding of the human condition was to be found in Prussia in the late 1900s. Husserl complains that the history of philosophy has moved nowhere in the last 2500 years and sets out to establish by rational analysis alone an absolutely certain foundation for modern thinking.

Alan McGlashan, in his delightful and provocative book *Gravity and Levity*, states that "the current conflicts of youth against age and authority are in essence a revolt against *smugness*, against the closed, superior attitude of mind which assumes that somewhere there is always a final truth to be found, if only reason is followed patiently to its conclusion. Youth in some unconscious or intuitive way has tuned in to the

---

* I have discussed this point of view at length in *Encounter With God*, the first chapters of *Afterlife*, and the first chapters of *Prophetic Ministry*. Having a world view that can stand in place of the materialistic one of our age is essential for dealing with the disbelief of our times, but the ability to help the intellectual disbelievers is a special ministry in which individuals need special training. All those doing modern physics must know some calculus, but then there are experts in mathematics who have a special ability; it is the same in spiritual direction.

physicists' discovery that there is no final truth to be found anywhere, that reality in the last resort is ambiguous, open-ended, a recurring balance of contraries."[3] The modern person, of whom the modern youth may well be a harbinger, is simply not convinced by rational arguments alone. Reason that does not point to and result in some experience has little meaning or significance for most modern men and women.

In spite of this, most Christian theology for the last eight centuries has been an attempt to provide absolute certainty by some system of rational thought. There are at least four clearly defined and much used methods of using reason alone.

The *Metaphysics* of Aristotle is an attempt to provide an absolutely certain proof for the existence of God, whom Aristotle conceived to be an unmoved mover of all things. This book should have been entitled *Theology.* Aristotle was a wise man and knew the uncertainty of the inductive method and the unreliability of sense experience. He wanted more certainty than these provided, *hubris* perhaps. He developed the deductive method, which became the bulwark of scholastic theology. Euclidian geometry is the perfect example of this thought. One starts with axioms and proceeds with syllogisms to absolute and certain conclusions. Right up to Vatican II, scholastic, deductive thought was the hallmark of Roman Catholic theology.

Immanuel Kant saw the logical fallacies in deductive thought and pointed them out with relentless clarity. He proposed another way of thinking. He looked for the necessary presuppositions that made possible the very existence of human experience. He saw clearly that logic does not unlock the secrets of either the subjective intellect or the objective physical world. Human knowing and reason come about by the interaction of two unknown realities—a subjective thing-in-itself and an objective thing-in-itself. All we can do is to describe our phenomenal experience, which is the result of this interaction.

Kant was one of the most influential thinkers of all times, and some of his brilliant intuitions anticipated the findings of Einstein. However, he was unconsciously caught in a materialistic world view, and it never occurred to him that there could be any experience not mediated through the physical world. There could be no experience of a spiritual, psychoid or psyche-like realm of being such as Jung suggests. There is only material reality and rational mind. Kant found any idea of extrasensory perception simply amusing, and he made fun of the visionary Swedenborg in his book *The Dreams of a Ghost-Seer.* The effect of Kant on liberal

Christian theology has been enormous. He provides a pervasive uncertainty and no hope of any experience to verify the tenets of Christianity. His attempt to develop a morality is almost humorous.

The uncertainty left by Kant stimulated Hegel to develop his own dialectic. Through this method we can start with any thesis and allow it to turn into its antithesis. This opposition is completed and transformed in a synthesis. This synthesis then provides a new thesis, and the process starts all over again. Through this method Hegel came to believe that all reality was spiritual in content, and that everything was the manifestation of absolute mind. He offered one of the most comprehensive Idealistic systems of thought ever conceived in the West. Marx used the same essential method to develop his theory of dialectical materialism, which is the basis of communist thought. Hegel's thought became the rage of the middle nineteenth century, a landslide reaction to the agnosticism of Kant and to the even more pervasive agnosticism of the naturalistic and materialistic thinking that was sweeping through Europe at that time.

This point of view was picked up and used by theologians against the threat of unbelief rampant around them. Von Hügel was nurtured in the theology of this German Idealism, but he realized in his study of St. Catherine of Genoa that there was no place in this point of view for the actual, concrete, discrete experiences of the Divine Love that St. Catherine undoubtedly had. And so he developed a new philosophical framework and a new method of using reason.

Within Idealism intelligence alone is significant, and much of what Jesus of Nazareth and the Christian tradition stood for was simply ignored. Sitting in his brown leather chair, the truly brilliant thinker like Hegel believed that he could spin out the final nature of the universe with absolute certainty. And there were few to cry that the Emperor was naked.

Still another method of coming to logical certainty about the final nature of things is found in thinkers who would analyze the very nature of experience. Descartes started the history of modern thought with his *Cogito ergo sum* ("I think therefore I am") and precipitated what L. L. Whyte has described as one of the most colossal blunders of modern thought. Husserl and the phenomenological existentialists who follow him—Heidegger and Sartre, Jaspers and Marcel—continue this tradition. Whitehead makes much the same sort of analysis from a background of mathematics and physical science. This kind of thinking has had a profound influence upon modern theology, upon Bultmann and Barth in particular. Again, the idea that there can be an experiential intrusion of the divine into human life and that this can provide the basis of a theology of experience is usually never considered.

The kind of rational analysis that we have been describing convinces very few who are acquainted with the thinking rising out of the developments of modern science. My experience of teaching young people with this background is the same as that of Dr. McGlashan. This dependence on reason alone is also subject to very severe criticism by logical positivists like A. J. Ayer. The positivist position is the logical refinement of the naturalism and materialism of the last century, and it sweeps most metaphysics, as well as most religious theological belief, into the dustbin. However, it shows clearly that we cannot prove the *existence* of any experiential fact. A. O. Lovejoy reveals the logical inadequacies of Whitehead's thinking in his book *The Revolt Against Dualism*.

Is there any alternative to these rational philosophies, which appear to many of us to be so much rational game-playing? Plato, von Hügel, and Jung, as well as many of the recent philosophers of science, think that there is an alternative. To find it, however, we must use our imaginations and break with the presuppositions of the last thousand years of Western thought. We can then begin to see that what we experience is real, but that our understanding and comprehension of what we experience is imperfect. Our knowledge is real, and it grows as we continue to use the learning process that we shall soon describe.

Our experience gives us *real* but indistinct knowledge. First we see the forest from a distance as a green mass. Then as we come closer we see the dark trunks against the green of the leaves. Then we see that the trunks of different trees are distinguishable, and then that no two leaves are the same. If we continue our analysis we come to the physical makeup of the trees and even to the incredible capacity of the chlorophyll to capture the rays of the sun and store the energy while giving off oxygen, which permits the development of animal and human life.

It must be noted that some of the religious thinkers of India came to another conclusion, to which we have already referred. The metaphysics of Hinduism and Buddhism has influenced a great part of the Orient. These religions came to the conclusion that all physical experience is illusion and the creation of mind and ego. Some even suggest that all inner images are illusory too, and only the imageless void brings reality and salvation. Others teach that the inner images are real, and that we can come to an ecstatic union with them as we learn to become detached from the outer physical world, which is produced by an illusion-making mind. This point of view has similarities to German Idealism and to the teachings of Mary Baker Eddy. It is popular today as many Westerners turn in despair to Eastern religion. As we have already indicated, but need to emphasize once again, the direction of spiritual training, education and guidance within these traditions is *very* different from what we are proposing.

Von Hügel, Plato, and Subatomic Science

Von Hügel had an encyclopedic knowledge of the world of the late nineteenth century. He was much impressed by the genuine advances made in nearly all the physcial sciences. He came to believe that the philosophers and theologians had tried to take a shortcut to knowledge, a shortcut that did not exist, and had landed in a bog, and that all of us could learn much by observing and imitating the *essential method* of the physical sciences. What is this method?

First of all, it consists of the slow, tedious, painstaking process of observation and comparison of the data on the subject under consideration. Then comes a second step, by which one comes to a hypothesis as to how and why these data are related. This is not done by reason, but by intuition and imagination. Paul Feyerabend, one of the most respected students of the philosophy of science, suggests that if we wish to produce creative scientists, the development of their imaginations is even more important than the development of their purely logical and rational capacities.

Once a hypothesis is framed we use our best powers of rational analysis and deduction to sketch out the implications of our theory. The painstaking observation and collection of detailed data are continued, often by scientific experiment. When some of the data of experience do not agree with the theory that has been formulated, and these facts continue to appear, then a new hypothesis is required. And the whole process begins again. A new hypothesis is "dreamed up"; it is subjected to further testing according to the logical implications; there is further searching for the data that do not fit, and so the growth of knowledge goes on.

Von Hügel suggests that this understanding cannot be given in the classroom alone, but must be experienced in the laboratory. A good liberal arts college provides the same emphasis. We learn more fully by going through the actual painstaking process than by reading or thinking about it. Actual study of the hard sciences is almost necessary to understand this process. Once we have broken free of dogmatic rationalism that has had a stranglehold on Western thought, we can begin to see that the data of the five senses do not exhaust the gamut of possible experiences.

A study of the development of science during the last century will show how inadequate the materialistic hypothesis really is. No study has summarized this development better than T. S. Kuhn's *The Structure of Scientific Revolutions*. Kuhn is both a trained physicist and the most influential living historian of science. For those dealing with the doubts and agnosticism of men and women in our age, this book is a must. Kuhn shows that modern science does not provide nearly the certainty that scientists had formerly thought. In his Gifford Lectures, *Physics and Philosophy*, Werner Heisenberg, one of the greatest revolutionaries of modern science, provided a profound study of the philosophical and religious implications of this revolution. He writes that science has become so skeptical that it has even become skeptical of its own skepticism, and has discarded many concepts that it thought were final and certain. I quote his impressive statement:

> One of the most important features of the development and analysis of modern physics is the experience that the concepts of natural language, vaguely defined as they are, seem to be more stable in expansion of knowledge than the precise terms of scientific language, derived as an idealization from only limited groups of phenomena. This is in fact not surprising since the concepts of natural language are formed by the immediate connection with reality; they represent reality. . . .
> Keeping in mind the intrinsic stability of the concepts of natural language in the process of scientific development, one sees that—after the experience of modern physics—our attitude towards concepts like mind or the human soul or life or God will be different from that of the nineteenth century, because these concepts belong to the natural language and have therefore immediate connection with reality.[4]

The work of Kurt Gödel, which is described in Nagel and Newman, *Gödel's Proof*, demonstrates that even mathematics does not provide absolute certainty. In 1933, as a young man of only twenty-seven, Gödel detected some flaws in what was considered the final word in mathematical theory, *Principia Mathematica*, by Russell and Whitehead. Using their methods, he demonstrated that two quite different answers can be obtained from the same group of mathematical data. The implications of this discovery, which has been replicated by several other mathematicians, are most impressive. I was first given Gödel's proof by a mathematician involved in computer programming. He pointed out that since computers operate on these very principles of mathematics, they sometimes spit out completely extraneous answers.

Gödel believed that mathematical concepts were perceived by intuition in the same way that Plato thought that the Ideas were grasped. If it is true that even our mathematical reasoning can be faulty and needs to be checked against reality and experience, how much more must we beware of rational speculation and metaphysics that soar off into intellectual fantasy. Those who would *reason* God out of experience and existence cannot be taken any more seriously than those who reason God into reality.

The work of Jerome Frank, Roger Walsh, Jung, and many others has shown the importance of faith and the value of spiritual disciplines for the health of the mind, emotions and body. We have already mentioned the sociological work of Andrew Greeley, who gave evidence of the correlation between emotional maturity and mystical experience. Modern anthropologists realize that one cannot observe a people or culture from the point of view of Western materialism and perceive all that is going on. The work of Loren Eiseley and Pierre Teilhard de Chardin have shown that natural selection does not account for all the data of biological development.

Parapsychology has finally come of age and gives further evidence of nonsensory data. In 1969, after years of rejection, the Parapsychological Association was accepted into the prestigious American Association for the Advancement of Science. This acceptance is an indication that the scientific community has come to believe that human beings are endowed with capacities to know in addition to those of the five senses. Charles Panati wrote one of the best descriptions of the research in that field in *Supersenses*. I have drawn out the implications of this data for theology in *The Christian and the Supernatural*. It is important not to reject some of the stories of the New or Old Testament as mythological, as some biblical critics have done, when the same events are discussed seriously at the present by students of parapsychology. One of the most delightful discussions of the findings of this field was written by the Dean of the Department of Engineering at Princeton University, Robert G. Jahn. It was published as a *Princeton Alumni Weekly Special Report* entitled "Psychic Process, Energy Transfer, and Things That Go Bump in the Night."[5]

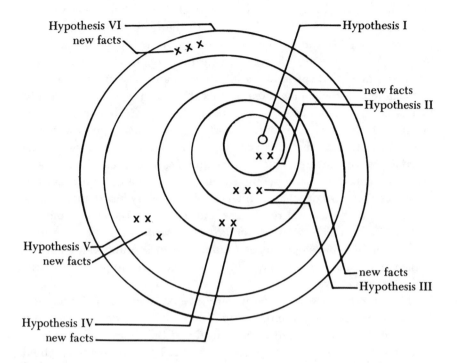

Hypothesis I: Greek science finds the universe composed of earth, water, air and fire.

Hypothesis II: Starting from alchemy, chemists, astronomers and physicists find various elements and discover principles of physical organization, seeing the universe as matter totally determined by laws.

Hypothesis III: Atomic physicists and others from Einstein on, find matter infinitely diverse in structure and organization, and see the universe as matter *and* energy governed by probability rather than by deterministic laws.

Hypothesis IV: Freud discovers psychic causation and, still holding to determinism, sees nonmaterial elements in the universe.

Hypothesis V: Teilhard de Chardin and Jung find that life develops in relation to an infinite variety of material *and* nonmaterial experiences, rather than being causally determined, and Jung suggests a new model of the universe to explain human consciousness and energy.

Hypothesis VI: The Risen Christ is the best description of the purposeful and healing reality that others have observed in the universe.

Freud was one of the great thinkers of all times. He showed the reality of the nonphysical realm by demonstrating that mental or psychic events can have an influence on each other without ever passing through the physical world. He also wrote late in life that if he were younger he would have taken up the study of parapsychology. Though he was still stuck in determinism, he had broken with the materialism of his time. Jung, following his lead, then went on to propose a vision of the universe in which both physical and psychoid (spiritual) realities have a place. He also maintained that spiritual reality is not meaningless and that anyone who will look at the data will realize that there is an aspect of this reality that is bent on helping us human beings come to religious meaning, health and wholeness. It is only a short step from this hypothesis to the Christian statement that this principle of love and healing was incarnated in Jesus of Nazareth, that he died and rose again from the dead and was experienced by many people living in that age and throughout the ages since. Teilhard de Chardin offers a similar theory based upon his anthropological studies and reflections. Huston Smith offers still another synthesis in his recent book, *Beyond the Post-Modern Mind.*

This complex development can culminate in a sound Christian hypothesis and can be diagrammed in a somewhat oversimplified way as I have shown on page 75.

This is the process by which we are given a more complete and detailed picture of the nature of reality. The Crucifixion-Resurrection also speaks to the reality of evil in our world and the necessity of having a place for it in our schema of the total universe. There are many psychoid contents, some of which appear to be autonomous and act like spiritual beings with a life of their own. These Jung called archetypes. Our task then is to move out of the control of evil in both the inner and outer worlds and allow ourselves to be reached and transformed by the Holy Spirit or the Risen Christ so that we can become ambassadors of this beneficent reality. Both the realm of sense experience and that of nonsensory experience are permeated by the creative influences of Spirit and by the destructive downdrag of evil. All of these elements are presented in the diagram on page 77.

Varieties of Disbelief

People reject the meaning that religion offers for many different reasons. It is very important in guiding people through the quagmires of agnosticism and atheism to listen to them and find out the reasons for their disbelief. I was raised in a household with a mother who continued to believe in spite of the agnostic ridicule and hostility of a

PHILOSOPHICAL AND RELIGIOUS WORLD VIEW

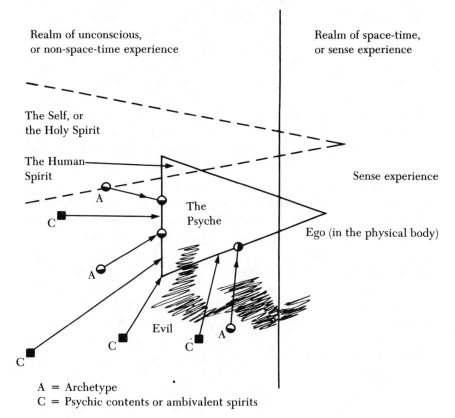

A = Archetype
C = Psychic contents or ambivalent spirits

father who was consistently enmeshed in the rational materialism of the late nineteenth and early twentieth centuries. I also found this kind of agnosticism rampant among the students at Notre Dame.

One student wrote the following reflection after a class in which we were dealing with the implication of modern science for religious belief: "I had received an excellent training in the sciences from grade school on, and I was operating on the assumption that science would inevitably discover everything that could be possibly known about reality. I was a positivist without knowing it." Then he was led by a physics teacher, "through Heisenberg's uncertainty principle, and in doing so the ultimate mysteriousness of reality, even physical reality, was revealed to me. It is significant that the intellectual experience that was probably the most important experience in allowing me to reconcile myself with my religion came not in a religion course, but in a physics course."

In dealing with students with this kind of attitude at Notre Dame I found that they had been given a materialistic point of view in their hard and soft sciences and meaningless existentialism in literature (Sartre and Camus); no one offered them a well-thought-out alternative. I discovered that the kind of understanding that I have sketched out above opened a way for many of them to return to the sacramental and religious life of Christianity. I had also discovered much the same enthusiasm on the part of the sophisticated adults for whom Ollie Backus provided this same kind of understanding in the parish in which I was rector for twenty years.

I also encountered a quite different kind of disbelief at Notre Dame. It was a defensive or reactionary agnosticism, common among the premedical students with whom I had a class entitled "Death, Dying and Suffering." Most of these students had been negatively conditioned by well-meaning but judgmental missioners, who had vividly described the agonies of hell. Consequently, the students ruled out all religious belief in order to be rid of the fear of the afterlife that had been conditioned in them. For these students the skeptical view of existentialism and positivistic science was actually a godsend, because it gave them a way out of being terrified! This kind of unbelief was quite different from that of those who were caught intellectually in a meaningless rationalism and could see no consistent way out. These students were reacting emotionally to unconscious *belief of the wrong kind*. Ministering to them required both the patience to uncover their basic emotional response and the intellectual tools to undo their positivistic attitude.

Still another variety of disbelief is well exemplified by a very intelligent minister who had been reared in a rationalistic and conservative church. He was in the depth of depression; he had lost his faith and was suicidal. He could not conceive how a God of love could permit all the evil in the world and in his own life. We worked together for many months, and finally he began to realize that physical reality does not fit into our neat logical categories. When he absorbed the truths that light has the inconsistent properties of both particles and waves and that even mathematics is not absolutely certain, then he could lay down his logical, religious bone and turn to the God of love that he had experienced. He could let that love lift him out of the evil that he could not understand but from which he could be delivered. However, until his thinking processes were straightened out he could neither feel a sense of meaning nor get well.

There is still another form of atheism common among those of the psychiatric profession who have drunk deeply of Freud's pessimistic view of nature. Although he believed that there was a psychic dimension of reality, it was either a blind downpull by a suicidal death wish, an irrational sexual desire or an unreasonable and repressive superego. Only human reason possessed any meaning or hope, and this died with our bodies. For him all religion was an immature, regressive return to the womb. He presented this point of view in his brilliant book *The Future of an Illusion*. Most in the counseling profession have been influenced either by the unconscious materialism of behaviorism or the conscious skepticism of Freud, and so few professionals of the helping professions offer much aid in combating disbelief. Rather, I have found that many of them need this help themselves.

In his glorification of the naked will to power and his ridicule of the traditional Christian virtues of humility and love, Nietzsche sketches out with clarity and force and beauty the ideal of making one's own will supreme and taking from life whatever one can get. This became the belief system of Nazism. I have already suggested that this kind of Christian disbelief is not so much total agnosticism as it is a worship of a power-hungry god like Wotan. Tragically, many of us on some level of our being have more than peripheral adherence to this deity. Most international politics (and much national politics) is based on an unconscious acceptance of this attitude. History shows us the futility and disaster in which this belief usually results. We can be grateful to Nietzsche for presenting so clearly what is so common among us.

The Healing of Disbelief

On the whole, most of us are more consistent in living out the implications of our fundamental beliefs about reality than we ordinarily realize. If our rockbottom view of the universe (whether held consciously or unconsciously) is that of deterministic materialism, it is almost impossible for us to take the religious life, and the Christian life in particular, seriously. We can opt for blind faith and throw away our rationality entirely, as is done in most fundamentalistic sects, but this is not mature Christianity. *It is possible* to present the Christian message in a way that violates no one's intelligence.

Paradoxically, I have discovered that angry and hostile atheists and agnostics are often far easier to bring to a vital Christian faith than most nominal and conventional Christians. These angry ones are at least facing the meaninglessness of the current world view and are aware of evil, which so many conventional Christians sweep under the rug in order to avoid dealing with their unconscious doubts. When approached with concerned caring and presented with a view such as we have sketched out above, agnostics often welcome the chance to bring meaning into their lives. The person who would accompany them on their journey of rediscovery needs to be wiser and more intelligent than the secular world and very patient and caring. Love alone is not enough for these people.

We conventional Christians often find ourselves faced with the shallowness of our religious convictions during times of personal crisis: at times of sickness, when facing our own deaths or the deaths of those whom we love, when confronted with financial ruin, rejection, jail, divorce or any of a thousand other disasters. How important it is to realize that there is a conventional Christian buried in the depth of each of us. If spiritual guides are known as people who are caring and not judging, people will open up to them. But again, caring is not enough. Unless these guides can provide some sound intellectual framework for belief it is difficult to rescue people from superficial, conventional Christianity. Abbé Huvelin,combined both of these qualities for many of those whom he directed, and his friend and follower von Hügel did the same for those who came to him.

If indeed there is such a world of spiritual reality, how do we get in touch with it? This is the next subject before us. It is an area of crucial importance for spiritual guides. There are many different ways in which the spiritual world breaks through upon us. Some are to be recommended, and some are to be avoided at all costs. Again, different people have very different ways and different needs.

NOTES

1. *International Herald Tribune*, Monday, June 14, 1982, p. 6. These are the important data, rather than the Gallup poll, in which the great majority of Americans state that they believe in God and do nothing about it. Most Europeans are more candid about their beliefs.

2. William James, *The Varieties of Religious Experience*, p. 204.

3. Alan McGlashan, *Gravity and Levity* (Boston: Houghton Mifflin Co., 1976), p. 33.

4. Werner Heisenberg, *Physics and Philosophy: The Revolution in Modern Science* (New York: Harper and Row, 1958), pp. 200 ff.

5. *Princeton Alumni Weekly Special Report*, Dec. 4, 1978.

Chapter 6

THE NATURE AND VARIETY
OF RELIGIOUS EXPERIENCE

Nearly thirty years ago I began to understand that we human beings have access to at least two quite different dimensions of reality. I also began to realize that Jesus and the early Church spoke of more than one dimension of reality. As I began to be more comfortable in both of these aspects of "beingness" and to see the naturalness of both, people began to knock on my door and ask me to discuss not only their problems with them, but also their spiritual journeys. Many of them complained, like St. Teresa, that it was difficult to find anyone who would accompany them on their spiritual journeys with understanding, someone who could give suggestions, encouragement, comments and warnings of danger.

I was a mere beginner on the inner journey, but I had started a practice of prayer and quiet and reading the Bible and the spiritual masters. In addition to this, I had been given a fairly good theological background by my reading of von Hügel and others. As I worked through some of my more glaring psychological problems, I began to see more and more clearly the wide and fuzzy line that separates psychological health from sickness. With the help of my Jungian friends, and again with the understanding provided by von Hügel, I was given a world view that made sense of what I knew about this the material world and what I was learning about the spiritual world. And last of all, I had come to see myself in depth; what I saw contained a large portion of ugliness, fragmentedness and evil. I saw how much I had missed the mark, and I realized that I was in no position to judge any other human being for anything.

I certainly hung out no shingle stating that I was ready to receive directees for spiritual guidance, but to my surprise people began to knock at my door. They wanted to tell me of their spiritual experiences. They wanted a companion on the inner journey, someone who knew that it was a serious undertaking, who knew that it was hard and dangerous work, and who realized that it could even lead into the destructiveness of the abyss. The numbers of those seeking fellowship increased over the years, until a major portion of my time was taken up listening to people on their spiritual journeys. From persons of all ages I heard about religious experiences of every variety and kind.

About the same time I came to know Agnes Sanford and was invited to lecture at the Schools of Pastoral Care that she and her clergyman husband had started. With the publication of my book *Tongue Speaking*, the invitations to lecture increased, and they continued to increase as my other books were released. One of the subjects that attracted the greatest enthusiasm was the gifts of the spirit, the various ways in which the experience of God and the spiritual world was expressed among us. These groups with whom I talked were eager to add new dimensions to the list I had, further ways in which the spiritual world is known to us. I am much indebted to those who have told me about so many of the experiences I shall describe. I started with five basic experiences, which I had culled from the twelfth chapter of St. Paul's first letter to the Corinthians. By the time I wrote *The Christian and the Supernatural*, the list had grown to seven. In *Transcend*, written four years ago, it had nearly doubled, and at present I have come to thirty-six distinguishable ways through which we come in touch with this spiritual domain. As a matter of fact, we have to make a solid effort to avoid the experience and knowledge of this dimension of reality.

A Theoretical Base *

Before we start to look at the list of experiences in detail, let us look back at the suggestion made by Aldous Huxley and described briefly in the second chapter. After experimenting with a mind-expanding drug and reflecting upon it (which most users of these drugs do not do), he concluded that we human beings are open to a vast array of experiences, but that our total preoccupation with sense perception blocks out most of these data and keeps us bound to the physical world so that we can survive biologically as animals and grow up as human beings. He also suggests that most of us are satisfied with the measly trickle of experience

* This section of several pages is somewhat technical, and if it is difficult to understand, pass on to the experiences themselves and return to this discussion later.

that remains after the total possibilities of experience have been funneled through the "reducing valve" of our sense organs, brain and nervous system.

Huxley then goes on to say that the problem is compounded as we express this reduced awareness of the universe in "those symbol-systems and implicit philosophies which we call language." Languages are both a great help and a hindrance: a help as they give us "access to the accumulated records of other people's experience," a hindrance in that they make us victims of a one-sided view of reality by confirming us in the idea that this reduced awareness is the *only experience to be had*. Also, we get into the habit of confusing concepts for data and "words for actual things."

As a matter of fact, different cultures have developed a variety of words for those things that are important to them and have few words for what they consider unimportant or "nonexistent" aspects of reality. The Eskimos have a great many words to describe different kinds of snow. The Greeks have twelve different words to describe their intercourse with a nonphysical dimension of reality. The Hindus have twenty to thirty words to describe various aspects of spiritual experience; on the other hand, they have few words to deal with different aspects of physical matter. People of European extraction have dozens of words for matter and have come up with over one hundred different elements of it. The English language also contains at least thirty expressions to convey psychological depression. However, English has only one moth-eaten and much abused word to describe our relationship with a spiritual dimension of reality: the word *mysticism*.

Huxley goes on to suggest that in the language of Western culture what "is called 'this world' is the universe of reduced awareness, expressed, and, as it were, petrified by language." There are other worlds of nonphysical experience, but our training and our language keep us from experiencing them. The Hindu, on the other hand, is oblivious of the different worlds of experience available within and through the material world. Each culture has its own unique "red six of spades."

"Most people, most of the time, know only what comes through the reducing valve and is consecrated as genuinely real by the local language. Certain persons, however, seem to be born with a kind of by-pass that circumvents the reducing valve. In others temporary by-passes may be acquired either spontaneously, or as the result of deliberate 'spiritual exercises,' or through hypnosis, or by means of drugs." Huxley enumerates only five categories of experience in his list of ways of bypassing sense experience, and it is surprising that he does not mention the dream, which is the most common and natural of all those experiences that circumvent the reducing valve. His description of these methods is important and suggestive, but it needs further differentiation.

Huxley concludes his reflections with these words: "Through these permanent or temporary by-passes there flows, not indeed the perception 'of everything that is happening everywhere in the universe' (for the by-pass does not abolish the reducing valve, which still excludes the total content of Mind at Large), but something more than, and above all something different from, the carefully selected utilitarian material which our narrowed, individual minds regard as a complete, or at least sufficient picture of reality."[1] It is important to realize that opening ourselves to the awareness of these other levels of experience need not dull our perception of this physical world. Indeed, just the opposite is often the case; these nonsensory experiences often give insight and understanding into the reality and complexity of our material world.

Mulling over the thirty-six distinguishable (although in some cases overlapping) experiences that have come to my attention, I have classified them in five groups in order to bring some order into their vast variety. The first category stands by itself. This consists of the *spontaneous religious experiences,* which come unsought and sometimes are not desired again, and experiences of discrete nonphysical "entities" other than the divine, as well as specific nonphysical contents. The second group I would describe as those "natural" and ordinary experiences that can carry with them an intimation or revelation of another dimension of reality. The third class of experience would include all those experiences that are sought for through the use of religious methods. Sometimes these religious experiences, even though we are seeking them, still have the quality of spontaneity. This is a large classification. The fourth category of experience is that of the neurotic and psychotic. These are "natural," but stand in a category by themselves. The last group consists of those experiences that are sought for, but which, unless well understood and hedged around with safeguards, can be quite dangerous.

Spontaneous Experiences

Nearly everyone knows some example of the appearance of the divine presence to someone who was not seeking anything of the sort. Sometimes this experience brought about a total change in the direction of the life of the one who experienced it. St. Paul and St. Francis of Assisi are classic examples. Andrew Greeley has shown how much more common these experiences are than we have been inclined to believe. William James gives case after case that resulted in the total transformation of the person who had this kind of "visionary" experience.

James called this kind of meeting with the divine a mystical experience, and he described four characteristics of these experiences:

1. First of all, they are ineffable. They are genuine experiences and not just ideas. Like all experiences, they cannot be described adequately to those who have never experienced them. However, two or more who have had this kind of experience can begin to communicate about them.

2. They are noetic; they are states of knowledge. They convey understanding, knowledge, illuminations, revelations and significance. They are a genuine meeting with something beyond the boundaries of our own limited psyches. They carry a strange sense of authority for most of those who have them.

3. They are transient. They seldom last for more than a few seconds or minutes, and almost never for more than half an hour. St. Teresa speaks again and again of the momentary nature of her deepest experiences. Those who try to remain continuously in this state can cause themselves innumerable psychological problems. When we repress our humanness to seek out such contact with the divine, we open ourselves to neurosis and worse.

4. They are passive. Those who have experienced them maintain that they are given, not achieved through our own effort. Like trees reaching for the sun, there is nothing that we can do until the revolution of the earth brings the life-giving sun. We are the responders in mystical experience, not the agents.

To these four characteristics I would add the two qualities of the holy, the *mysterium tremendum,* that Rudolf Otto provides in *The Idea of the Holy.* Otto calls such experiences numinous.

5. There is an overwhelming attraction that we feel in the presence of this "other." We are drawn towards the reality in spite of ourselves. It satisfies something within us that we did not know existed. Through this encounter our lives can be transformed and raised to a new level.

6. And there is also a holy fear. That which we encounter is more than we can cope with. We are dizzy, as when we look into the depth of the Grand Canyon for the first time. Our sense of nothingness becomes oppressive, and our faultiness seems infinite. We are overwhelmed with awe. I conclude this description of mystical experience with three categories of my own.

7. This experience can be experienced as a dazzling darkness or in quite clear and distinct images. It may come as a resplendent Risen Christ, or an overpowering light, or a sense of presence or even an imageless merging of ourselves with "holiness." The experience can be perceived either as imageless or through the clearest of images, depending upon whether we are at that moment at the focus of detachment or of attachment, as suggested by von Hügel. These two aspects of experience are complementary, not opposed to one another.

8. For many within the Christian, Sufi and Hasidic traditions, there is an experience of ravishing love, of meeting a Divine Lover whose justice is consummated in self-giving love. St. Catherine of Genoa cries out in her deepest mystical experience, "Oh, Love, Oh, Love, Oh, Love. . . . "

9. There is yet another quality of this love. In my own deepest experiences and in the many conversion experiences described by William James there is a sense of being saved from something by this love. When in darkness and inner torment I found myself lost in the pit and set upon by darkness, I have experienced a compassion that responded to my expressed need and lovingly lifted me out of my inner torment. Those whose primary experience is one of detachment seldom express their mystical perception in this way.

There is little reason to multiply examples of this kind of experience. In reading the lives of the saints, both Eastern and Western, in reading the writings of the religious masters that have been compiled and published under the editorship of Richard Payne by Paulist Press, in listening to the experiences of ordinary people seeking companionship and in examining our own experience, we find innumerable examples. One of the most helpful exercises in making ourselves aware of the vast number and gamut of our experiences is to take several periods of an hour or so, and one by one list all the experiences that seem to carry many of the qualities that we have described above. In a later chapter I will give a personal example of this kind of saving experience.

Some of these spontaneous experiences break in upon us whether we want them or not. Acknowledging them often helps us be more open to the spiritual-psychoid realm of experience. These experiences can be essentially ambivalent, innocuous, deeply destructive (demonic) or divine. Having such experiences is not as important as how we regard them, how we discern them and which ones we open ourselves to. Much of religious practice in meditation and ritual is designed to help us open ourselves to the creative aspects of this dimension. The final value of all positive experiences of the Holy, of God, is how we integrate them into our lives and what fruits they bear in us. From the Christian point of view, experiences of God that do not bear the fruit of increased love are either from the wrong source or have been misused. We shall see that psychosis can open us to this dimension, but the psychotic is neither able to discriminate among experiences nor to integrate the creative ones into their lives.

Four More Spontaneous Experiences of the Beyond

One of the pitfalls in discussing mystical experience, one into which William James himself slips at times, is the idea that mysticism and experience of the nonphysical dimension necessitate an abandonment of our personal, subjective, perceiving selves, and that all such experiences are essentially incommunicable. There are four other experiences of nonphysical reality that can be clear and distinct and that still exhibit at least the first seven of the qualities I have described above.

These have been described by Raymond Moody in *Life Beyond Life* and by Karlis Osis in his book *At the Hour of Death*. I have summarized them in *Afterlife*. During one single day three people came into my office at St. Luke's Church and described experiences of this nature.

The most common spontaneous experience of the nonphysical realm after the specifically religious ones is an encounter with the deceased, who from the point of view of any decent materialism should not be experienceable at all. If these individuals exist, they certainly do so in no known physical way. They can be experienced in dreams, in visions of sight or sound, or even smell or touch, or in a sense of presence. These meetings often have all the profound reality of a physical meeting, and they often make a tremendous impact on those who have them. They are sometimes accompanied by the sense of an electric, awe-inspiring numinosity that so often goes along with the experiences of this nonphysical dimension of reality. Indeed, one of the ways to distinguish imagined encounters with the deceased from the real McCoy is by the presence of this sense of numinosity. Those who would deny this kind of experience because it does not fit into their materialistic world view are misguided and unfortunate folk who are caught in the superstition of materialism. Examples of these meetings with the deceased are found from Plato to Tolstoy to Jung. The person interested in further data should read the section devoted to the subject in *Afterlife*. It is far better, however, to allow these experiences to be spontaneous rather than to seek them through mediums; dealing with seances can get us into very muddy and dangerous water.

The spiritual guide certainly needs to be aware of these common experiences and should treat them as a matter of course, neither denying their reality nor attaching too much importance to them.

And then there is another group of encounters that can come through dreams, visions, automatic writing or similar activities, or through imagination. Sometimes simple facts unrelated to the individuals having the experiences emerge: people, places, dates and apparently irrelevant pieces of information. Those who believe in reincarnation believe that these facts and people relate to the former lives of those who have these experiences. We can explain these occurrences, however, by the simpler hypothesis of the collective unconscious offered by Jung. Experience reaching into all time and space is available in the inexhaustible bank of the unconscious or spiritual realm. Those who are open to this data bank often receive experiences of this kind, experiences which may be meaningful or not.

In still another kind of encounter, we can come into the hands of spiritual "guides" who speak to or through individuals. Most of the time they speak rather banal things, but sometimes they produce material sounding very much like a kind of watered-down Hinduism or theosophy. Sometimes whole religious systems are given this way. The Koran was dictated to Mohammed in much this way. All such "guide-given" material should be treated with careful discernment, and *never* swallowed whole.

Still another category could be described as archetypal experiences, to use Jung's word. These are ambivalent power centers of the psychoid realm, which can give incredible power and wisdom and which, on the other hand, can possess us and make us demonic. The Greek Gods are perfect examples of archetypal power, as are Shiva and Kali in the Hindu pantheon.

One last category of this kind of encounter is that of meeting and being overwhelmed and terrified by the numinous darkness. We find this in the terror dream, with its sense of a destructive presence. We awake knowing we have encountered evil. As Jung once said that he did not need to believe in God because he *knew* him, so I would say I *know* this dark reality. It is well portrayed by the colorful dancers in the Balinese Barong Dance or in the fearsome deities in Hindu and Buddhist temples, as well as in the blood-curdling descriptions of *The Tibetan Book of the Dead*.

Because of our Western refusal to believe in such dark reality we are all the more subject to its ravages.

The near-death experience is well described by Moody. Jung wrote a full chapter concerning his own experience of this state in *Memories, Dreams, Reflections.* Here individuals at the verge of death suddenly find themselves in an out-of-the-body state. They often describe a similar progression of experiences: hearing themselves declared dead, a loud noise, being led through a tunnel, being able to observe their own lifeless bodies. Sometimes they then meet their deceased friends and family and find themselves in a place of indescribable greenness and beauty. Some of them report meeting a "being of light" expressing love such as I have described above. Then they come to a boundary, and they know that if they pass beyond that point they can never return to their bodies. Often, when they wake up, they have a sense of life's meaning and value and ongoingness that most of them never had before, and they never lose it. Quite obviously, one cannot recommend this experience as one to be sought.

I once visited a young man in the hospital during a serious illness. Many years later, when I described the data of the near-death experience about which I had written in *Afterlife*, he smiled and told me that he had experienced just such a series of events at one point when the doctors thought he had died. Accounts of this kind upset people caught in a superstitious materialism, and their only recourse is ridicule. Consequently, most people will not talk about such experiences unless they know that their listeners have open minds. Books continue to pour out from scientists and medical doctors convinced against their wills of the authenticity of these experiences.[2]

Although some people have had these openings to another dimension when they only *thought* they were in danger and were actually unharmed, most people have known this kind of invasion of nonphysical reality in an acute physical crisis. This leads us to the fourth kind of encounter with psychoid reality. This is known as the out-of-the-body experience or the OOBE. People with this experience seem to be able to detach their psychic natures from their bodies and wander around in physical and psychic "space." Sometimes they simply observe physical things that the ordinary person cannot observe: the tops of moldings, the reverse side of a bulletin board, or an event some miles distant. However, at other times they report meeting with the souls of the deceased or other spiritual entities. I have had close contact with a young man who was invaded by such experiences and who was much relieved when Agnes Sanford gave him a method of releasing himself from these spontaneous experiences. As long as he could not control these states he had a sense of being quite strange and different. There are some people who offer methods of inducing these experiences. However, except for experimental use and under closely supervised controls, we may be teasing a tiger if we just play around with OOBE.

Twenty Natural Experiences of Nonphysical Reality

I have already indicated that the barrier between the physical and the psychoid aspects of experience is far less distinct than we ordinarily think. Once we have a view of reality that has a place for a spiritual dimension, we can begin to see that many people are touched by this dimension in quite common and ordinary experiences. Many of these experiences have been used by the religions of humankind as an aspect of their deliberate practice, but they occur and bring intimations of something beyond their ordinary banal meaning whether they are part of religious ritual or not. In some cultures, of which the Balinese is an excellent sophisticated example, the religious and secular aspects of life are so intermingled and intertwined that it is difficult to say which aspects are secular and which are religious. Indeed, these words have little meaning. The Christian culture of the high Middle Ages had the same quality. Some Muslim societies share in this interpenetration of the religious and secular. These religions use images and rituals to convey the divine and are highly kataphatic.

We are far less entirely materialistic than we usually believe. The following list enumerates many of the ways in which we participate in more than purely materialistic existence whether we seek it or not, whether we like it or not.

1. Those who will take the trouble to examine the data will find that *psi* phenomena are a fact of experience and that nearly everyone of us has had some experience of one or more of them. There are first of all experiences of extrasensory perception, known in alphabetic lingo as ESP, and psychokinesis, in which the human psyche apparently can have a direct influence on matter. Dr. J. B. Rhine, the first serious researcher in this area, recently said that there was no need to do further experimenting to show that such things happen, but only to find out what they mean.

ESP consists of five different kinds of perception:

Telepathy is the most common. It is thought transferred from one mind to another without being conveyed by any known physical means. Most of us have written a letter to someone who is not a regular correspondent, only to find that a letter has crossed in the mail to us from them, or we have picked up the phone to find the person whom we were about to call calling us.

Clairvoyance is the experience of observing events separated from us by some distance. There are numerous common examples of these occurrences, and they have also been checked through rigorous experimentation by Rhine and others. The experience of *déjà vu* (French for "already seen") is probably related. It is the sense of seeing a scene for the first time and feeling that it is already familiar, perhaps because we have seen it before through clairvoyance.

Retrocognition is the experience of perceiving one event or a series of them out of the recent or further past and living through them as if they were present at this moment.

Precognition is the experience of perceiving events before they happen. While other experiences are difficult to understand within a strict materialism, precognition simply blows the materialistic mind, and yet these experiences are frequently recorded and have even been produced experimentally.

Perception of nonembodied contents and personalities has been discussed at some length in the last section.

Psychokinesis can be observed in plants and animals, but particularly in some human beings. PK, as it is known in ESP circles, can be consciously willed by some gifted people. When the experience occurs unconsciously it is called a poltergeist. Psychic healing is the release of psychokinetic energy directed towards the restoration and healing of some diseased organism, human or animal.

In *The Christian and the Supernatural*, I have gathered together some of the more important data from this field and tried to point out the significance of them. The implications of this data are devastating to a materialistic determinism, to say the least.

While I was teaching at the University of Notre Dame, which was operated by the Order of the Holy Cross, it became known that I had some knowledge in this area. I often received referrals from priests of that order who ran parishes in South Bend. Sometimes their parishioners had experiences of this kind. The priests were at a loss to know what to say to them, and so they often sent them on to me. These people found their experiences frightening and needed reassurance that there was nothing wrong with them and that these experiences were not of the Evil One. It was particularly frightening when they foresaw the death of someone close to them, or even a stranger. My usual advice was to pay as little attention to these experiences as possible, to realize that they were perfectly *natural* happenings, and to come back if they found the experiences oppressive. Usually that was all that was required.

In discerning the nature of this kind of experience it is wise to see how well the individuals relate to space and time. When the person has good contact with the environment and has real relationships with other people, there is little or no danger, but one sign of psychotic breakdown can be that patients report ESP abilities and enormous powers of the mind.

It is important to treat these experiences as a matter of course, neither rejecting them out of hand (or looking for psychosis) or being overimpressed with them. When put in proper perspective within an adequate world view they can be meaningful, and even helpful experiences. Gerald May offers excellent advice in *Care of Mind Care of Spirit* about the spiritual direction of those with these experiences. "Extrasensory and parapsychological experiences need to be evaluated not so much on the basis of their actual validity or nature as in terms of how seriously one takes them." He goes on to say that they are increasingly developed and noted as people grow in spiritual practice: "Usually such experiences are more distressing than exciting for the individual because they provide extra information without any real guidelines as to how to use this information."[3]

2. Powerful emotion can frequently open us to more than the physical dimension of experience. Undoubtedly the appearance of deceased people at the time of their deaths is in part due to the tremendous emotional charge that dying releases. When the experiments of Dr. Rhine were being checked in various places around the world, only some experimenters were able to replicate his results. He was accused of falsifying his data. Then it was discovered that subjects were only able to keep up outstanding *psi* results as long as they were interested, as long as they were emotionally involved. One of the variables necessary for the production of significant *psi* data is emotional involvement. Strong emotion appears to break us out of a total encapsulation in the material world.

3. This brings us to the dream, which has been called by Charles Panati the natural altered state of consciousness. The dream is indeed our

most common and natural exit from purely materialistic existence. It can provide us with nine different kinds of experience.

a. First of all, it can report and comment (sometimes very sagely) on yesterday's events.

b. The dream can draw upon the deepest level of memory and present scenes from fifty years ago with the clarity of a wide-vision cinema screen, with all names and colors intact.

c. The dream can dredge up the contents of the personal unconscious—those aspects of our memories that have been repressed. One young man protested to me that he had never been involved in any sexual activity, and I took him at his word. Nearly a year after we began talking he had a dream in which a certain person appeared, and when I asked him to tell who it was, he turned beet-red and stammered that it was the person with whom there had been a sexual adventure. This was the turning point in our counseling.

d. The dream may speak in symbols that portray the very structure of the psyche itself, of the collective unconscious manifested in my discrete psyche. We are presented with symbols and images that describe the universal nature of the psyche. This is a highly technical aspect of dream interpretation, which Jung discovered. It has been elaborated by many of his followers. Jung does not clearly distinguish this experience from the experience in category *f* below.

e. The dream may also present us with any of the aspects of extrasensory perception that we have described above. Some fascinating studies have been done by Montague Ullman and Stanley Kripner demonstrating the ESP capacity of dreams. *These ESP experiences form a very small portion of our dream experiences, and nothing is sillier than most dream books, which only look at dreams as a way of unlocking the future.*

f. The dream can also bring us into touch with any aspect of the entire objective psyche *outside* our own personal psyches, and so can give us all those experiences of disembodied contents and personalities and more than human realities that we have described above in some detail. At this point the dream becomes religious, whether we like it or not. And here we need to find religious methods of dealing with this data or we may become inundated with the unconscious. These dreams often have a numinous quality like that described in the experience of the deceased.

g. There is the clear dream, which speaks its message not in symbols or hints, but straight out, in plain English, if that is our language, or Japanese if we are Japanese. When I hear complaints that the spiritual world and those who dwell therein don't speak more often in this manner, I recall that both Basil the Great and Edgar Cayce suggested that the reason that God didn't speak more often in this way was that he was more interested in our company than in giving us information.

h. There is also the dream that tells a story using images from the present, from the past, from all levels of the unconscious. Often these dreams are like letters that come from a wisdom greater than our own. This wisdom knows all about us, knows where we have gone off the path, where we should be going, and how we can get back upon the path toward our destiny. Developing methods of interpreting these dreams is one of the main accomplishments of Dr. Jung and his followers; his method of understanding them is similar to the traditional religious understanding of dreams. I have discussed this correspondence in several places.[4] Many people have found their dreams one of the most confirming, jolting, startling and helpful methods of finding their way to meaning. Dreams have been used as part of devotional practice by many of the Church fathers and the doctors and saints of the Church. Many Christian leaders have believed that God often speaks through dreams.

i. And then there are those dreams in which it seems that the heavens have opened and we are given an overview of reality and its meaning or an encounter with the very source of Divine Light and Love. Some of my own deepest and most profound religious experiences have occurred in dreams. I have discussed some of these in *Christo-Psychology*.

4. Young children live between two worlds. It takes years of training in our materialistic culture to brainwash them into believing that only the physical world is real. Young children do not distinguish between outer reality and inner reality, as the imaginary playmates of many children demonstrate. Their imagination is for them as real as hard, cold, physical reality. When the Rorschach (ink blot) test is given to children the results have much the same characteristics as those from adult psychotics. Psychotics are like young children in that they are not able to distinguish between what is considered real by society and what seems real to them. Thus they get in trouble with society and are usually put out of circulation because they won't play the game by the rules. The trick of adulthood is to recognize the reality of the inner world, both personal and transpersonal, and that of the publicly accepted physical world with its customs (such as wearing clothes, not defecating in public and paying taxes) and never getting these two mixed up. The psychotic denies the overriding reality of the physical world. The consistent mate-

rialist denies the reality of the psychoid dimension. The mature adult lives in both. There are few better descriptions of this aspect of childhood than Frances Wickes' *The Inner World of Childhood.*

Watching, observing and playing with children can bring us back to the naturalness of living within the spiritual dimension. Most young children take to prayer and meditation as birds take to the air. Perhaps this is one reason that Jesus set a young child in the midst of his disciples and told them that until they became like one of these they could not enter the Kingdom of Heaven.

5. Children share naturally in the world of plants and animals. The world of biology can reveal for us some of the same divine surge toward meaning that we find in children. The unfolding, growing, instinctive nature of birds and animals often reveals a purpose that certainly seems divine. Loren Eiseley has written profoundly in this area. For those who can observe it, like Teilhard de Chardin, the divine shines through the living world, the biosphere.

6. One of the most revealing characteristics of children is their capacity to play. In his book *Behold, the Spirit*, Alan Watts has written a paean of praise celebrating playfulness:

> The trouble is that we are too proud to be children and appreciate the playing of God. It is just this pride which brought tragedy into the universe, marred the happiness which God created us to share and made necessary a redemption through the cross. For sin is precisely the adult, unplayful action of taking one's self seriously . . . by sin man kills the child in himself, thinking the playful will of God beneath him and desiring to be God in his own right, working out his serious, weighty schemes. But if you give yourself weight you fall down to hell. . . .
>
> [Children] are the happiest when they are doing things that have no particular purpose, playing with a capricious pup, making up lunatic stories with friends, walking aimlessly through fields and hitting at old stumps with a stick, whittling hunks of wood just for the sake of whittling, drawing wayward and aimless designs on scraps of paper and mixing horrible concoctions of all various types of household liquids from paint remover to codliver oil. . . .
>
> Music at its highest as in Bach or Mozart is pure play. The preludes and fugues of Bach are simply a complex arrangement of glorious sounds, entirely sufficient in themselves. . . . Inferior music, however, needs props and commentaries, since it proceeds from human purpose rather than from that playfulness of divine perfection which the arabesques of Persian miniatures, and illuminated margins of medieval manuscripts, the wind-swept bamboos of Chinese painting, and the entirely satisfying and purposeless figures of the dance as it may be sometimes seen in Russian ballet. Such playfulness is the very nature of divine wisdom.[5]

In his book *Homo Ludens* (translated as "man, the one who plays"), Johan Huizinga has suggested that the essence of being human may have more to do with our capacity to play than our capacity to think! Plato in the *Laws* lays down legislation that all older statesmen must be accompanied by youths so that they do not lose the perspective of playfulness. Whenever we play games, whether golf or tennis, chess or bridge, we enter into an imaginary world with rules of its own and with its unique sacred space. We can become so involved in this imaginary world that we can do bodily damage to those who let us down or we can smash our tools of play with anger at our mistakes. Play brings us into another dimension of reality. Religious ritual must contain some of the spontaneity of human playfulness or it loses its power and no longer feeds the soul.

7. Long ago, Aristotle noted that drama, particularly tragedy, could touch and purge the soul. Mary Renault's novel *The Mask of Apollo* shows how closely related drama was to Greek religion. The great dramas of Euripides, Aeschylus and Sophocles were originally staged, not in some secular place, but in the temples of Dionysius. The dance-drama of the Hindus of Bali, in particular, are secular and religious at the same time. In great drama we step into another world and are introduced to a deeper dimension of life. In Göethe and in Shakespeare we are given access to this dimension. Jung once said about Shakespeare, "There is one who knew God."

In a class on the significance of religion for modern men and women we concluded each semester by enacting T. S. Eliot's *Cocktail Party*. It summed up and made present to us this nonphysical dimension of reality in a way that no purely cognitive statement could have done. Most religious ritual, the Christian as well, has its roots in dramatic reenactment, in reliving sacred events so we can participate in them. In the Eucharist we step by divine play into the drama of redemption.

8. Plato stated in the *Phaedrus* that we are given experiences of the spiritual domain through four kinds of divine madness. First there is prophecy, then there is cathartic madness, through which healing is given, and then there is artistic madness, which can open the very gates of heaven. Last of all there is love. We shall look at all of these categories before we are finished. Real art is an expression of the unconscious spiritual-psychoid domain, which speaks to or reveals an experience of universal appeal.

We cannot create art by reason or will. Real art is indeed the gift of a kind of madness that the crass, materialistic world can hardly understand. Important art can portray the evil aspect of reality, as well as the divine, but the greatest of art, as in Dante, Göethe and Shakespeare, presents the very same message we find in the most optimistic of religions, the message that there is a divine and reconciling love that has overcome evil and is overcoming it now and that we can be in touch with it.

Poetry, incense, beautiful cloth, stained glass windows, architecture, music, sculpture, painting, dance, storytelling (novels), and fantasy can each usher us across the boundaries of the purely physical world and give us a real encounter with this other dimension. Religious ritual uses all of these artistic methods to enable us to participate in the positive aspect of reality that can renew us and give us a taste of the divine. Methodist hymn writing and singing can open the gates of heaven, as can a great choir or organ. For some persons poetry is a way *par excellence* to share in the divine experience. For others it is the sculpture of Michelangelo, for others a Raphael. The icons of the Greek and Russian Church were seen as windows into heaven.

Reading the fantasy novels of Charles Williams gave flesh and blood to the vision of reality that was growing out of my study of the unconscious with some of Jung's followers. Somehow the novels of Williams let me live for a while in this other dimension. Reading the *Four Quartets* of Eliot while listening to the late quartets of Beethoven was another experience I shall never forget. The children's stories of C. S. Lewis touched me as well as my children when I read them aloud, and I found that adult and very sophisticated graduate students at Notre Dame were sometimes opened to meaning through these children's tales.

Jung and his followers have shown that much of the inner lives of novelists is revealed in their stories. Stevenson was instantly popular through his story of Dr. Jekyll and Mr. Hyde, which revealed Stevenson's problems and also the psychic split in Victorian England, as well as the inevitable struggle between good and evil within all of us human beings. Great literature, as well as great drama, carries us on its wings beyond the limits of a purely materialistic world.

Artistic inspiration is one of the most important natural ways in which we are given a taste of the spiritual world and its importance. It is no wonder that religion has relied upon it so heavily in seeking to open us to this reality. Except for some sects of Buddhism such as Zen and some groups in Christianity like the Quakers, nearly all religions of every variety use these artistic expressions to mediate their experience of the Holy.

They use this natural avenue to the psychoid dimension of experience in order to direct the individual to the creative and positive center and source or sources of things. They use the stories of mythology, music, which so often takes us out of ourselves, poetry, which the circle of Lewis and Williams believed was a particularly open doorway to the spiritual realm, dance, in which music and movement and story are joined, beautiful cloth and embroidery, flowers, painting, stained glass, incense, sculpture and architecture.

9. In his book *The Psychopathology of Everyday Life*, Freud points out how our mistakes and our humor open us to a realm of experience beyond the ordinary. Real humor has an ecstatic quality. Suddenly we are able to see things as whole, from God's point of view. Our tense human strivings can be seen for what they are. Not only do we see, we feel the picture of the whole, and we laugh. The laughter may be hearty or only a quiet inner chuckle, but it tells us that we have been released from looking at things from a purely practical and materialistic viewpoint.

The positive effects of humor and laughter have been noted from ancient times right up to the writings of Norman Cousins and Raymond Moody. Comedy may be an even higher form of soul cleansing than tragedy. In the last three comedies of Shakespeare, *The Winter's Tale*, *Cymbeline*, and *The Tempest*, the forces of evil are confronted and defeated through forgiveness and love. T. S. Eliot's *The Cocktail Party* is tragedy that is redeemed by a supernatural perspective. D. M. Thomas' *The White Hotel* transforms utter tragedy in the same way. The name Dante gave his greatest work was in Italian simply *Comedia* (*The Comedy*). Within the Christian world view an optimism pervades everything. Evil has been defeated and only the mopping-up action still remains. It is my firm belief that this God who allowed Christ to give himself on the cross for us while we were still in sin will not cease seeking and searching until all have been redeemed.

Closely related to humor is joy, joy that is found in the lives of nearly all of the most authentic followers of Christ. Jesus tells us that we need to be able to pipe and dance with the happy as well as to mourn with the sad. Von Hügel, following the wisdom of Huvelin, points out that a Christianity that is not characterized by joy misses the mark. We see joy in the great troubadour of God, Francis of Assisi, in St. Philip Neri and in most genuine saints. These people are able to see things from the ultimate point of view of the Kingdom, in which the love of Abba prevails.

The derivation of the word humor shows its significance. It comes from the word for the four basic bodily fluids, and was then identified with the wet fluid that enabled a person to have a joyous outlook on life.

10. One of the finest studies of insight ever written is Bernard Lonergan's book *Insight*. We have a capacity to perceive things as a whole, to see beyond the fragmentation within our world and grasp essences. Plato speaks of a mathematical intuition by which we perceive the structure of reality. It was through insight of this kind that Sir Isaac Newton was given his monumental vision of the order within the cosmos. Kurt Gödel speaks of the insight through which we can perceive the truths of mathematics and compares this to Plato's understanding of how we encounter the Ideas. This "seeing through" ordinary reality, if carried far enough, can bring us to a religious understanding, but it can also stop short of this apprehension of reality in its essence.

11. Related to insight, but much more common, is our capacity for intuition, the perception of meanings and realities other than those perceived through the five senses. Jung, in his important psychological analysis of human beings, *Psychological Types*, writes that we have two quite different ways of taking in data: one through the five or six senses, which he calls *sensation*, and another that he calls *intuition*. Through intuition we can sometimes learn about the physical world and nonphysical world within or beyond our psyches. It would be possible to classify many of these thirty-six methods of opening into the dimension beyond the purely physical as intuition.

Nearly all of us have simple intuitions—hunches or vague momentary flashes of understanding. This is a capacity in which all of us share. Perhaps those who develop it most highly could call their ability insight. But all of us are given these momentary and natural openings beyond the realm of the physical experience. The Meyers-Briggs Type Indicator is a psychological instrument by which, among other things, we attempt to determine how much we prefer to use our capacity for intuition. All intuitions need to be carefully checked and tested if they are to provide knowledge of either reality.

12. The contents of the unconscious break through into our lives in still another way, as Freud showed in his clear and delightful book on the psychopathology of our ordinary life. Our mistakes often reveal parts of us that we would rather keep hidden. Our missed appointments often tell us our feelings about certain people and situations, feelings of which we

had not been fully conscious. Our delayed reaction times in the Word Association Test developed by Jung shows how we cannot think of associations to words about which we have queasy feelings. Likewise, our bodies sometimes respond in sneaky ways when we try to lie; it is upon this fact that the polygraph or lie detector test is based. We do not have total control of our psyches or bodies, and often our mistakes, misspeakings, lapses of memory and bodily reactions reveal the world of the unconscious, a different domain from the physical.

13. As much as I don't like to admit it, suffering can be a gateway beyond the confines of a purely material universe. Max Zeller once told me that depression (as intense psychic suffering as human beings can endure) can be the abscess on the soul that requires lancing and in some cases shows us that we have cut ourselves off from transpersonal meaning, from the divine. Physical suffering can also be so intense that we perceive another dimension of meaning. Some of the martyrs actually experienced ecstacy in their heinous deaths. This may be the action of the loving God who also seems to give to the dying at the time of death (quite contrary to the observable physical responses) a sense of peace and freedom and joy that is quite inexplicable. Many of those who have had near-death experiences tell of this experience of release and joy. Those who minister to the dying often report a sense of euphoria in the dying, when from a physical point of view the opposite should have been experienced. Karlis Osis has provided data on these states in his book *At the Hour of Death.*

William James tells of a woman who experienced the divine through suffering: "I wondered if I was in a prison being tortured, and why I remembered having heard it said that people 'learn through suffering,' and in view of what I was seeing, the inadequacy of this saying struck me so much that I said aloud, 'to suffer is to learn'. . . .

"While regaining consciousness, I wondered why, since I had gone so deep, I had seen nothing of what the saints call the love of God, nothing but his relentlessness. And then I heard an answer, which I could only just catch, saying, 'Knowledge and Love are One, and the measure is suffering'—I give the words as they came to me."[6]

There has been a widely accepted practice, a brand of asceticism, which offers the body as a sacrifice through self-inflicted suffering. I do not dignify it with the name of religious practice because it appears to me to be a deformation of the religious impulse whether among gnostics, Hindus, Moslems, or Christians. It occurs in many forms: sleeping on nails, wearing hairshirts, cutting down on sleep, self-flagellation, sitting on pillars for years, or courting the presence of lice. Some of these practices have been known in Christian religious orders during the last twenty years. After a catalogue of some of the wilder excesses of this kind of asceticism, William James makes this sage comment: "For in its spiritual meaning this kind of asceticism stands for nothing less than for the essence of the twice-born philosophy. It symbolizes, lamely enough no doubt, but sincerely, the belief that there is an element of real wrongness in this world, which is neither to be ignored nor evaded, but which must be squarely met and overcome by an appeal to the soul's heroic resources, and neutralized and cleansed away by suffering."[7]

There is still another element in this immolation of the body and psyche. It can come from the gnostic rejection of the body as evil and be an attempt to escape from the snares of an evil physical world or an illusory one. Again, this may stem from the actual experience that some people have of finding the divine through suffering. Out of the deepest level of my interaction with God has come the conviction that seeking suffering is misguided and that it is as wrong to torture ourselves as it is to torture other people, no matter what the motives. Some of my most real experiences of grace have come to me as God has lifted me out of the pit of inner suffering; however, to seek out such suffering deliberately would align me with the destructive side of reality, and not the divine.

14. There is still another strange method of achieving ecstasy, which has been known in many places and times. Constant, rhythmic physical activity can send the human being into a trance-like state and produce an altered state of consciousness. The most common example of this is in running. There is a point, after two miles or so, when the body seems to run by itself and there is a euphoria similar to that which is sometimes obtained through some drugs. This phenomenon has been used in some religious groups. The whirling dervishes of some Islamic groups keep up a kind of dance-like movement until a trance occurs. The same phenomenon has occurred among the Hindus of Bali, where young women danced until they dropped in a trance. In both instances it was believed that through the trance state so induced the divine spirit would speak. Some chanting produces the same effect. In Bali it was an accompaniment to the dancing. Hare Krishna chanting produces something of the same condition. And at the opposite pole from this deliberate religious exercise is continuous disco dancing. This also can provide a sense of well-being, similar to that produced by some drugs.

15. And then there is the capacity for wonder. Wonder is that state of mind in which we are open, expectant. We have not scaled the universe

down to fit into our petty understanding and our pettier language. Wonder is not being "stuck in cement." It is being open for change. In this frame of mind and being we are open to surprise, to astonishment. We can see red sixes of spades. We don't have everything accounted for. We are still open to a spiritual dimension.

This is a quality, like playfulness, that is found in nearly all children unless they have had it stamped out of them. The insatiable thirst for learning emerges out of wonder. Perhaps another reason Jesus said we need to become as little chidren in order to come into the Kingdom of Heaven is that children possess this sense of wonder and openness. The world for children has a magical quality, and it is still possible to have faith in Love. We also find the same quality in the greatest scientists, such as Einstein, Heisenberg, Jung, Madame Curie and Gödel. This quality is also the essence of scientific discovery.

16. The next three natural methods of ecstasy are related, and we can only begin to hint at their nature in this brief description. In *Caring: How Can We Love One Another?* I have tried to offer an understanding of the nature of human love, a very foolish thing for a human being to try to do. John Sanford once said to me that he knew a lot about transference, a lot about love, and a lot about sex, but when he added all this knowledge together, he knew absolutely nothing. In the matter of love we enter into a mystery. Long ago Plato saw love, concrete human love, as one of the supreme and most adequate methods of giving us ecstasy and of opening us to a knowledge of the Ideas, of the spiritual world.

Our word *love* carries many different meanings. I will separate three of its meanings into three different ways of opening ourselves to the psychoid or spiritual realms. The Greeks had many different words to distinguish the different kinds of love. There is, first of all, falling in love, which is known in psychological lingo as transference, and which contains an element of projection. Then there is the deep loving of another in which we behold the divine through the other person. And last of all there is sexuality, in which two persons come together for an ecstatic union in which the inner love relation is lived out physically.

In order to justify speaking on the subject at all, I refer to the delightful words of Aldous Huxley's book of essays, *Tomorrow and Tomorrow and Tomorrow*: "Of all the worn, smudged, dog-eared words in our vocabulary, 'love' is surely the grubbiest, smelliest, slimiest. Bawled from a million pulpits, lasciviously crooned through hundreds of millions of loudspeakers, it has become an outrage to good taste and decent feeling, an obscenity which one hesitates to pronounce. And yet it has to be pronounced, for, after all, Love is the last word."[8]

Plato described the various aspects of love in *The Symposium*. One of the participants at the wine bust (for that was the meaning of the word *symposium* in Greek) tells a myth explaining the reason for the relentless power of love. We human beings were once whole beings. We became a threat to the gods, who never wish competition, and so the very essence of our wholeness was split into two parts. Each single whole human being was made into two persons. Love, then, is the desire of each half to find its other half, and an unquenchable desire it is. There is no greater desire than that for the return to a state of equilibrium and wholeness.

Psychologists have coined the word *transference* to describe this astonishing quality of falling in love. The idea contained in this word is that we project onto other people aspects of ourselves of which we are not aware, and we *think* that the other people embody them. Of course seldom, if ever, does any other person contain all the elements of our unconscious religious and other strivings. Some people do, however, provide a hook upon which we can hang our projections. If, on our part, we provide a hook for *their* inner projections, then we have a double whammy and enter the state about which so many dramas are staged and so many novels written and so much music composed. This is the Romeo-Juliet state of being. People are simply taken out of this world and live on a different plane. This state seldom survives reality testing for very long. When the people concerned begin to have to accept what the others really are, the attraction often dies down.

The classical Greeks called this aspect of love *eros* and saw it as coming from the god of love, Eros. Plato believed that as we fall in love, we first of all fall in love with a beautiful body and then move on to the beautiful soul that shapes that body; then the searching soul seeks the god who has made such beauty of mind and soul, spirit and body. This kind of seeking desire, *whether or not it is physically consummated,* can drive us onward to seek for the best things in the universe, or it can, when it is misused, bring us to demonic destructiveness. It certainly reveals meanings, values, and feelings that are different from those of the ordinary world in which we live. For those truly in love the world has a deeper and richer shade of green, and it is easy to believe in the divine. The word *eros* is not found in the Greek New Testament, but the word *agape* sometimes carries the same sense of longing.

Dante fell in love with Beatrice when he was a young man. He worshipped her from afar. She became for him a symbol of divine purity, holiness and beauty, and then she died. She became his guide through the many mansions of heaven in *The Divine Comedy*. In his book *The Figure of Beatrice: A Study in Dante*, Charles Williams speaks of the role of this kind of love, which is the driving desire for wholeness, for the divine. I doubt if it is possible for the person who has never been able to fall in love to know the kind of self-forgetfulness and self-giving that is part of the essence of this genuine ecstasy, this standing outside of oneself. There is little question that this kind of love, when understood in depth, can reveal the divine in and through another, but few people love with the depth and consistency and maturity of Dante.

17. And then there is the self-giving love that is more concerned with the growth and development, the welfare and wholeness of the other person than it is in finding those qualities for itself. This is what the Greeks called *agape*, and it is the word that is used in most of the New Testament to speak of God's love for human beings. Erotic love can burn out and continue in blindness (breathtaking as it is). The goal of a real relationship, and particularly of marriage, is to develop the attraction that has drawn people together into this self-giving love without losing the magic of eros.

In the Sermon on the Mount and in Luke 6:27–36 we are told by Jesus that we become perfect and become children of God as we have this kind of love towards the good and the evil, just as Abba does. Agape is the essential quality of the follower of Jesus of Nazareth. In John's Gospel, Jesus tells his disciples that they are his followers when they love one another as he has loved them.

When we come to this attitude we no longer see others as the world does. We can see the divine even in the worst of human beings, and we can turn even to our enemies with caring concern. This is a quiet ecstasy, in which we look at the world from God's perspective, and it has something of the quality of divine humor and joy about it. Like most of the important qualities of life, it is both worked for and given. It certainly gives access not only to the spiritual world, but to the central creative heart of this realm of experience and being.

There are some modern theologians who oppose *eros* to *agape* and make them mutually exclusive, one a human striving and the other a divine self-giving. The New Testament does not oppose them one against the other. They are rather like twin peaks rising from a great plateau, and they have the tableland in common. Seldom do we human beings come to agape, to self-giving love, until we have first of all been set on fire by the longing and desire of eros. One of these peaks is an inactive volcano while the other may be a dormant one ready to explode, but both have risen from the mystery of the divine fire. Eros that has not been tempered and matured through agape can be selfish, destructive, and even demonic. Agape untouched by eros can be distant and cold.

18. The last of these related experiences is sexuality. Many Christians have been caught in the gnostic myth that tells us that creation was a cosmic tragedy and that our only hope is to free ourselves through knowledge (*gnosis*) from the binding ugliness and snares of evil matter and return to the perfect bliss of pure spirit, the *pleroma*. When we do not try to return to our purely spiritual home, we are lost indeed. But it was believed among Manicheans that worse than not trying to return is the physical act of conceiving a child, which traps more spirit in matter. This sect believed it was permissible to have sexual relations with girls before puberty since no conception could take place. Even the Roman emperors were shocked. Conception is the ultimate in evil, and naturally intercourse (the usual means of conception) is tainted with the same horrible stain. As long as sexuality is viewed in this light, either consciously or unconsciously, it can only be an ecstasy leading to hell! This was the view of Augustine who had been for nine years a peripheral follower of the gnostic Manichean sect. This attitude toward sexuality has contaminated Christianity, both Catholic and Protestant, and has been an underlying unconscious attitude in the life of many religious orders.

If sexuality is separated from love, then its ecstatic quality does turn negative. Some writers, like those in the recent book *Human Sexuality* (published by some theologians of the Roman Catholic Church), try to discuss sexuality without reference to love. I can't blame them, for love is a slippery number, but they fall into absurdity. On the plateau of love there is a third peak, smaller in size, which is constantly smoking and often erupts; sexuality is its name.

Throughout the history of religion, except in gnosticism and some totally world-denying forms of Buddhism, sexuality has been understood as an ecstasy. In many ancient cultures there was a sacred sexuality performed in the temple (if one calls it prostitution one has already prejudged the case), in which one came to union with the mother goddess through her priestess. Much Hindu erotic art is found within the temples. The Chinese developed the *Tao* of loving, in which human sexuality was seen as a symbol of the union of the feminine principle (*yin*) and the masculine principle (*yang*). Within this point of view, so different from that in which most of us have been raised, the proper use of sexuality actually brings about the transformation of both human beings and brings them spiritual, mental and physical wholeness and health.[9]

Those who avoid all contact with their sexuality must be very aware if they are to avoid serious consequences. Freud has certainly demonstrated that a society that represses sexuality often plunges its people into the negative ecstasy of neurosis, as well as cutting them off from what can be a positive participation in the psychoid realm. I have listened to several people who told me that some of their most vivid experiences of the divine came at the time of fulfilled sexuality. I am not suggesting that sex should be indulged in promiscuously or for itself alone. Any aspect of life that is separated out of the whole usually becomes evil. What I am suggesting is that sexuality properly used (and this always involves tension and conflict sooner or later) should not be rejected out of hand, but seen as one possible symbol that God gives us of coming to wholeness and the divine. How much this can add to a committed relationship or a marriage if both persons strive for it.

On the other hand, there is a place for celibacy, as St. Ambrose pointed out long ago. Visiting the nuns at St. Scholastica's convent in Chittagong, I realized that the work they were doing, taking in and educating orphans, children who would otherwise have died, would have been impossible in that culture if the nuns had not accepted the celibate life. There was no way they could have been married, grubbed for a living, and done this work. They consciously sacrificed their sexuality for a greater good. Sexuality, in spite of some current voices to the contrary, is not the final good, and like everything else, it needs to be subordinate to the greater good.

19. This brings us to the last, and one of the most common and unpleasant ways of being spontaneously confronted with the psychoid or unconscious aspect of reality. After the dream and the whole complex of love, falling in love, and sexuality, the most common intrusion of the psychoid realm into our lives is through mental illness of one kind or another, through the various forms of neurosis and psychosis. Indeed, most of us suffer from inner tensions that manifest themselves in neurosis.* In

---

* It is true that the words *neurosis* and *neurotic* are no longer used by the American Psychiatric Association in their *Diagnostic and Statistical Manual of Mental Disorders*, Third Edition (published in 1980 and often referred to among the elite as DSM–III). However, there is still some value in describing those disorders in which there is a tension between the ego and the unconscious as neurotic and those in which the ego gives way to the unconscious contents, either personal or collective, as psychotic. I have discussed this matter at greater length in *Christo-Psychology*.

both situations there is a lack of harmony between the conscious personality (the ego) and the depths of the psyche, whether caused by repression or psychic trauma or coming from the structure of the unconscious psyche or from the psychoid realm beyond it. In *Christo-Psychology* I have described the difference between these two in the following way: In neurosis the afflicted person cries out, "Two and two is four and I can't stand it." Psychotic people faced with the same proposition quietly say, "Two and two is twenty-two; isn't it wonderful?"

Another comparison tells us that neurotics build castles in the air and are most upset that they can't manage to live in them. Psychotics, on the other hand, take up residence in them, and the psychologist collects the rent. In neurotic problems the tension and conflict with the inner depth are maintained and endured. In the psychotic, the personality is fragmented and gives way to the intrusions of the psychoid realm.

Every one of us who would guide and be a companion to others on the spiritual journey needs to have some basic knowledge of the kinds of mental disorders we humans suffer. Often neurotics exhibit religious compulsions and obsessions, which are called scrupulosity in religious language. Psychotics often have experiences of the spiritual domain for the simple reason that they are so open to the unconscious. For some neurotics sexuality and religion get all mixed up. Some neurotics become inflated and believe themselves mouthpieces of God. Some psychotic people think themselves a divine figure out of the past or think that their bodies and minds are puppets of God. There is no reason to go into a long description of the common mental disorders. Gerald May has made a clear and detailed analysis in *Care of Mind Care of Soul*. Any one of us dealing with other people on a one-to-one basis should have this basic knowledge so that we are never surprised and so that we can discern between the two states with some confidence. I know of no better analysis of the material for spiritual guides than that provided by Dr. May.

Many people have visited professional psychologists who either were reluctant to deal with religious issues or who gave psychiatric labels to religious experiences. This is very dangerous, as May points out again and again. He also notes that few psychiatrists have a world view that can deal with these experiences. This is one reason why May separates so completely spiritual and secular psychological counseling.

In *Christo-Psychology* I have pointed out that Jung's greatest contribution to psychology and religion is providing a world-view in which these two areas can be discussed from a common point of view. Naturally the behaviorist, whose universe is limited to physical reality, will have no place for visions, religious dreams, religious experiences or ecstatic states. These are simple aberrations of the mechanical machine. I have already noted Dr. Roger Walsh's critique of this narrow, dogmatic approach. From a Freudian point of view religious experience is regression, a return to the womb, and so it cannot be viewed as a creative and positive contact with another dimension of reality without breaking with Freud. In a recent article on Freud in *The New Yorker*, Bruno Bettelheim emphasizes the point that Freud never changed his mind on this subject, and Bettelheim, as a Freudian, goes along with his conclusion. If we are to be able to listen to people and not be surprised, we need to have a view of the universe into which both the psychological and the religious facts fit without excluding each other. The world view that we sketched out earlier provides such a base; I have elaborated it in *Christo-Psychology*.

In a later chapter we shall show how psychology, psychiatry, pastoral counseling, pastoral care and spiritual direction are related. It is my firm conviction that we need to have a good basic acquaintance with the discoveries and conclusions of modern psychology if we are to be effective as spiritual companions, friends and guides on the spiritual journey. This knowledge cannot be obtained from books alone. In addition to being up to date with the material presented in summary form in *Care of Mind Care of Soul*, we need to have had some experience with the mentally ill. There is no way in which a physician can learn to diagnose heart conditions except by listening to thousands of hearts. Some firsthand contact with mental illness shows us in what a different way from most of us people with severe mental disorders deal with religious experiences. It is also wise to know ourselves well enough to be aware of our own neurotic problems and tendencies, as well as our lack of wholeness. Fortified with this objective and personal knowledge we can give maximum companionship and guidance and be least in danger of doing damage to anyone. I personally have found it most helpful over the years to have a close relationship with a psychiatrist with whom I am able to discuss puzzling situations and to whom I can refer cases that are beyond my competence. I also find it helpful to have psychologists and others engaged in the cure of souls with whom I can interact and have fellowship.

All of us have our psychological quirks. These do not inhibit us from being creative Christians and effective spiritual companions. The important matter is that we are aware of our problems and working on them, and not projecting our problems onto those who come to us. The totally adjusted person might be frightfully dull and give us horrible inferiority problems.

Deliberate Religious Practice as an Entrance to the Spiritual World

Religious practice is so common the world over that it might well be called a natural way of being open to the wider world of spiritual or psychoid experience. We shall see that some religious groups, as part of their practice, use nearly all of the doors out of a complacent materialism that we have already discussed. Most religions deliberately set out to make contact with the "spirit world," that aspect of experience that refers to something beyond the material world. Although there are certain black shamans who seek to invoke the destructive side of spiritual reality and use it for their own designs, the great majority of developed religions are an attempt to come into contact with a creative, caring and beneficent aspect of this domain, to embody it and release it.

In this whole area of relating to the divine our words are unclear, and different people have quite different meanings for the same words. God can certainly be thrust upon us with little or no conscious desire on our part, but our participation in religion begins when we consciously make an effort towards relating to these more than human powers, expecting some response in return. Sabatier has described this well in these words:

> This intercourse with God is realized by prayer. Prayer is religion in action; that is, prayer is real religion. It is prayer that distinguishes the religious phenomenon from such similar or neighboring phenomena as purely moral or aesthetic sentiment. . . . This act is prayer . . . the very movement itself of the soul putting itself in a personal relationship of contact with the mysterious power of which it feels the presence—it may be even before it has a name by which to call it. Wherever this interior prayer is lacking, there is no religion; wherever, on the other hand, this prayer rises and stirs the soul, even in the absence of forms or of doctrines, we have living religion.

William James quotes these words and then goes on:

> This intercourse is realized at the time as being both active and mutual. If it is not effective; if it be not a give and take relation; if nothing be really transacted while it lasts; if the world is no whit different for its having taken place; then prayer, taken in this wide

meaning of a sense that *something is transacting* is of course a feeling of what is illusory, and religion must on the whole be classed, not simply as containing elements of delusion,—these undoubtedly everywhere exist,—but as being rooted in delusion altogether, just as materialists and atheists have always said it was.[10]

There is a practically limitless number of ways through which people have sought to make this motion toward these nonphysical powers, presences and realities that can make a difference in their lives. I shall discuss ten of the more common of them, ten that I believe can be used by people in our culture today as means of facilitating this transpersonal transaction. I shall conclude with three that I think are quite dangerous and to be avoided by most of us.

1. Throughout the world the most common method of religious practice is participating in religious rituals or symbolic religious acts. They can range from the Christian Eucharist sung to the Bach B minor Mass to the ritual feeding by devout Moslems of the sacred turtles in a holy lake within the confines of a mosque in Chittagong, in Bangladesh (the turtles are believed to be incarnations of certain saints and effective at healing). The catalogue is endless—from amulets, to prayer wheels, to sacred buildings, to bones of saints, to inscribed replicas of limbs, to prescribed worship of sacred snakes, to the golden calves that caused the Hebrew prophets such concern. Spiritual directors who ignore or look down upon sacramental practices, who do not understand them and know how to help people use them to open themselves to a fuller experience of God, are likely to have an inadequate psychology and at the same time to cut themselves off from the great majority of people who are religiously seeking. My only criticism of Dr. May's book, to which we have referred several times, is that it has no place for the continued use of rituals and sacraments, nor suggestions as to how they may be used in spiritual direction.

We human beings are sacramental creatures. We live and move through symbols and sacraments. Hans Schaer has written a fine study of the psychological and religious value of symbols, dogmas and rituals in *Religion and the Cure of Souls in Jung's Psychology*. One of the finest discussions of the importance of our religious rituals and how they open us to the nonphysical dimension through use of the right brain is written by neurosurgeon Eugene d'Aquili, and sociologist Dr. Charles Laughlin, Jr.; it is burdened with the title: "The Biopsychological Determinants of Religious Ritual Behavior."[11] Jung's paper "Transformation Symbolism in the Mass," in *Psychology and Religion: West and East*, is also a fine discussion of the universal meanings imbedded in the Eucharist.

The task of the spiritual guide is not to turn people away from participation in rituals, but to lead them to that which most deeply meets their needs. There is truth value in mythology and in the ritual that allows us to participate actively in its meaning. All rituals are not equally useful in bringing us to an effective transaction with the divine, however. Some rituals are quite destructive and immoral. Both the Eucharist and the Aztec human sacrifice stress the importance of sacrifice. However, in one case we are led through the voluntary sacrifice of the God-man to sacrifice ourselves *inwardly,* so that we may be transformed and rise to a new level and so give of ourselves lovingly to others; in the other we use our *power* to sacrifice another person to placate the gods.

The spiritual guide also has the task of helping individuals integrate their lives into the meaning that their highest ritual symbolizes. Daily communicants at the Eucharist can be guided to live in such a way as to allow the actual life of Christ to be more effective in and through them. This is not the place to discuss this matter in detail. It is my hope to write in the near future on the importance of the Eucharist in the Christian spiritual life and on how this sacrament can be used as a means of religious growth, as well as a measure of how mature our transaction with God has become.

There are several guidelines that the spiritual guide and companion may use in enabling people to understand the place of outer religious symbols and to participate creatively in the rituals of their faith.

a. Whenever we see any ritual or outer symbol, or inner vision or experience, as containing *all* of the divine mystery and reality, it has become idolatrous. When we think that we have God securely in our own grasp we debase religion and usually exhibit prejudice against those who do not believe *exactly* what we do. Thus we become bigots. At this point a hearty dose of critical thinking is a good prescription.

b. On the opposite hand, those who reject all outer symbols and rituals can become equally dogmatic. In the *Mystical Element in Religion*, von Hügel carefully sketches out the dangers of quietism, in which the individual who has experienced the inner way of imageless communion with God rejects and looks down upon all participation in outer religious actions. The smashing of religious images common among the more radical groups during the Reformation demonstrated a onesideness and bigotry as great as that of any exclusive sacramental sect. An understanding of the natural symbol-making nature of the psyche is helpful at this point. It is seldom an expression of love or good spiritual friendship to deride or destroy images that are helpful to some people.

c. Images and rituals can carry a wealth of meaning and understanding for a religious tradition. We have already noted the enormous dangers that can arise when we fail to see how much we owe to our historical roots and how much we need them in order not to wander off into the innumerable religious quicksands and dead-end streets. Our tradition is helpful in calling us back to those elements of the religious way that we would like to ignore and forget.

d. Within Christianity the essential message is carried by four *events:* the Incarnation, the enfleshment of God; the Crucifixion, the death of the God-man; the Resurrection, the reappearance of the glorified God-man; and Pentecost, the giving of an empowering spirit. The Seventh Ecumenical Council, the last one in which both Eastern and Western Christianity participated, decreed that total disregard or rejection of images denied the Christian dogma of the Incarnation. If that doctrine is true, then God has quite a predilection for images. This council put an end to the iconoclastic (image-breaking) controversy, which had troubled the Church for over one hundred years in the eighth and ninth centuries.

e. Some kind of ritualistic practice is necessary if people are to share in a meaningful fellowship. The silent Quakers have developed a highly effective and careful *ritual* for their practice of silence. When there is no communal worship there is usually a lack of understanding of the horizontal outreach of Christianity, a diminishing of the emphasis on love. My wife and I have discovered that our very different individual practices of private prayer can come together and reinforce each other at a daily Eucharist.

f. For over twenty years I was involved in or the leader of a prayer group in which we practiced the inner journey as a group. The practice that we found most balanced and helpful consisted, first of all, of the Eucharist, then the laying on of hands for healing, followed by a period of quiet and then intercessory prayers for others (horizontal outreach), and then a meditation guided either by the leader or one of the group. We concluded with a discussion of what we had experienced, relating this to a study of some book of the Bible or a devotional classic.[12] These people often formed deep friendships within the group and often tried to bring this quality of relationship to people outside the group.

2. There are two essentially different *emphases* on the inner journey: the way of affirmation, the kataphatic, that is, the use of images, on the one hand, and the way of renunciation, *via negativa,* the apophatic, the dismissal of images as inadequate to the mystery of God, on the other hand. I have said earlier that *both of these emphases are true and complementary.* I use the word *emphases* quite deliberately to indicate that they are two aspects of one process and not two contrasting and opposite ways, as Harvey Egan points out in the article to which we have already referred. The apophatic emphasis, as it is described by St. John of the Cross, St. Teresa and the author of *The Cloud of Unknowing*, was largely developed for the Christian monastic community, and it *presupposed that those using this method were also daily in attendance at the Eucharist and the offices.* The kataphatic emphasis nearly always starts in silence and detachment, then moves into imagery. At the same time it is well to be aware that no inner vision or image of God exhausts all of this mystery.

In chapter 8 we shall describe these two emphases at greater length, but we mention them here briefly in order to be comprehensive. There is a great divergence in the way these two aspects of the inner way are named. I call the way of using inner images *meditation* and distinguish it from the traditional meaning of the word. Historically, meditation was the conscious and rational consideration and elaboration of religious images and ideas. I use the word to mean the deliberate attempt to use the inner image as a means of opening us up to spiritual reality. I use the word *contemplation* to signify the silent, more or less imageless, communion with the ineffable core and heart of spiritual reality. Again, I wish to make myself very clear, at the risk of unnecessary repetition, that these two approaches are not opposed to each other and that neither is *higher* or more advanced than the other. Probably our type structure and basic psychological make-up will determine which of these two ways is more congenial and helpful for us.

We who would be spiritual companions need to be comfortable with both of these approaches to the inner way and to know people who are more competent than we in the complementary approach. It is important to make referrals when we see that we cannot lead others as far as they wish to go. Centers for developing and fostering the spiritual life would do well to provide expertise in both of these approaches.

3. The deepest levels I have reached in my own religious practice have been achieved through meditative use of inner images. My wife

finds very little help in this method. She discovered the approach of Sr. Rita Anne Houlihan, a sister of the Cenacle, to be very meaningful and creative. She developed her own practice, and when we lecture together on the ways of inner prayer she presents the following suggestions for contemplative prayer.

> The basic idea is that the spiritual and physical worlds are *one* in the sense that they totally interpenetrate each other. Whenever we touch the physical we are also touching the spiritual. Contemplation (from this point of view) is an attempt to deal with our spiritual lives in the same natural way that we human beings handle most situations in life. This is a threefold process: 1. We experience something. 2. We mull it over or think about it. 3. We try to discern what implications this experience and our consideration of it has for our lives.
>
> As a method of religious discovery, we need first of all to become aware that we have lived all our lives in a society that has given us a sensory overload of noise and smells and colors. We have become desensitized to sensory experience, and we need to learn to truly *experience* once again. We need to concentrate *totally* on a limited area of sensation for a short period of time without blocking any aspect of it and without thinking about it—just experiencing the *what* as it is now. We can usually enter that sensory experience and stay with it for a short period of time. Any analytical thought at that time immediately turns off the process.
>
> The process begins with relaxation, quieting of the body and the mind as much as possible. After a few minutes of experiencing and concentrating on the sensory data that is presented, we can then withdraw further into the silence, into the absence of any sensation, and rest in it, just experiencing whatever comes. What comes may be a dazzling darkness, a sense of presence, a deep sense of peace, a cessation of struggle, or we may be presented with a word, a thought, a number, a color, a musical sound, etc.
>
> As we pull out of the depth of the quiet we begin to mull over that which has been given, thinking about it, seeing where this experience leads us. This can go on for several minutes or an hour. The last stage occurs as we pull out of the depth of quiet and try to understand what the experience means to us, how it applies to my everyday life, where I am now, what it tells me about my relationships with God, with other people and with the world around me, and finally what I am going to do about it.

Zen Buddhism represents probably the most total expression of pure imagelessness in the practice of the interior way. The practitioner comes to sensory deprivation by "just sitting" and finally is opened to *satori*. This tradition is similar to the one found in Christianity arising from the inspiration of Evagrius, the writings of Dionysius the Areopagite, *The*

Cloud of Unknowing, and in the works of St. Teresa and St. John of the Cross. Gerald May describes this kind of practice and experience with great care in chapter 3 of *Care of Mind Care of Spirit,* and Tilden Edwards provides an understanding of this practice in chapter 6 of *Spiritual Friend.*

4. In many religions and cultures revelation has been given through the trance state to which we have referred above. The shaman was the person who was able to go into trance at will. Among some people it was believed that the soul of the person in that state left the body and was able to find the causes of sickness of the diseased and also to be a guide and companion to the deceased who entered the world of afterlife. Sometimes religious ritual was deliberately directed toward inducing this state. Mircea Eliade has written a definitive study of this phenomenon and shown how it is to be found in nearly every human culture. This practice appears to be native to human beings, and not only transmitted through cultural influence. There are similarities among people and cultures as diverse as the aborigines of Australia, the ancient people of the Kalahari desert in Africa described by Laurens van der Post, the tribes of Siberia, and the American Indians. Some aspects of the present-day charismatic renewal are also similar. Obviously sleeping is similar to the trance state, and the dream is often valued as a revelation among these people. Trance and dream are seen as gateways to another level of experience. Eliade provides a fifty-page bibliography of relevant material in his book *Shamanism.*

There is a basic difference between the priest, who carries out rituals and is an expression of a law and an institution, and the shaman, who offers a direct contact with the other dimension of reality for the immediate and specific use of the person seeking help. There are white shamans and black shamans; the white seek to bring the individual in touch with the creative forces, the beneficent realities on the other side, while the black seek to bring us into contact with the dark and destructive forces, through which we can wreak havoc upon our enemies. Voodoo is an example. It is only a short step from black shamanism to witchcraft.

Often there is a conflict between the priestly community, which has codified religion and has everything decently in order, and the shaman, who is trying to bring about an immediate relationship with the powers that be. No human institution can capture all the divine for every situation. What God will do next with the human soul almost always has an element of surprise and mystery. When a culture is living in *participation mystique,* as described by Levy-Bruhl, the state where individual consciousness is little different from that of the social group, the ritual dance or service can often provide individuals with this contact. As individual consciousness grows there is a tendency to reject the group ritual. We often forget that we need both our own individuality and a deep groundedness in the social group, which can only be forgotten at our peril. When we are cut off from a sound historical group consciousness, even educated people can fall prey to "isms" like Nazism and Communism, or we can be taken in by some person seemingly possessed by "spirit and power."

No person or group at the height of classical Greek culture made an important decision without consulting one of the oracles, where the prophet or prophetess gave an answer while in a trancelike state. The guilds of the prophets described in the Old Testament used all sorts of methods to induce this kind of state. Some of the great Hebrew prophets spoke out of trance-like states and had visions; some of them believed that the voice of God spoke through them. They believed that this was a particular gift for a few instruments of God. However, when Jesus said that the Kingdom of God is within you, he democratized the prophetic role. All Christians may have some share in the shamanistic role by their participation in the Kingdom.

The Christian priesthood that developed through the first centuries of our age had two functions: on the one hand it interpreted the sayings and life of Jesus and the religious framework that he accepted, and it provided the life-giving sacraments. On the other hand, the priest had the role of shaman and certainly was one who had contact with the Kingdom within. The Christian priesthood has combined both roles when it has been true to the teachings and practice of Jesus and his disciples. The priest became the mediator of both the tradition and the direct experience of the divine. Those who act as mediators of God are priests, whether ordained or not. This is one meaning of the priesthood of all true believers. The Church usually hedges the performance of rituals around with certain requirements, but within the Christian framework those who would lead others along the way to God (and this is the essential function of spiritual guidance and companionship) need to be well versed in the tradition, have their own experience of the spiritual world, have a well-developed common sense (a developed critical intelligence), know something of the working of the human psyche and be representatives of the *love* that makes us genuine followers of Christ.

In most societies becoming a shaman requires a long period of training, of learning what it means to be dismembered and brought to wholeness again and coming to deal with the powerful realities, both positive and destructive, of the spiritual world. This kind of training is what is so much neglected in our education for Christian ministry today. It is necessary for some people if there is to be sound spiritual guidance available for all kinds of hungry men and women today. In every period of Christian history there have been saints who were revitalizing centers of the life of the Church and who brought a new sense of the immediacy of the Kingdom to the people. We need to know well the lives and practices of these people if we are to be guides and companions on the inner way.

5. We have already described the gifts of the spirit, the charismata, in chapter 4. The charismatic renewal is an expression of the immediacy of the Kingdom now. These gifts of proclamation and revelation and discernment, of wisdom and knowledge, of faith and healing, are considered outward and visible evidences that the Kingdom is exploding out into the lives of ordinary Christians. In some groups there is even an encouragement of a trance-like state known as being slain in the spirit or resting in the spirit. I have described this phenomenon in detail in *Discernment*. Speaking in tongues is often seen as *the* sign of having been touched by the spirit, and prophecy is encouraged, as well as sharing of visions and dreams. At the risk of being repetitious *ad nauseam*, I must say again that these experiences should not be squelched, but rather interpreted within the context of a sound historical and liturgical tradition, in the light of the lives of the saints, sifted through a critical evaluation intellectually and psychologically, and evaluated by the *love* they produce. If love rather than law, is not primary, the movement is not of the Holy Spirit.

6. Although healing is usually described as one of the gifts of the spirit, there is almost more interest in healing through faith or healing with a spiritual dimension outside the Church than within. The body can produce its own opiates (many times more powerful than the opium derivatives) and healing substances, which are released by the faith and confidence of the patient. These are the endorphins. The materialism of our time has silently eroded away the healing practice that was common in the history of the Western church, a practice that remained common in the Eastern church, as I have shown in *Healing and Christianity*. The fact that the healing movement was embraced by the somewhat suspect

charismatic renewal has not made the practice more popular among the mainline churches.

Psychologists like Lawrence LeShan in *The Medium, the Mystic and the Physicist* and nurses like Dolores Krieger in *The Therapeutic Touch* have pointed out the mystery of healing and the *fact* that prayer and sacramental actions like touching and anointing still produce healing. Psychiatrist Jerome Frank speaks of the healing power of faith in *Persuasion and Healing.* Following the discoveries of Candace Pert, physiologists have discovered that we have many inbuilt healing systems that faith stimulates.

If there is anything that can lift people out of the realm of disbelief and open them to the reality of the Kingdom it is being healed of illness. In the experience of being healed we know the reality of a loving Abba. When we are lifted out of depression, anxiety and inner psychic agony through Christian meditative practice we are less doubtful about the victory and power of the Risen Jesus. Likewise, the experience of acting in obedience to the instruction of Jesus and going out to preach and teach and heal can bring a new level of conviction about the closeness of spiritual reality as we observe healings taking place through us. The healing ministry can be an effective way of mediating the reality of the Kingdom, as Paul states in Romans 15:18.

7. The use of the oracle is an attempt to determine the meaning of the time in which we live, to discover the will of God or to get a hint of the way we should go into the future. This is a religious practice that has been used by nearly every highly developed religious group. Many ways have sprung up to assist us to discern our path through this often dark and murky life. Astrology, the reading of stars, dream interpretation, the examination of the entrails of animals, the sacred lots of the Old Testament, the method of I Ching, tea leaves within a cup . . . the list is nearly endless. All of them are attempts to read the meaning of inner reality through events within this world. Gideon used such a method. The apostles chose the successor to Judas through lots. Mennonite bishops are still selected that way, and most of us have opened a Bible at random and put our finger down upon the page to see if it can provide light in our perplexity. In these kinds of action we are trying to understand the world of spirit or *Tao* as it shines through this material world. Somehow the depths of our being and the outer stimulation often produce hints of wisdom that we do not find otherwise. Let us not reject out of hand that which has been so much a part of our deep and ancient religious tradi-

tion. It was the thinking of Dr. Jung that snapped me out of my total rejection of all such practices and offered the idea of synchronicity to account for them.

8. The word *asceticism* has a bad connotation to most people, and many feel that any ascetical practice is world-denying and to be relagated to the dump in which we deposit outmoded superstitions. We shudder when we read descriptions of the excesses of fasting, self-punishment, lack of sleep and both mental and physical self-torture that are described by William James in his study of religion. Much of this nonsense has been the result of gnosticism, which has viewed the world and the body and sex (in particular) as evil in essence.

Asceticism need not mean this kind of thing. It is helpful to see that the word comes from the Greek and simply means a discipline or an exercise that enables us to become more proficient in what we are doing. As a matter of fact, any human development requires that we give up some things and do other things. We are limited human beings. Discipline is absolutely central to the development of any kind of skill, whether it is in sports, in scientific discovery or in learning to love or pray. Richard Foster's *The Celebration of Discipline* calls us to the disciplines of meditation, prayer, fasting, study, simplicity, solitude, submission, service, confession, worship, guidance and celebration. The very popularity of the book is an indication of the need we human beings have for discipline, for asceticism. The Christian Church, and we its members, have reacted so strongly against the world-denying nonsense that it erroneously professed for so long that we have neglected the place of healthy asceticism.

There is a need for freedom and spontaneity, but sometimes this freedom and openness to another dimension is given us through our disciplines. Fasting can be to the body what silence is to the mind and soul. As a matter of fact, few of us can do much in the way of real meditation on a full stomach, as all practitioners of yoga know. Disciplined exercise on a regular basis can actually open us up to the beauty of the body and physical things. Of course, fasting should never be undertaken in depression, and exercise should always be done within our physical limitations. We need definite times for prayer, quiet and Bible reading. Richard Foster gives us an excellent introduction to a modern asceticism. Without it few of us will achieve the communion with the spiritual world of which we are capable.

9. It is only in recent years that the power of group process has been

studied in depth by psychology. The discoveries that resulted from this work, which began in Bethel, Maine, have had a profound effect upon our culture. Out of this have developed the many different organizations that have used this dynamic to mold people in one direction or another or to open them to an experience of the nonphysical realm. Encounter groups, EST, group marathons and long prayer meetings use the same principles. Within a group that meets together over a long period of time ego defenses tend to break down, and we become more open to one another and to the experiences of the psychic domain in general.

Some years ago the Episcopal Church conceived the idea that Christian education was essentially a matter of group process, and that as we opened ourselves to it, the Kingdom would automatically be invoked. Parish leaders and ministers were advised to attend Group Life Labs, in which we were initiated into the mysteries of the cult and then could share the secrets of this experience with our parishes. I had been in analysis for some time when I thought of participating in this venture. I was somewhat deflated when my analyst responded to my plan with these words: "I think that you are strong enough so that you will not be damaged by the experience." She went on to remind me that the Hitler youth groups, as well as the Nazi party, derived their power from group dynamics.

I attended the sessions. The experience was a powerful one and a watershed time for me. I realized much about myself that I had not seen in many years of analysis. It was indeed an opening to a new level of psychoid reality, but I realized that it could be an instrument of evil, as well as of the divine. The experience does indeed break down ego defenses and open us up to deep levels of ourselves and to the spiritual world beyond our own discrete personalities. Without help in assimilating these experiences on a one-to-one basis, though, the experience can be extremely destructive. These experiments in Christian education had to be abandoned because so many people were tragically injured by them. They were unable to integrate that to which they were opened, and no opportunity was provided to facilitate that integration. Many of the leaders were simply unaware of the depths and troubles within us human beings or to the negative as well as the positive side of spiritual reality.

Through the wise guidance of Dr. Ollie Backus, who worked with our parish for many years in using group dynamics as an educational tool, I have come to see that the leader of any such program will determine its quality and nature. If the leader is unconsciously hostile or destructive, the group will reflect evil and destructiveness. When the leader is led by the Holy Spirit and love, the group can be unbelievably creative. The fellowship of the Church of the first three centuries had this spirit. Wesley revived the same spirit in the small groups of early Methodism.

For many years I was a leader of a prayer group that met weekly for an hour or so. Again and again we discovered that people who were not able to become quiet and reach through to another dimension by themselves were able to do it in the presence of others who were trying to be open to spiritual experience. There was an actual contagion of a positive kind, which enabled some people to break through the barrier of our materialistic consciousness. They could then carry this experience over to their private prayer times. I myself find it easier to be quiet and open when in the presence of others engaged in the same process than when alone.

10. In nearly every developed religion there have been groups of people who have desired to live in community with one another. The monastic tradition is found in most Eastern as well as Western religions. The Book of Acts speaks of this kind of community. Monasticism has been an attempt to provide group living in total dedication to the practice of the faith. When the growing Church accommodated itself to the world that accepted it, many people sought refuge in communities in order to have a more vital Christian life and practice. Unfortunately, this movement was often contaminated with a gnostic rejection of the body and sexuality. With this attitude, monasticism spread throughout the Church until there was a pervasive belief (quite contrary to Jesus and the early Church) that we could be *truly* religious only if we were sexless celibates living solitary or community lives. In his writings concerning religious communities St. Ambrose never suggests avoidance of sexuality as the reason for religious orders. Rather, he sees that women who lived in the Roman society of that time were either playthings or slaves of their husbands and were not free to follow fully their Christian profession. Men were caught up in a similar lack of freedom. The religious order was actually a liberation for them.

During the Middle Ages in Europe life was a struggle, and except for the rich, there was no hope of service except through monastic life, just as in Bangladesh today. There is no question that one of Jesus' clearest commandments is that of reaching out to the poor and those who have been crushed down by life. Reaching out to these people can necessitate celibate life.

One of the finest communities I know is that of the Benedictines at Pecos, New Mexico. They attempt there to provide for all five of the elements of spiritual guidance and maturity that I have suggested. There are parallel living situations for men and women, so that they can meet at meals and work and pray together. Few are the men and women who can grow to their full human or spiritual maturity without interaction with their inner, unconscious contrasexual side. And for most of us this is impossible without some interaction with flesh-and-blood people of the opposite sex.

The loving religious community can provide for discipline (asceticism) and for an atmosphere in which spiritual growth and openness to the spiritual domain are possible. It can also provide a knowledge of the Christian tradition and foster a critical intellectual attitude. There are some religious communities in which married couples live together in order to free themselves for both prayer and service. Bethany Fellowship in Minneapolis is a fine example, one which has been in existence for many years. The same kind of community living has been tried by many of the charismatic groups. Living in community and interaction in service and in worship may enable people of certain psychological types to be more open to the spiritual dimension. *It is so important for the spiritual companion to be aware of the enormously different ways in which we are most creatively opened to the boundless realms of spiritual reality and to encourage others on their way, not ours.*

Three Dangerous Doors

There are three common practices that enable people to break out of their total preoccupation with the physical world around us but they can be very dangerous. I question the use of all three of them for the same reason: there is a total abandonment of our individuality and little attempt to view these experiences critically. Often there is a naive sense that there is no evil that can touch us from the other side, the attitude of the once-born Christian described by William James. It is very important that those of us who would be companions on the spiritual journeys of others and who are basically optimistic and of this once-born make-up at least be aware of the inner darkness and evil with which many people deal. What is not dangerous for some can be deadly for other people. Naivete is almost never a qualification for a spiritual director or guide.

There is a kind of hypnosis that can be very dangerous. The word *hypnosis* has a variety of meanings; it refers to very different actual practices. There are national associations for the use of hypnotism in which hypnotism means a gentle suggested meditational experience, the kind of experience that Assagioli recommends in *Psychosynthesis*. This kind of practice can be very helpful, and I have used it for years in prayer groups with no ill results. We are always making suggestions to others, and it is nearly always better to offer positive suggestions than negative ones, particularly for doctors, counselors, and psychologists! There is a many-pointed scale from this kind of "activity" to the type of hypnosis that is described so well in Charles Tart's *Altered States of Consciousness*.

In this latter kind of hypnosis, which is typified by the practices of Svengali or Rasputin, another takes total control of our personalities. I very seriously doubt if any person has a moral right to take total control of another's life. This is the essential evil in slavery and prostitution (which is slavery for a limited time). One of the essential manifestations of evil is that it desires to possess, whereas the divine and the holy seek to encounter and relate. Between these two there is a great gulf fixed.

There are several old-wives' tales about hypnotism that need to be corrected. The idea that people will not do anything under hypnosis that they would not do consciously is simply not true. William Sargant, in *Battle for the Mind*, tells that many people were hanged in England for crimes they did not commit. The actual murderers showed up later. In nearly every case the individual, under the stress of police investigation, the "third degree," had signed confessions that resulted in their deaths. This kind of interrogation is a kind of hypnotism, as is intensive brain-washing.

Those who are unconventional and have their own firm, individual point of view, are least open to hypnotism. The people who live and act almost totally within the conventional point have already shown how suggestive they are. They have been hypnotized by society already.

As legal proceedings have shown, some physicians have used hypnosis for purposes other than the removal of pain. There is also a real danger in using hynosis to get rid of minor bad habits such as smoking or biting fingernails or overeating, as these can be ways of coping with deeper and darker things. Once they are removed, it is possible for some people to be thrown into the deeper problem, sometimes an overwhelming one. On the whole, the more radical kind of hypnosis should be used only in controlled experimental research and in situations where pain or behavior problems must be dealt with and there is no other way to do it. The only person whom I would trust totally to take over my soul is the Risen Christ, and he wishes to relate to me, not to possess me.

Mediumship has been very common in the history of religions. Mediums are those who give up conscious direction of their own psyches in order that some other spirit may control and speak through them. Undoubtedly this is possible, but it is dangerous for many reasons. First of all, the total abandonment of our autonomy suggests that we *should be* so used by others. This is not the way of Jesus of Nazareth or mature Christianity. Second, there may be evil or ambivalent spirits that can speak through us and can do much harm. Third, thinking of ourselves as mouthpieces of the divine or of discarnate spirits can give rise to inflation or *hubris.* And fourth, statements that come via this method are often taken by people as authoritative. This is particularly true of those with a materialistic background who are overimpressed with this kind of phenomenon. All ideas and statements that come through mediumship need careful critical evaluation. And last of all, when mediums are not in contact with the other dimension they often fabricate and falsify. One student of the subject said to me, "Some mediums lie all of the time, and all mediums lie some of the time." They are expected to produce whether anything comes through to them or not.

It is one thing to receive spontaneous experiences of the deceased or precognitive flashes; it is quite another to seek out those who can provide these for us. C. S. Lewis once remarked that God has taken such trouble to keep the future from us that most of us would be wise to live in the present and leave the future to God.

There are two common practices that have many of the characteristics of mediumship: automatic writing and use of the ouija board. In both cases there is an attempt to release ourselves from the conscious direction of our personalities and allow whatever comes to take over. Often something does come, and it is seldom the Holy Spirit, because (and I am being purposely repetitive for emphasis) the creative aspect of spiritual reality wishes to *encounter* us and not to *possess* us. One of the real dangers of keeping a religious journal is that writing in it can slip into automatic writing, and we can be uncritically and unduly impressed. The real use of an ouija board is not child's play, but is serious confrontation with the spiritual dimension of reality. Beware!

The last way of opening ourselves to the psychoid dimension is the use of hallucinogenic drugs, which we have already discussed as being so common within our culture. Many religious groups have used drugs as part of their religious ritual; however, this is quite uncommon among the more developed religions. Even Don Juan used no drugs with Carlos

Casteneda until this shaman had exhausted every other means. The use of these drugs outside of well-developed religious traditions can be dangerous, particularly for people with personality problems and little discipline.

It is a tragedy that in a church that does not offer the more creative types of spiritual experience that I have been describing, people come to believe that the use of hallucinogens provides the *only way* to this inner experience. The church that does not believe in and provide methods of spiritual encounter is driving people into dangerous alternatives. There is a deep instinctual need for experience of both dimensions of reality, and if the religious institutions do not provide it, people will find nonreligious and dangerous methods of achieving this kind of experience. One of my students at Notre Dame remarked in a concluding paper for a class that he had been in church schools for sixteen years and that our class on the phenomenology of religious experience was the first time he had heard the suggestion that meditation could provide a deeper and more significant experience of spiritual reality than drugs.

When the milder hallucinogens are used regularly there often develops a dissatisfaction with the mundane world of physical existence. The more potent hallucinogens can fling us into the depth of the unconscious, into the vast ocean of spiritual reality where there are both destructive and creative elements. Our ego standpoint has been dissolved chemically, and our situation can be likened to that of being on a wild sea in a rudderless boat. Again, it is one thing to find ourselves there and another to throw ourselves into that situation. The bad drug trip is like being caught defenseless in a stormy sea, usually far from a guide who can help.

The spiritual director dealing with young people who have had experience with drugs needs to be knowledgeable, charitable, nonjudgmental, and equipped to show that there are better ways of entering into the spiritual depths of life than drugs offer. They also need to be aware of ways to rescue people from the psychic storms and the abysses into which many fall in the drug experience and elsewhere on the spiritual journey.[13]

NOTES

1. Aldous Huxley, *Doors of Perception* (New York: Harper and Row, 1970), pp. 23, 24.

2. Kenneth Ring, *Life at Death: A Scientific Investigation of the Near-Death Experience* (New York: Coward, McCann & Geoghegan, 1980), and Michael Sabom, *Recollections of Death: A Medical Investigation* (New York: Harper and Row, 1981).

3. Gerald May, *Care of Mind Care of Spirit*, p. 36.

4. In *Christo-Psychology* and *God, Dreams and Revelation* I have described the difference between Jungian and Freudian dream interpretation. In *Dreams, A Way to Listen to God* and in *Adventrue Inward* I have presented a nontechnical method by which the person with little or no training in psychology can come to some understanding of their dreams.

5. Alan Watts, *Behold the Spirit: A Study in the Necessity of Mystical Religion* (New York: Pantheon Books, 1947), pp. 176, 178, 179.

6. William James, *The Varieties of Religious Experience*, pp. 392–393.

7. Ibid., p. 362.

8. Aldous Huxley, *Tomorrow and Tomorrow and Tomorrow, and Other Essays* (New York: Harper and Row, 1956), p. 68.

9. An excellent description of this Chinese Taoistic teaching is found in Jolan Chang, *The Tao of Love and Sex: The Ancient Chinese Way to Ecstasy* (New York: E. P. Dutton, 1977). It concludes with a sermon given by Joseph Needham, in his address for Caius Chapel, Cambridge University on Whitsunday, 1976. It offers an understanding of sexuality within Christianity similar to what I have given. Norman Pittinger stated in a series of lectures many years ago that D. H. Lawrence's *Lady Chatterley's Lover* was an example of redemption through sexual love.

10. William James, *The Varieties of Religious Experience*, pp. 464–465.

11. Eugene d'Aguili and Charles Laughlin, Jr., "The Biopsychological Determinants of Religious Ritual Behavior," *Zygon*, March 1975.

12. In chapters 12, 13, 14, 15, and 16 of *The Other Side of Silence, A Guide to Christian Meditation*, I have examined in detail the relationship between ritual, image, tradition and the inner way. The reader who wishes further development of these ideas is referred to those pages. I know of few other discussions of this material.

13. An excellent presentation of religious experiences of alcoholics as they have bottomed out and turned to God is found in *Came to Believe* . . . Alcoholics Anonymous World Services, Inc. Box 459, Grand Central Station, New York, New York 10017.

Chapter 7

THE PERSONAL JOURNAL AS A
SACRAMENT OF THE INNER JOURNEY*

Which of all these doors to the inner world is the most helpful in facilitating our journey toward the center of life and reality? How do we pick and choose among these sometimes confusing opportunities? There are several practices that I have found most rewarding and creative over the last thirty-five years. I have found the worship and fellowship of a church necessary to keep my bearings. In recent years the sacraments, and particularly the Eucharist, have become increasingly important to me. I have found honest sharing with trusted friends and guides crucial at times. I have found it helpful to have a small group of people with whom I can pray in order to receive confirmation of my inner way. I have found it important to have those with whom I could discuss ideas, with whom I could share my study and thinking. Reading of the Bible and the great devotional masters have fed my soul. And then I have had my times in silence, in prayer, in dialogue, in contemplation and meditation, which have been a central and stabilizing factor within my life. My practice of keeping a personal religious journal has tied all of these elements together.

The personal journal has been a great help to many people as they have tried to deepen and enrich their religious lives, both outwardly and inwardly. For many it has become almost a sacrament of their religious

* Those who wish to pursue the ideas in this chapter in more detail are referred to my book *Adventure Inward*, which is a practical guide on how to use the journal as a companion on the inner journey. In *The Other Side of Silence* I have presented the theoretical basis upon which this Christian method of meditation is based.

way, a symbol of the religious quest. Some of the most important Christian devotional reading is little more than a reproduction of the journals of outstanding religious leaders. Augustine's *Confessions* begins a new genre in religious and psychological writing; he writes from a uniquely Christian perspective. Within the Christian theological framework each individual has unique and ultimate value, and so the reflections upon each life convey something of that divine value. These thoughtful musings over our lives may also give help to others on their religious journeys.

The *Journal* of John Woolman provides a dramatic insight into the beginning of the abolition of slavery in the United States as well as giving a clear picture of the Quaker religious way, which inspired his social action. René Descartes kept a careful journal, and in it is recorded the dream that brought him from chaos to clarity and gave him the inspiration for his *Discourse on Method*. Some of the most helpful of Thomas Merton's writings are reproductions of portions of his journals. If we wish to discover the real John Wesley we need to read the selections from the many volumes of his published journals. Most Christian masters of the inner way (those who could read and write) found it necessary to keep some record of their pilgrimage toward God.

My own journal-keeping practice started some thirty-five years ago as I began to take the religious way seriously. I realized that I needed to reflect upon my life, that I needed times to bring my life and activities into focus. Even before this, I kept lists of the people I had called upon and the engagements I had in parish life. I realized how easy it was to have life run me when I did not try to take some control of it. How was I to fit my parish activities, my wife and children and family events together with my own needs and desires? I certainly can't hand the reins of my life over to God until I have them in my own hand. This level of journal-keeping was largely rational, conscious, and reflective, attempting to bring order and sense into my life. However, having developed the habit of reflection I discovered that on occasions something of a deeper nature emerged out of the depth of me. For instance, one day I felt that my life and everything around me was dull and uninteresting. I stopped in the church and quietly sat in the "grayness" with my journal open before me. After some time the thought popped into my head that grayness means that the sun is shining somewhere, and it is much better than blackness. After I had meditated quietly in the grayness for about twenty minutes, gradually the gray fog lifted, and I found myself bathed in the bright light of God's presence. I remember writing this down. I also discovered that the insights that I recorded stuck with me and were more likely to be integrated into my life than those ideas and experiences that were not written down.

The big change in my journal keeping came, however, when I was introduced to the writings of Fritz Kunkel, and I began to realize that dreams might have great significance for my psychological and religious life. When I began to take the dream seriously and record it I realized that there was a lot going on within me of which I had not been aware. As I opened my life to this level I realized that I had received no training in the nature or the depth of the human psyche nor how to deal with it. I was caught within a materialistic world view and did not see how God could help. For a clergyman this alone can cause deep anxiety. There were other factors involved, and the time came when I knew that I needed some help in dealing with these forces at war within. Taking our inner lives seriously can result in our facing deepest conflicts and may reveal hideous monsters within. We may find we need help with these things. People who start to keep journals on the inner journey should always recognize this possibility.

During the next six years I learned a great deal about using the journal as a catalyst in growing toward wholeness. I recorded experience after experience giving evidence of another dimension of reality. I used my journal to sketch out and elaborate a new schema of the total world in which I lived. Max Zeller gave me encouragement to use the journal to work with the conflicts and images that had risen from the depth. Then I learned to use the journal to mobilize the imagination, to bring me in contact with the divine and to defeat the forces of darkness that I found within. During the latest phase of my journal keeping I have concentrated on the journal as part of the religious process and have found Ignatius of Loyola, John Woolman, C. G. Jung, and other religious writers of tremendous help. In these last years I have shared my journal with my clergyman-psychologist friend Jack Sanford and with my religious-psychotherapist friends Andy Canale and George Lough. As I shall show later, a deeply personal inner journey that is not recorded and shared can be dangerous. It is a perilous path to go alone.

Outside of my friends and guides along the religious way, my journal keeping has helped me more to bring my life together and set me upon the religious way than any other one religious practice. It has kept me honest, given me companionship and allowed me to listen to the deepest levels of myself, allowed me to vent my deepest anger, and brought me into creative, saving relationship with the heart of reality, whom I have found to be a Divine Lover, Love Divine, all loves excelling.

In order to show how a journal can reveal some of the ways toward psychological and spiritual growth and can actually be a source of guidance upon it, I shall first of all outline the many different uses of a written daily record of our lives. Then I shall get into the nitty-gritty of how to start keeping a journal. I shall then describe some of the material a journal may contain. This will lead us to a personal log's most important use, to find relationship with the center of reality, to understand its message for us and to integrate our lives around this center. I shall conclude with a few words about the dangers of journal keeping and how to avoid them so that the log may provide its greatest potential benefits without the pitfalls.

What is a Journal For?

Before we set out to examine the religious use of a daily log, let us look first of all at why so little has been written over the years on the value of journal keeping for ordinary people. If people believe that we are of no value in the cosmic order, or if they think that these specific and individual egos and lives are illusion, it cerainly doesn't make much sense to spend time recording the events and reflections of our lives. We must also realize that even in the West universal education is very recent, and in the rest of the world the ability to read and write is more greatly limited. Also, only in the last few hundred years have writing materials been cheap enough so that anyone could afford them. To make journal keeping a highly valued part of the religious way in such a situation would have excluded a great portion of the populace. The very value of the journal can be another reason for bringing literacy to people.

People have been keeping records from the beginning of time. We find them everywhere, scratched on stones and monuments. People want to be remembered. They are afraid of being forgotten. But people have also kept records for themselves, and it is this kind of record we are talking about.

1. The first use of the diary or personal log is to record things so that we do not forget them, in order to keep track of money and property, of ideas, events and relationships. How fallible our memories are. Events

we thought would never grow dim can fade, get garbled, and be lost. Several years ago I had an amazing series of dreams. In one of them I found myself pierced with a beam of light that revealed the darkest and deepest hidden uglinesses within me. Then suddenly the light became an ordinary human being, who reached down and lifted me from where I was kneeling in the light. I wrote the whole experience out. I thought that I could remember all the details, but when I went back two years later I discovered that I had totally forgotten some of the most significant details and had avoided some of the obvious implications of the experience.

In addition, keeping a log gives continuity to our lives. Here is something solid and real about us, which we cannot change at will. This kind of record anchors us into space and time and shows their reality as well as our own.

2. Most of us like to talk about ourselves when others are interested. The journal gives me a concrete and creative way of talking to an unseen friend. In his play *The Fall*, Arthur Miller portrays the hero as often addressing the "listener," who is offstage and never appears. We can't always find a friend who will listen, but the journal will. We become more of who we are when we express what we experience ourselves to be.

3. Most of us have the urge to create, and as we create we move toward realizing our potential. The journal gives us a place in which the creative fancy can be let free. We can tell stories, write poetry, record insights and ideas. We can draw pictures or cartoons, or we can quote meaningful passages. We have already seen how this artistic madness often opens the door to the inner world.

4. The creative urge usually involves imagination. Few things can stimulate the imagination more for some people than a blank piece of paper and a pen or a typewriter. Some people find the same stimulation with paints and an empty canvas, others with cloth, still others with stone to be hewn into shape. The journal is something that we can always have with us, and it is one of the best ways in which imagination can be stimulated. Through imaginative play we can step across the threshold out of our purely materialistic existence.

We can learn in this way to express ourselves and be more creative and imaginative. This may well be more important than learning logic. Unfortunately, most school systems turn the torrent of natural creativity and imagination into a trickle by emphasizing unnecessary precision and order. Writing becomes hedged in by barriers of spelling, proper margins, legibility, and neatness. One of the most creative teachers I have known was able to stimulate a child defeated by a rigid education by realizing that he could tell better stories than anyone else in the class. She wrote them down, duplicated them, and used them as the reading book for the entire class. This let loose the natural torrent waiting to be released in this child.

5. When our emotions surge through us, emotions of fear or anger or love, it can be dangerous to give way to them, dangerous both for ourselves and for those who might be standing close by. Sometimes we do not even know the depth of an emotional conflict until we write down what we feel. This writing provides a *via media* between repression on the one hand and explosive action on the other. These emotions and feelings about others can be very harmful for them (one reason for writing and taking thought before expression), and so the journal, which really expresses our inner being, should be kept private and never casually left lying around. This privacy sometimes requires a code, for people are naturally very curious.

6. The journal not only gives us a safe way of dealing with the feelings that are often ready to burst out of us, but offers us objectivity about them as well. How different ideas seem as they lie naked on the page before us than in the moment of "inspiration." Sometimes they appear less and sometimes even more inspired. How much less powerful the emotions that consumed us on one day are when we look at them with a calmer disposition the next day. I have found that writing my fears down one by one can often remove the panic I feel when they are invading me like a hostile army. When we can look at them lying helpless in black and white on the pages of our journal, they often assume their proper size.

7. Most of us suffer far more than the people living next door realize. And most people around us really don't want to know about our sorrows and inner struggles. The journal can be an invaluable therapeutic instrument. It gives us space to deal with our inner turmoil. We can bring problems and fears, infatuations and hatreds into the open and deal with them face to face in honest combat. We can distinguish between friends and foes. In his book *No More for the Road*, Duane Hehl describes with utter honesty how he used a journal to live out and integrate the twelve steps of Alcoholics Anonymous. Later we shall show how we can deal with inner situations that seem to overwhelm us by expressing them in images and then introducing a savior figure to change the picture.

8. *Growth* is a slippery word. The question is: growth from what to what? Nonetheless, the journal is one of the best tools and aids in the process of inner development, in increasing self-knowledge and in spurring us on to fulfilling our maximum potential. Indeed, such movement toward wholeness and maturity is sometimes impossible for educated people without the use of some kind of continuous, recorded reflection.

In his book *At a Journal Workshop*, Ira Progoff provides an excellent set of practical exercises in this growth process, exercises that are taken from the actual experiences of his journal workshops. However, Progoff fails to express very clearly the goal toward which the process is leading.

I have found the journal a great help in teaching classes with students of various age groups, but particularly with college students and adults. Education can be the process of assimilation and changing through new insights and experiences. George Simons' *Keeping Your Personal Journal* shows how students can use a journal to help them in the learning process.

9. There is another, quite different reason for journal keeping: to deepen my relationship with that center of spiritual reality of which all the great religions of humankind speak. My goal in this kind of journal keeping is not so much to forge a chain of growth by my own effort as to bring the totality of my inner being to the blacksmith and cooperate with the forging. I return to Roy Fairchild's description of prayer: "paying full and fervent attention to all the god that you know—in Jesus Christ— with all of yourself you know." There is no doubt that a well-kept journal will provide deeper and deeper knowledge of all levels of ourselves, areas that need to be related to our personal experience of God. The journal also helps us to open us to deeper and deeper revelations of the nature of God as we reflect on scripture, on the religious experiences recorded throughout history, and on our own personal experience of God through our prayer and meditation.

It is not a matter of using a journal *either* to seek a relationship with God *or* to help us grow in our self-knowledge and effectiveness in the inner or outer worlds. *We begin to realize our potential when we use the journal for both reasons.* If my goal is to bring all of myself to God for redemption, renewal and transformation, I will need to use all of the nine practices that I have outlined above. If, however, my primary reason for using a journal is only my personal growth, I can quite easily avoid the demanding and sometimes painful experience of relating to the divine center of reality. I may even keep a journal for superficial intellectual reasons. And then I may avoid my maximum personal growth without even knowing it, because my vision is limited. C. G. Jung believed that none of us could attain our maximum wholeness except through the agency of a suprapersonal and objective center of love and meaning and wholeness that was more than our personal psyches.

10. Few people ever try to tie together their ideas or their lives until they stop and reflect and then record their reflections. There is a place for thinking and waiting upon the insights given by God, insights that show us how all these diverse aspects of our lives fit together. Clear and communicable expressions of our world view are practically impossible unless we write them down again and again and check them against all that we know. This is particularly important for preachers, teachers and spiritual guides who wish to share with others.

Starting a Journal

The first step in keeping a journal is action: going out and buying a journal. As long as reflections and dreams and insights are recorded on scraps of paper or the backs of envelopes, we are screaming aloud that we do not place much value on the inner journey and the recording of it. The log book need not be as complicated as Progoff suggests: sixteen carefully differentiated sections. I find that such complexity turns most people away from journal-keeping. Any looseleaf or bound composition book will do. I use the front of my journal for conscious reflection and lists and the back of the journal for those aspects which come more from the unconscious, from the depths of me and beyond. I also find it helpful to keep a mechanical pencil containing a large amount of lead exclusively for the journal. Thus the journal is always available for use at any time. I prefer a journal small enough so that I can carry it with me wherever I go, and large enough to last six months or a year. Some people prefer to do their journal work on a typewriter and bind the typed pages. I find typing a helpful adjunct to my notebook journal, but not the main medium of journaling, as I can always have my journal with me and my typewriter is somewhat bulky. I have found tape-recorded journal keeping cumbersome; it is also difficult to find information that we may desire to retrieve.

In the front pages of the journal I keep lists of various important pieces of personal information: the phone numbers and addresses of people whom I call often and with whom I correspond. I keep a list of people who are in my regular prayers, friends and enemies all mixed together, for obvious reasons, records of people that I have seen for counseling and what they owe me, lists of things that need to be done. I wrote the outlines for most of these chapters in this section of my journal. I do the first drafts of letters and book reviews or articles. I plan my schedules and speaking engagements and keep a calendar of events ahead.

This kind of recording may sound quite pedestrian, but at least all of my concerns are in one notebook, and I don't have a multiplicity of things to carry around with me. But there is also a value in having my ordinary life in the same book as my deepest prayers and reflections. This reminds me that all of my life, even my accounts with clients, belongs together as a part of my religious venture.

In the back of the journal and moving forward, Chinese style, another dimension of my journal takes flesh and life. First of all, I make a daily *dated* entry of where I am and the time of day. This is important. This practice locates me firmly in space and time and reminds me quickly when I have neglected my journal keeping.

Whether first thing in the morning or in the middle of the night, I first of all *always* record any dreams that I have just had. One reason for having the journal available with a pencil attached is that most dreams disappear within five minutes of awakening. If they are not recorded immediately they will usually be lost. If any meanings pop out of the dreams I will jot them down, but usually I find that I have further work to do if I am to understand them.

Then I reflect upon my general state of being, what might be bothering me, any particularly important experiences, anything noteworthy that happened the day before. I look at the day ahead and assess any situation that may appear difficult, and I try to gain perspective and objectivity. I reflect to see if there is anything that I need to pray for or about specifically.

Then, in quiet, I try to come into the presence of Abba or Jesus the Good Shepherd, or the inner voice of wisdom and love, the Holy Spirit. This inner wisdom personality is a palpable reality. One of Jung's most important contributions to the study of dreams and the understanding of the religious way was his theory and evidence that in many dreams a reality wiser, more concerned, and more kindly than our petty little egos is trying to get our attention in order to get us off the wrong path and onto the best one for the fulfillment of our personal destinies. Working with my dreams over many years I discovered, through the help of several people who knew the symbolic language of dreams well, that my dreams were indeed pointing the way out of one dead-end street after another. No one tried to force a meaning of dreams on me. These people revealed their meanings. Something clicked, and I knew the interpretation was right. No dream interpretation is correct unless it does inwardly click sooner or later with the person who dreamed it.

The idea that *something* nonphysical and outside of me knew me and was *interested* in me to the point that it staged a continuous series of dramas on the platform of my soul made the idea of providence concrete and real for me for the first time. Here was flesh and blood to put onto the theological bones that von Hügel had provided. The idea that *someone* or *something* wanted to communicate with me opened me to the next level of my daily prayer-journal experience.

After recording my dreams I then try to listen in the quiet to the inner voice of wisdom and love and hear what it has to say to me: words of correction, comfort, peace, love or direction. I did not learn to do this from any religious guide, but from a psychological one. Most of my religious teachers in the seminary, and few of them would have been comfortable being called guides, did not believe that such listening and talking with a helpful center of caring nonphysical power was a real possibility. No one had ever suggested it to them.

I remember clearly how this process of listening to God began. I came into Max Zeller's office one day feeling like death warmed over. He asked me why I was feeling so awful, and I replied that I couldn't sleep. I would wake up at two or three in the morning and then toss and turn the rest of the night with a fourteen-hour day of work facing me when I got out of bed. He asked me if I knew why I couldn't sleep.

I growled a "no," while thinking that it was his business to have the answer and that this was what I was paying my money for. And then he said, "The reason that you can't sleep is that God wants to talk with you." My answer was a sarcastic "Now really, you know I went to seminary." And then he said very calmly, "This is the way that God got in touch with Samuel. Do you think he's changed?"

If we are hurting enough and someone offers a sensible reason for some action we will even do something that seems as foolish to the world as getting up in the middle of the night and trying to talk to God. I did get up that night, and something spoke back that assured me of love and concern and pointed to a way of courage and discipline. After my half hour I went back to bed and went to sleep. I have continued this practice five or six times each and every week over the last thirty years. This practice, more than any other, has been the source of my contact with a cosmic carer, the source of the thread that has led me through the mazes I constantly keep falling into. This time of quiet has been the source of the best insights and inspirations and ideas that have come to me over the years. I find that I need at least twenty minutes to an hour each day for this reflecting and listening process.

This kind of deep listening and centering reflection does not have to take place during the night. It can take place any time during the day or night; it needs to occur, however, during our prime time, when we are most alert, not during the tag ends of our time when we are capable of doing nothing else. I find the nighttime helpful because when I awake I am already quiet; there are few interruptions between two and five in the morning, and I wake up bright-eyed and bushy-tailed. It is absolutely essential that we first come to quietness before we begin this listening process, or else we will reach only a superficial ego level of our being, and what comes will not be very significant or valuable. But even reflection in busyness is better than no reflection at all. I find that during about half of the times that I sit before the wisdom of the Kingdom something from beyond my own intelligence and knowledge breaks in upon me.

Journaling in Depth

I personally find that I need at least three different kinds of time in which I use my journal intensively. This is in addition to trying to practice the presence of God during the day as Brother Lawrence and Thomas Kelly suggest. First of all, I need the daily half-hour or so that I have already described; however, I have come to realize that I can only go so far and so deep in that brief daily time. I often call these daily occasions for reflection and listening my daily "love letters" to the Divine Lover, although sometimes they contain anything but loving sentiments. They form the basic foundation of my adventure inward toward an intimate relationship with God.

Secondly, I find that I need a period of two to four hours every two or three weeks *in which I have nothing else to do.* I focus my entire being upon my inner journey.

I also find that it is necessary to stop whenever the inner darkness or inner pain becomes intense and deal with it immediately. I find that I am more likely to experience this darkness when I have not had my regular longer times of quiet, when I have been sick, and when I have not had adequate sleep. Most of us who travel this path will find guilt and pain and darkness. I doubt if it is necessary to stay within it for any prolonged periods, particularly if it interferes with our outer effectiveness. It is easy to glory in our dark night of the soul in a masochistic way. Some spiritual leaders may not have known the way to pass through these dark periods. Others have found them as congenial as their hairshirts and lice. We can continue to be very humble without remaining in a dark night. Indeed, if bringing the darkness and anguish and dryness to the one who has conquered the prince of darkness does not help me after one or two or three attempts I seek out a spiritual guide who may be able to see in me what I cannot see within myself and help me through the darkness.

It seems to me after deep reflection and reading many books on spiritual guidance that many people who write about the dark night of the soul have never experienced or known the depth of agony it can produce and how easily it can slip into real and destructive depression. I have had some experience in this area within myself and as a companion to many others in this condition, and I know that every spiritual guide needs to realize the dangers of the dark night, which are described so well by William James in his Gifford lectures. Spiritual guides who do not know or appreciate the dangers of the dark night may very well unconsciously shut out those who are experiencing them and leave them high and dry without help or guidance in a worse state than before they started the journey.

Every companion does not need to be an expert in this area, but everyone needs to be sensitive to it. This is simply Christian charity and love in action. If guides have never experienced such darkness it is imperative that they know someone who has experienced and passed through it, to whom people in *persistent spiritual darkness may be referred.*

I also find that at least once a year I need a period of at least thirty-six hours of total quiet and reflection. After a very busy time I may need longer, sometimes a week, or even a month. I have found that after many months of intensive work it may take several weeks before I can unwind and the depth of me begins to be revealed. Jung said that after three months of continuously listening to people in their agony and confusion he needed a month away to unpoison himself. It can also be helpful for others whom we are counseling or guiding to learn to get along without us, and good for our humility to realize that they can. This does not mean that we leave our family and other personal responsibilities behind. Rather we are given a fresh look at these aspects of life.

During this period we are sometimes given entirely new perspectives on who we are and how God wants us to serve. We may need to draw up a new list of priorities. When students come to me worrying about which profession they are to enter, I have found it helpful to remind them that one vital person may live through two or three or even more different professions in one lifetime. It is in these times of lengthy encounter with God that we can be given the courage to change the direction of our lives. During the time of writing this book I found it necessary to spend a lot of time with myself, and a very new and different set of priorities appeared to be necessary for my life.

If I am going to have a transforming and renewing personal, spiritual encounter I must first of all learn to be silent and to listen. I need to stop all outer doing. This kind of inner *work* cannot be done while knitting or doing the dishes. Then I try to stop the inner chattering that goes on in most of us most of the time. With this I often discover that my inner rages and storms begin to quiet down and I am looking out on a calm ocean with the silver pathway of a sinking full moon. If I feel any tension I need to release it by relaxing the muscles from my face to the top of my head, through my neck to my torso and limbs. Tension is congealed action, being ready to spring. I will usually find that I am breathing slowly and rhythmically when I relax. If not, I can bring my breathing to slow, even, deep inhalations and exhalations. This quieting of my whole being brings a kind of detachment from outer sensations and involvements that alone often opens me to another dimension of experience.

Once we are in this state we can move in one of eight different directions. I can give only the barest outlines of these practices in this chapter. However, anything real can be summarized. Those who wish to be spiritual companions need to have some knowledge of each of these processes. They need to know those who are particularly gifted in each of them so appropriate referrals may be made.

Since the dream is the natural altered state of consciousness, something nearly everyone has experienced, I will first suggest methods by which it can be understood. I have already mentioned keeping a record of dreams, since most of them are forgotten if they are not written down shortly after they occur. Seldom do they get written down unless we keep a journal. Once we have become quiet we can reenter a dream, live within it and listen to its meaning. Once reimmersed in the dream there are several different directions we can follow.

We can merely savor its quality, and sometimes a meaning will spring out of its structure and story as out of significant events in our lives when we reflect upon them or out of a good drama when we think about it and listen to its message. Or we can bring the dream before the dreamer within, that source of the dream and the wisdom that seems to know more about us and our destinies than our conscious egos know. We can ask for a meaning and message, and often in the quiet listening understanding will come. We can pray for the understanding of dreams as we can for the meaning of troublesome events in our lives.

And then we can dialogue with the various characters within the dream, from a deceased brother to the carpet on the floor, from an ape to an angel. We can ask them who they are, what they are doing there in our dreams, and what they have to tell us. Until we have tried this inner conversation (and some people have a far greater aptitude for it than others), it is difficult to realize the range and depth of information and meaning these inner figures can provide; often they provide content that our rational minds would not have considered. It is important after *becoming quiet* (nearly always the necessary prelude) to approach these images in an attitude that is a combination of *playfulness and seriousness.*

I remember being awakened one night by a very vivid dream in which I sensed an intruder at my bedroom door. Even now, writing about it twenty years later, the dream comes back vividly. I was frightened and in the dream slammed the door shut and locked it. I realized that I needed to find out who the intruder was. I spent some time in conversation with him after bringing the dream back to reality in my imagination. The dream had a numinous quality. As I confronted this intruder I discovered that he was not negative. He was a positive presence, the Risen Christ figure, who playfully reminded me that I had been praying for his presence and didn't like it much when he came. I have also discovered in working with some of the negative characters—bums and thugs and others who were attacking or pursuing me—that as I confronted them they often turned out to be parts of me that had been repressed. They had turned hostile and negative in order to get my attention and regain their rightful place. For many people this kind of practice is very helpful in enabling them to bring all of themselves to God for transformation.

We can also step into a positive or numinous or significant dream and let it move on and take us with it and show us how it can be actualized. Dreams are neither good nor bad. We make the dream valuable by our action. We give the dream its value by what we do with it. The dream is creative if it is either a positive dream that has been actualized or a negative, warning dream that has been heeded. Both can lose their value if we do nothing with them.

Many years ago I dreamed of a large and wise-looking turtle, which came up out of the ocean onto a sandy, palm-studded beach. The turtle was imparting a wise lecture, which I forgot before I awoke. I felt that its message was important, and so I returned to the dream-beach, and the turtle obligingly came up out of the ocean once again, but it wouldn't speak. However, it did lead me over to the rock wall that towered up behind the beach and knocked three times at the stone cliff. A door opened, and I entered. For two years I spent several hours each month exploring this inner world that the turtle had revealed, and I discovered most of the great myths of humankind spinning themselves out within me.

We can also step into a dream that troubles us and live with it. Slowly and *playfully* we can nudge it to a more satisfactory solution. Sometimes this kind of action can actually change the quality of our psyches, making us more mature, and even change our relationship with the world around us. Sometimes, in the strange working of synchronicity, this practice can even change the objective world outside of us. How different the world looked after I spent some time with a recurring dream in which my childhood home was on fire. Someone suggested that I enter back into this dream, which had happened many times (those dreams that come again usually suggest that we have not yet heard their message), and instead of trying to put the fire out with the garden hose or calling the fire department, just let the house go up in flames. This was a pivotal experience for me, one in which I realized that I needed to let my childishness be consumed. The fire was of the Holy Spirit, not of hell.

In yet another way we can step through imagination into a dream. When we seem to have no power to turn a dream around we can invoke the presence of an inner saving figure (for me usually the Risen Christ) and let him or her bring about the creative resolution. One of the finest examples of this process I have used before, but it is so fine that I repeat it here. I had been working for some time with a very creative woman who had been damaged by an authoritarian religious sect, which her family had accepted in entirety. Finding a sense of worth was very difficult for her. She had the following dream:

I was with a group of women; it was some type of party, but very boring to me. I decided to leave early, but before going I noticed a small baby lying on a couch. The poor child looked as if it hadn't been fed recently.

I decided to breast-feed the child, knowing full well that I wouldn't have any milk. Well, to my surprise, the milk began to flow. The baby became very cheerful, laughing and happy.

The mother came; she looked like an irresponsible young thing. I thought she was going to take the baby and go home, but she preferred to party. And in leaving, she told me that the baby was retarded anyway.

My friend realized that this dream spoke of her own vision of herself. It portrayed her inner idiot. A few days later she wrote the following fantasy, which lifted her mood and gave her a real sense of value once again. Seldom have I seen a better example of the process of turning a dream around in imaginative prayer, and it was a turning point in her growth process.

I am sitting and cursing myself for being such a fool! "I am nothing," I tell myself. "Unintelligent, worthless—an idiot!" How I hate myself. Who would ever want and care for me?

The more I tell myself these things, of course, the gloomier I get. The world is horrible! No redemption, happiness, nothing!

The time passes, and I feel there's no hope. Hopelessness completely takes over. I am temporarily shaken from this mood, for a knock comes on the door. I open it, and there before me stands a most hideous-looking hag! She is holding a bundle. The bundle is, of course, a baby.

She tells me to take care of it for a while. "No one will," she said. She had been door-to-door, but each person had refused her.

The hag told me just to care for the child a while.

Well, certainly I thought of refusing. I don't have time to care for any baby. And what right does the ugly creature standing in front of me have to tell me to take care of a brat!

The hag's eyes looked as if they were reaching to my very soul. I began to tremble. "Well," I said, "Don't be too long." She said, "I won't be long, and I thank you." She handed me the baby and left.

It scarcely weighed anything, and I thought maybe the woman had fooled me and handed me nothing but blankets.

I began to take the blankets away from the child. I gave a scream of fright, for I was holding a most deformed-looking child. It was the most hideous of idiots. I put the child down and ran away from it! "What has this woman done to me?" I dared not enter into that room again.

After a while, the child began to whimper. It was probably hungry, but I dared not feed it, let alone touch it. What was I to do?

The child then began to cry. A pathetic, desperate cry of complete helplessness. No one wanted it, no one loved or cared for it. One would rather have it rot than touch it.

The crying increased! What was I to do? I began wringing my hands in desperation. The child needed help, and I was the one left to do it.

I went into the room to the child. I looked into its face. How revolting! How horrible! I picked the baby up, and it quit crying. I could barely look into its face.

I had no bottle with which to feed it; it was too young to drink from a cup. What was I to do? My breasts began to throb. They felt hardened and full, like the breasts of a woman who nurses her child.

My blouse became soaked with milk that was pouring out of my breasts. How could this be? I have no baby myself.

I put the idiot to my breasts and he eagerly began drinking from my life. I looked down at the deformed head and little body, its twisted arms and legs. The color of its skin was not even normal.

"How pathetic," I said. "No one to care for the wretched creature. No one to love it."

I began stroking its head and arms. Its claw-like hand grabbed one of my fingers. It had finally found someone.

I began to cry! Tears of compassion, tears of hope, tears of joy, tears of love, tears for this baby. I had reached out and touched someone who needed love. I quickly forgot my own helplessness, uselessness. I was looking down into the face of my own inner idiot, who until this time I dared not look at and recognize—this inner idiot who needs love, nourishment, and care. If I don't care for this idiot, I will be thrown into despair and inner death.

My tears washed the child's head. He turned from my breast and looked into my face and smiled and laughed. His face no longer looked ugly and frightening. I was looking into the face of the Christ Child. The Christ Child in me.

I turned and looked at the open door. There standing in the doorway was a beautiful woman. She told me that she had come to take the child, and appreciated what I had done for this little one. I realized that this beautiful woman was the hag that first brought me the Child.

The possibilities for this kind of work, as well as for other kinds of imagination that I shall describe, are innumerable. However, as Barbara Hannah said in a lecture many years ago, we can find a million lousy excuses for avoiding this kind of creative work.

Other Imaginative Dialogues

Once we realize that we can step into the dream world and dialogue with its characters, we begin to see that we can dialogue with any aspect of our inner lives. Ira Progoff gives excellent suggestions for this kind of dialoguing in *At A Journal Workshop*. Christina Baldwin also gives concrete creative suggestions in her book *One to One: Self Understanding Through Journal Writing*. We can dialogue with our bodies or any part of them. We can hold a *tête-à-tête* with any period of our life histories: the inner child, the inner youth, the lost lover, etc. We can dialogue with angers and fears and opportunities, missed and accepted, or we can even converse with our marriages. Many different schools of psychotherapy recommend this kind of imaginative work, and the Simontons, in *Getting Well Again*, prescribe it as a way of helping retard cancer growth.

One of the most important things to realize is that we never finish dealing with the depth of our inner lives. There are always new doors opening, new vistas available, new journeys to make into the illimitable land. In *Adventure Inward*, I described dialoguing with the inner child within me and how helpful this practice was for me. During a recent time of introversion I realized that although I had dealt with the child and with the younger adolescent who still lived in me, I had never dealt with the older youth in me who had taken hold of life and repressed much of his fear under a display of rational ego strength. I became quiet as I sat at the typewriter. The picture emerged of myself as a college student in his room in a boarding house.

I walk into the room. He is studying at the desk by the window from which he wrote his frequent letters to his sick mother at her home across the country. He realizes that someone is present and turns to me and speaks:

YOUTH: And who are you? I did not hear you open the door. You look friendly and like one with some background. You do look familiar. Should I know you? Come and sit down.

(*He motions to a chair. I sit down in the comfortable chair that I so well remember buying, and then I reply:*)

ME: I should have visited you long ago, but it was only the other night that I realized that you were still here within and frightened and alone, that you had remained here isolated and in panic. I wonder if you have any idea of how much I care for you and how sorry I am that I have not visited you before.

YOUTH: I really have no idea what you are talking about. You know me well, for I have been through a terrible time, a ghastly time, but I am trying to pull myself together and forget that—to take my life in hand.

I don't know what happened. I had had a cold and then got the doom-filled letter and I fell apart . . .

ME: No one has ever explained this to you, have they? And here you re-main in panic, not knowing what to do and trying to be brave, caught in a wrinkle in time. But you want to know who I am. I am you forty-six years later. I have come to be the father you never had, because he was frightened of himself and of you. He projected his fears upon you. He half worshiped you and half rejected you and loused you up.

YOUTH: All I know is that there is deep resentment and anger in me to-ward him and toward my brother for writing so coldly about mother's impending death . . . but what does this have to do with my falling apart?

ME: Morton, don't you see, *you are alone,* and you feel alone, and you see no hope, no way out. Until you face what you feel you cannot over-come it, and you remain stuck here in the depth, and then neither of us is free. No, I know you don't understand. Let me try to explain. I am what you have become: a writer, a retired professor, a lecturer who has some success in life. And because we have not become friends and I have not helped you with your inner panic, your panic still rises up from within me, and I fear that there is no one to love us or care for us.

(Tears well up in the kid's eyes as he speaks:)

YOUTH: You are so right. Hardly anyone has ever asked me how I feel, how miserable I am, even Mother. Indeed, I have not even allowed myself to see how miserable I am and have been. I haven't allowed myself to look, and I've pretended that these feelings were not there. I feel ugly, unattractive, never knowing when I'll be sick again. I am alone against a hostile and meaningless universe. I can't believe in my mother's hope, and Father is so confident that there is no meaning or future to individual lives, and he is so intelligent and makes fun of Mother's attitudes.

ME: I know how you feel, but I can honestly say as I sit here with you that I find you one of the most beautiful, sensitive, creative and loving people that I have ever known.

(I stand up and open my arms to him. He stands there questioning, not knowing what to make of all this. He alternates between wanting to be-lieve me and anger. Finally he speaks:)

YOUTH: How can I believe you? Why have you left me alone, left me here in my agony?

ME: It is the fault of both of us. You wanted to do it on your own, and I forgot that you were here. I am sorry that I did not realize that we needed each other. Come, receive my embrace. You want it as much as I; we both need it, but it has to be freely given and received.

YOUTH: How do I know that you will not just use me and drop me? I doubt if anyone could truly love me. At least I have seen no evidence of it yet.

ME: Give me a chance. I cannot force love upon you or anyone, but I know that you want what I have to give.

(*He rises slowly from the desk and comes toward me. He is crying now, sobbing. We embrace, and he lays his head against my shoulder and clings to me and I to him.*)

YOUTH: O God, how I have yearned for this, wanted someone to truly father me, someone to lead, understand, guide, teach, and I did not think it was possible. I thought that I had to go it all alone. Even if you throw me over it has been worth it. I do feel cared for.

(*We talk on for a while, and finally I suggest that we invoke the Risen One, who has saved me again and again in spite of all my blindness and unconsciousness, my lust and hatred, my violence and my fear.*)

YOUTH: Invoke such a one if there be such a one. I have tried to find someone to help, but have had no help or guidance. I needed such a one, someone who would lead me to that one, but no one knew how.

ME: Come, Lord Christ, come and bless this inner union, come touch this hurting youth who fears that he lives in a meaningless universe and that there is no abiding love, this one who troubles me in the depth when I have ignored him, who has dwelt there only half known for nearly half a century.

(*A voice is heard, a voice coming from some source we cannot see.*)

INNER VOICE: I am here with you, children, beloved. Thank you for inviting me to be present consciously in your lives, where I am always present. But I cannot come to you fully until you allow it. I force myself on no one.

ME: We hear your voice, but where are you?

INNER VOICE: In the bright sunlight of this desert country it is difficult to see an even brighter light. Pull down the shades.

(*We pull down the windowshades, and still a light remains, as bright as the desert sun. It is frightening, and we kneel on the floor and cling to one another. The intensity of holiness is there. The light is electrifying in power and penetrates both of us so that we close our eyes. How long we stay like that I do not know. Then we feel a touch on our arms. The light has changed into an ordinary-looking man, who lifts us to our feet. He embraces each of us in turn with tenderness and love, and then he puts his arm around the two of us. And then it is as if the youth and I were each the only one and this one was embraced by the Christ. Then I stand alone, and then I am sitting at the typewriter here on the ship. I feel whole and refreshed.*)

The third method I suggest is very closely allied to the one I have just discussed, but it is different enough and so important that it needs a separate section to describe it. It is the practice that I have already referred to above as the inner dialogue with the caring, creative inner wisdom. We may believe that there is such a wisdom that would relate to us, but until we step out in faith (or on the strength of an hypothesis, if we prefer that phrase) and actually spend some time in such a conversation, we will not know that reality, which wishes to speak to us more than we do to Him/Her.

Throughout the early history of the Church, right up through the time of Ignatius of Loyola, it was taken for granted by most Christians that such conversation was not only possible, but necessary in living the Way. Ignatius of Loyola gathered together the practices and suggestions current in his time and passed them through the creative crucible of his genius to elaborate one of the greatest methods of praying ever described. He tells us how to have a colloquy with Jesus on the cross, with the resurrected Jesus in the garden, with the Blessed Mother, with our favorite saints. Or the dialogue can be with any religious figure from any tradition, with Moses or Zarathustra. Of course, such a dialogue must be discerned when it is completed. The third book of the *Imitation of Christ* is a superb example of this kind of interactive prayer.

This kind of imaginative practice can open us to levels of meaning and understanding and insight that are hardly available to us in any other way. Such journaling can bring us into relationship with a highly creative level of the objective psychoid or spiritual world quite external to our own personal psyches. Very recently I came into the silence wondering why I kept myself so busy when the outer circumstances of my life did not require this kind of franticness. Many rather personal reasons were pointed out to me for why I kept myself in an overload of doing; then the suggestion came that I should do what I tell others to do and take an afternoon to make a completely new list of priorities. I did this the next day and found that my view of what was important in my life had shifted a full ninety degrees. I knew with certainty that the new way was right for me. I felt freed and unbound.

A fourth method of entering into the psychoid domain creatively and safely is by religious ritual. By imagination and ritualistic action we can step into religious myth. I again use the word *myth* as C. S. Lewis and Charles Williams have described it: a pattern of reality that can be revealed in imagination, in history, or in ceremonial rites or actions. By stepping into the biblical or mythological story imaginatively (and such getting into the story often involves our actual movement and action) we can often share in its power and transformation. Generations of Christians, ancient and modern, have found that drenching themselves in the stories of the Bible brings renewal and openness to the spiritual realm. Liturgy can be an archetypal acting-out of a mythological reality. Real liturgy can be religious play, in which the participants step into the reality of the pattern. One reason why many people get so little value from reading the Bible or other religious literature or attending the Eucharist is that they participate only with their logical minds and so fail to enter imaginatively and actively into the story and action.

We can imagine and step into any part of any real myth. We can go with the very pregnant Mary from Nazareth to Bethlehem and on to the flight to Egypt. We can walk with the other Mary into the garden of the tomb and share her transformation as the reality of the Resurrection penetrates her entire being. We can step into the story of the Samaritan and the man who fell among thieves, or into any other story about Jesus or parable of Jesus. Since most biblical stories are moving toward the victory of love in the Resurrection, stepping into them can often facilitate personal transformation, as Walter Wink shows so clearly in *Transforming Bible Study*.

Jung discovered a fifth way of dealing with the imagination as he was passing through his own dark night of the soul following his break with Freud. He found that he could allow his emotions, moods and affects to express themselves in images, and then he could begin to deal with them. The greatest difficulty about our moods and emotions is that they are so amorphous and uncontrollable. In his penetrating study of human affect, *Emotions*, James Hillman has shown how deeply related our emotions are to our inner images. As we are able to allow the mood or emotion to express itself in an image or a story, we can sometimes get a handle on our emotional situations. We can then gently lead the imaginative situation toward a more positive outcome. When this occurs often the worst of the mood of anger, fear or depression is dissipated. One friend discovered that only as the novels that he was writing could be brought to a nontragic conclusion did his own inner emotional situation begin to heal. We can seldom become what we have not first of all conceived as a possibility. Jung found he frequently needed an inner wisdom figure to help him through the darkness. Often we realize that we cannot handle the darkness by ourselves. We learn to invoke a saving power imaginatively.

Dante's *Divine Comedy* is a magnificent example of such imaginative work, written in superb poetry. Dante moves from the dark wood of his inner turmoil and confusion to the white rose of paradise, as Helen Luke shows in her study *Dark Wood to White Rose*. Goethe makes the same transition in *Faust*, and John Bunyan's *Piligrim's Progress* is a magnificent working through of religious and psychological problems, as Esther Harding has shown in her study *Journey Into Self*. St. John of the Cross portrays the same experience in poetic images in his incomparable poem *The Dark Night*.

We do not have to be John of the Cross to express such experiences in poetry. At a conference some years ago Dorothy Foesten handed me a poem that she had written, which expressed the same kind of experience in a modern and feminine idiom. She called it "St. Brigit Talks About Courtship." Here it is:

> I do not trust myself alone with God.
> He is so quick to garner me.
> I do but glance His way and faith
> He swatches off my clothes—
> Those garments which I need
> To cover up my soul.
> And there I stand before Him—naked to the core,
> Ashamed and blushing—horrified.
>
> Would that I could—some fair and favored day
> Find courage to approach Him—utterly,
> Dropping each loosened figment of disguise,

And there in swift surrender to His gaze
Know love—and offer simply what I am.

'Tis not for sham—He keeps on wooing me,
'Tis me—myself—my Lover-God would have.

Here is an example of actualizing the reality of one's inner experience of God, integrating the experience into the fabric of our being.

When darkness overcomes us there is no better method for dealing with it than allowing it to be expressed in images and then calling for the help of the Risen Christ. And we must realize our helplessness and let go of our pride if we are to call out sincerely. The beginning of wisdom is to realize that we cannot encounter the deeper darkness alone. Repressed parts of ourselves can cause anxiety and pain. There is also the darkness not only of an aching void, but also of an assailant, such as the one who tempted Jesus in the temptation narrative, and which William James describes in so many conversion experiences. Only the one who has defeated Death through love can help us in that ultimate struggle.

Many of the most experienced in the spiritual struggle have told us that the same darkness attacks again and again, and the further we go upon the path, the more subject we become to attack. The victory is not something that occurs once and for all. We need to appropriate the victory of Christ and pass through the confrontation again and again. We are not meant to remain in darkness. The Christian Way is indeed a journey with many perils. It is not a safe refuge. I have given several examples in previous books of passing through the darkness, but two recent examples will clarify my meaning for those who have not read them. We can encourage others to do this work and let them share it with us.

The first was written by a very gifted young man who was opened to the dark side of the unconscious through many factors. When he was a senior in college we came to know each other, and he discovered that he could use the imagination creatively to invoke a saving power. He wrote me the following letter when I was out of the country and another friend in whom he could usually confide was in Europe. He had an ugly dream, and the darkness attacked again:

> I awoke and quickly felt panic seize me. Deep dread and the worst fears grabbed me—I would go insane . . . I would find out all the progress I had made was a mockery. All signs of the presence of that hellish destructive force. As I said in my last letter, I think that it has its big guns out after me! . . .
> I want to put in writing that I know I can't face that destructive

force alone and that I need my friends to help me. I'm sure that the dream presents a legitimate challenge for new understanding on my part; but the weight of the destructive force I feel is all out of perspective. That force just wants to smash me, and it will lie, cheat, twist the truth, and play on my weaknesses to do so. And it's much stronger than I. It looms before me, pure malevolence. And now in imagination I see the Christ between it and me—he turns to me and smiles, and in his smile is the hope I had thought was lost. Around me he places a ring of light—it sparks with angelic energy—the love that moves the sun and other stars. The light sings—even in the face of the malevolence it sings a song of joy; I know I am surrounded with an energy that can defeat death— protected by the very energy that coursed through Christ in the tomb and raised him. "For such is my love for you," says Christ, laughing. "When you hear that voice whispering in your ear, call me. The thief comes to destroy; I come to protect my flock; by these words I first entered your heart six years ago. Remember them and call me. I will come—and I am with you always. . . . Now share your dream with Morton—and if the darkness threatens, feel the ring of light around you. You are not required to defeat the evil one! Only to face your tasks honestly and try your best! Leave the evil one to me.

This restored his equilibrium and put his life back into perspective, and he sat down and wrote to me.

On our recent freighter trip to Southeast Asia we visited several countries where the poverty and misery and overpopulation were staggering. In one country we visited an orphanage where children were taken in and nurtured. They had been abandoned because their mothers could not support the lives of the children and their own. And then in Sumatra we visited a leper colony, where the Salvation Army had a church and ministered to those living there. Some of the families had been there for thirty or forty years. To enter we drove down a long road built through a swamp, passed through a locked gate, and here was an ugly, flat island surrounded by the swamp, the tide flowing in and out each day. Often outer darkness will trigger the presence of inner darkness, which has caused the outer horror, and we must confront the reality of evil and then move through it to the redeeming center. I wrote the following dialogue a day later.

The thunderous, murderous voices are at it again and again. They must be confronted. . . . The feeling of utter worthlessness, helplessness, valuelessness in the face of all this evil, and then feeling like the crud, the scum at the bottom of the barrel . . . the pounding of lostness, my inner being receiving lashes, being punished just for existing.

What is it like?

Being captured again by the enemy? While I was asleep they came and seized me, bound me, and carried me away to their cave. I lie in their secret lair on the hard rock with the stones eating into my flesh. They have dropped me there. I'm gagged and bound. They laugh and joke. They will roast me alive and consume me.

In the back of the cavern stands the dark and ugly one, the leader, the concentration of evil and darkness, envy and hatred, violence and terror. Finally he notices that they have brought me in. He strides over and kicks me in the side and sneers:

DARKNESS: Why do you try to avoid us and seek help. We always bring you back. You belong to us, fool; you belong here with us, with the forces of hell and deception, of hate and vileness, of corruption and power. Join with us or the torture begins. Take the gag off him. I want to hear him scream when he can't stand the pain. It won't take much. He's a coward and weakling with delicate sensibilities

. . . and he bursts out laughing.

ME: Why do you bother with me, dark one. I know I am nothing. What good does it do you to make me suffer and scream. Why do you pursue me and try to break me?

DARKNESS: Because I hate you with an eternal hate, you vile fraud, deceiver, monster, ugly misshapen thing.

ME: What have I done? Who am I that you attack me again and again? What good does it do you? What are you trying to prove? Why do you hate me?

DARKNESS: Because you remind me of love and goodness and I can't stand it. I can't be comfortable while you are free and speaking lies, while you are free to try to be conscious and to care. I hate you because you try to follow one who has defeated me, and I can get back at him through you . . . swine, stinking, rotten one

. . . and then he kicks my face again and again and cries out:

DARKNESS: I've said too much. Heat the fire ten times hotter, and we'll roast him and listen to him howl. Then he'll know the power and delights of hell.

ME: (*Even though my face is smashed I cry out:*) Lord, come and deliver me from the pit of darkness, from this monstrousness. I don't know how I've fallen here. Come ...

DARKNESS: So you weasel out and call in the big supernatural guns, can't deal with me yourself ... weakling. This time no one will save you. There is no one to save. No one would want anything to do with you, vile animal, but to destroy you, step on you.

They bring a long pole to which they bind me, but within my heart and as much as I can outwardly, I continue to call out:

ME: Lord, Come. How or why I got here I don't know. Come, Abba, Come, Abba, Savior, Love Divine.

The cave is glowing with the blazing fire. It is a cruel, dark, crimson light. And then into the dark light there comes another light—white and pure, a light of pure love. It radiates through the place. The Dark Lord screams and lashes out at the light, and turning to me he screams out:

DARKNESS: This is why I hate you; you bring the light that torments me. I always think I can destroy you, and it does not happen.

The light throbs through the dark pit and becomes a glowing ball that encircles me. I close my eyes and feel all the evil and futility and hurt within me, my sins and ignorance and pride and lack of love, my comfort in the midst of this miserable world. This is pain, but a clean pain, a pain of birth and new life and healing, the pain of a limb that has fallen asleep and is coming back to life. How different from the binding and the beatings and the kicks and the fire of their furnace. Then I feel a hand on mine and another behind my head, and there is someone who would lift me to a sitting position ... gentle, loving, healing hands. I open my eyes and see him there, the Lord of Life. I look him full in the face, and there is love in his eyes and in his smile. He bends over and kisses me on the forehead, and my head glows; its pain is assuaged. Out of the deepest gratitude I whisper:

ME: Lord, thank you, but why do you bother with me when there are so many starving and frightened and broken people in the world? I feel so unworthy, almost as though I should not have your comfort and your saving help when there are so many who live and die in misery.

RISEN CHRIST: I love you, silly child. My love is not limited, and I can love you all. Perhaps you can let others know that there is hope, saving power.

ME: But why am I again and again and again dragged back into the depth, captured, beaten, defiled, played with, blinded, tortured?

RISEN CHRIST: You have been exposed to the misery of the world; you do not have very high defenses against it, and it seeps through. It is good for you to see this poverty and misery and pain. This is the way of the world; this is why I died on the cross. But you absorb it, and this opens the door for the Dark One.

ME: Should I have written before this?

RISEN CHRIST: The important thing is to deal with the inner darkness and its attack when it arises and as soon as you recognize it, and this you have done.

ME: I don't understand, but my heart is bursting with gratitude.

RISEN CHRIST: It is more than you can understand, the misery of the world, but you can help assuage it. The love of God is also more than you can understand.

ME: There is so little I can do. It seems hopeless . . . futile. What can be done? After two thousand years Christians are less than a third of the world's population, and most of them lukewarm in their practice or fighting among themselves.

RISEN CHRIST: Remember that you were not called to be successful, but faithful. You have looked into the outer darkness and into its source within. It captured you, you are saved again, and you are trying to explain to others that there is hope.

ME: And sometimes I don't believe it myself and doubt.

RISEN CHRIST: But you keep on trying in spite of your failures and faults and doubts, and you get rescued again. This is all that mortals can do.

ME: Lord, hold me, that the wounds may be healed and the pain and fear may subside.

He picks me up like a weaned child and holds me close to the heart of caring, compassionate, self-giving love. Hours go by, and I sleep and awake and sleep again. Gradually the pain diminishes, and the fear begins to fade way. Finally I speak again:

ME: Lord, it is painful to live in the midst of this aching, hurting world and to be able to do so little. And then when we become somewhat conscious of our own inner confusions and conflicts and contradictions we are so vulnerable.

RISEN CHRIST: All this is true. There is great evil and destructiveness, but there is also hope and love, and you are trying to side with them in spite of your vacillations and faults.

ME: I wish I might have this kind of time with you when I didn't need it, when I was just coming because of desire for you, as Bonhoeffer suggested.

RISEN CHRIST: You expect too much of yourself. You are a broken human being living among other damaged humans. Keep on trying. Use these times for coming close. Survive and share your survival with others. Enough of this, let's up and out of this dungeon, out into the fresh air.

He sets me down, and then we are of the same stature and size. We walk up the tortuous pathway from this den of darkness. We come to the light, which blinds me for a while. He has his arm around my shoulder. I feel supported and cared for. As my eyes become accustomed to the light I see before us the secret valley in which we have walked before. The great spring breaks forth from the rock and falls into the pool, surrounded by a meadow filled with fruit trees, which are always in bloom and still carry the ripe fruit. It is the garden. And yet so close is this place to where the Dark One dwells.

The pool flows out into a stream and moves down toward the sea. I am very quiet, and I can hear the distant breakers pounding against the great cliffs. And perched on the rock above the sea is the cabin where we have been before. Slowly we walk toward the cabin, down along the river bank, down to the sea with its great sandbar, and then ascend the steps chiseled into the stone up to the cabin. The cabin is warm from the setting sun. My friend and master lights a fire and sets the table and we sup. The healing darkness falls, and we lie down to sleep listening to the pounding of the waves in the sea caves below.

Within a few hours the heaviness has passed, and I go about my work again, refreshed and with new hope and conviction!

Sometimes the spiritual companion can just sit with another person in this kind of darkness, and this helps the other to bear it. Sometimes we can help people invoke this imagery or can suggest to them the redeeming image. But we cannot help others with this darkness unless we have experienced it and dealt with it ourselves.

Three Other Ways

Starting with the quiet, which is essential in all of these methods, some people can become still enough to open themselves to the flow of their own inner psychic lives. Either by sensory deprivation or through concentration on a symbol, a mantra or some physical sound or object, many people can step out of ordinary sensory experience and observe the incessant and meaningful flow of images and stories that can ordinarily only be experienced in dreaming. We are more conscious during the meditative state than in dream and so have more conscious control. We can direct and alter the flow of images more easily within this state. This state of being consciously aware of the unconscious or psychoid realm, called active imagination by Jung (to distinguish it from merely passive entrance into fantasy) is described by him in his book *Analytical Psychology: Its Theory and Practice*. This process can open some of us up to the very depths of ourselves. An unfinished story or an incomplete picture, ink blots or clouds in the sky can be the initial stimulus, as well as inner emptiness or a mantra.

These images then can be understood through the same methods of interpretation that we have suggested in dealing with dreams. These images may arise from each of the different levels of personal or collective spiritual or psychoid reality that we have discussed with reference to dreams. The important thing is not having the images, but coming to understand them and learn from them. Some people can become overawed by these images and fail to do anything with them. Gerald May makes this point with force and clarity in *Care of Mind Care of Spirit*. Taking an interest in these inner images in preference to the realities of outer life can lead us into real trouble. Psychosis results when the images take over and we can no longer distinguish between them and physical reality. The separation between inner and outer worlds becomes blurred and confused. We are unable to decide what is our inner world and what is the outer one.

When we spend time dealing with these inner images, some of which have great power, it is important that they be discerned, understood and valued. We need to look carefully into apparently negative and hostile ones and actualize the positive. Some of the hostile images turn out to be rejected parts of our natural selves, which need to be integrated. Others are essentially evil, and we need protection from them. The positive ones need to be actualized in some form. We can write in our journals about them; they can inspire some outer action of concern or caring. They can move us to tell stories, write poetry such as the examples we have provided, or they can be expressed in drawing, modeling in clay, sculpturing in stone, weaving, dance, drama. Through this kind of creative play (and taking a bowl of chicken soup to an invalid can be play) we can often come into touch with the deep and hidden aspects of psychoid or spiritual reality and in this process be changed and deepened. The meaning of these events and experiences is usually more totally integrated if we make some kind of written record of what we have experienced and reflect upon our encounter.

There is a real danger in entering this state just for fun and without realizing the dangers that are inherent in it. This is a *real* world, and we will find not only peaceful mountain valleys with lush meadows and babbling brooks, but also quicksands and jungles with venomous serpents and hungry tigers. If we refuse to confront these apparently hostile psychoid contents, we may be rejecting those creative inner, personal contents that are simply rising to capture our attention. Then our lives will probably be shallow, and we will most likely project these inner contents out onto other people. Projection is the source of much of our social and moral evil. It is very difficult to face the inner darkness. It takes courage to stand up to it and differentiate between that part of the unconscious depths which is pure gold and that which cannot be redeemed by our efforts, that part which is malignantly evil and from which we must be saved.

If we come into confrontation with this essential evil, this destructive side of reality, and have no theory, hypothesis or belief that there is a creative power that can deal with this darkness, then we can be in peril. We have the "bad trip" often described by LSD users, or we can fall into existential depression, in which we are helpless before the menacing meaninglessness or retreat into ourselves in horror.

One of the main purposes of religion is to provide a way to deal with the reality of evil so that we are not destroyed by it. The resolution is provided because good has conquered evil. If, indeed, we can bring in some savior figure who has met the darkness and overcome it, for example, the dying and rising god of ancient Asia Minor, or Ganesha, the resurrected son of Shiva, who can rescue us from both Kali and Shiva, or the Risen Christ, then we are not intimidated by the darkness and can be delivered from it. I find the historical risen Jesus the best exemplification of this reality. Jung called this creative, reconciling, victorious, saving, objective psychic reality the *self;* he maintained that it could be observed by anyone with an open mind. The introduction of this content can change the essential direction of the inner story and also the quality of the personality of the one who has used this religious method. It can even synchronistically alter the outer shape of things. It is very dangerous to open ourselves to whatever psychic contents may appear unless we realize the perils involved and unless we have a possible religious solution to the devastation we may encounter. Again, this victory over darkness is not like a problem in algebra, solved once and for all, but more like finding our way through an uncharted jungle.

Most of the classic spiritual directors, including Abbé Huvelin, Abbé de Tourville, Scupoli and others, stress the suffering that is involved on the inner way. Jung once said, "These talks with the 'Other' were my profoundest experience; on the one hand a bloody struggle, on the other, supreme ecstasy. [They were] an annihilating fire and an indescribable grace."[1] The question is how to get from one to the other. It is masochism to remain in the suffering any longer than necessary. The saint who wore an iron chain around his waist with spikes on it turned inward may also have glorified in the dark night. The goal is not the suffering, but the joy on the other side of suffering. Jung provides some methods of passing through the darkness. Good spiritual guides of all ages have done the same. Those without some hope in a creative solution, without a method of employing it, and without someone to whom they can turn when it doesn't work should not enter this inner world. If, however, they find themselves thrown into the abyss, they need to seek out someone who has methods of dealing with the inner destructiveness. A way of victory does exist and can be used. This is one important aspect of spiritual direction.

We shall not say much more about the method that we described as contemplation in the previous chapter. In this practice, after we have come to quietness and relaxation, we take up some aspect of the outer world and pass through it to its inner meaning. This can result either in imagelessness or in images. It is important that once the actual experience is concluded that we reflect upon what we have encountered. Most of those who teach this method usually tell people to come out of the silence if they discover something dark and forbidding. This method reflects the conviction that this outer world and the inner one are intimately related to each other and that through the outer we can find the inner. This expresses the thinking of Teilhard de Chardin. Those who advocate this method should certainly have resources available for dealing with the destructive encounter that can be triggered by this method.

The last of the methods I wish to examine is one that is widely used and very helpful for those who do not need to or should not go the route of confrontation with the full gamut of psychoid reality. This is the way of the once born, as described by William James in *The Varieties of Religious Experience*. It is a method that stresses imagelessness, the apophatic way. After we have achieved quietness, using relaxation and deep breathing, we try to come to a state in which the self-image is abandoned and other images that come into the field of consciousness are allowed to float by without capturing our attention. The desired and usual state is described as union. Transcendental Meditation (TM) speaks of the soul being dipped into the divine dye like cloth until it shares the same hue. Basil Pennington has described this way in his book *Centering Prayer*. The best, most complete and most sophisticated descriptions of this method are by Tilden Edwards and Gerald May in their books to which we have referred. Their description is based on a carefully monitored project of spiritual direction using this basic approach.[2] May writes, ". . . it is of value to recognize the two essential and fundamental qualities of full unitive experience, that *all* self-definition is suspended and that awareness is clear and *wide open,* excluding nothing." These experiences "constitute the basic form of spiritual experience, one in which a person, however briefly, actually experiences the reality of being rooted in oneness with all creation."[3] It is immoral to try to force people who need this method into confrontation with evil. It is also tragic to use only this way when people require the intervention of a savior.

There is no question about the wide use of this method both in Eastern religions and in some traditions within Christianity. This method almost always requires a director or guru who has learned to experience this state and so is able to guide the seeker toward it. Under skillful guidance a person can go very far spiritually using this pathway. The very use of the director, however, brings in a nonapophatic element, and both May and Edwards use a great deal of content in their training of directors. Everyone acting as a spiritual companion should know how to use this method. I repeat: the person who finds meaning with this method should almost never be jolted out of it into a confrontation with evil. Only God has the right to do this; humans can become demonic when they see their task as forcing people to confront evil, as was the custom in some religious orders. Training in this method should be available in all seminaries and retreat and renewal centers.

However, if this method is viewed as the *only* way inward or the *highest* spiritual practice, and no value is given to history, the use of images and sacraments, and psychological growth, then this way is beset with the following dangers:

1. This way can act as a spiritual tranquilizer, erasing concern with the horrible evil rampant in us and in the world around us. The Quakers have avoided this pitfall by their social conscience and group direction; skillful spiritual direction can also prevent this danger. TM is open to this criticism. At the University of Notre Dame I taught a course entitled "Practicum In Religious Experience." In it we shared in a variety of Christian and non-Christian religious experiences, one of which was directed by a TM leader. He had found a way through TM to overcome his anxieties and was quite comfortable, but his *unresolved* psychological problems stuck out like a sore thumb. The relaxation and relief from tension provided by TM enabled him to ignore these problems. Also, in monastic houses where the unitive experience is valued inordinately people can suggest themselves into it and so bypass their problems (which are usually expressed in images and dreams) and actually develop serious psychological conflicts.

2. A tendency to spiritual pride and superiority can also result, a looking down on those who find their contact with God through images and sacramental means.

3. Some practitioners of this method tend to view people who find it necessary to use images and confront the abyss of evil as immature or even psychologically disoriented.

4. People trained only in this method are not equipped to deal with existential depression or with the kind of devastating encounter with darkness and evil that is so often described in spiritual literature East and West. Jung's comments on *The Tibetan Book of the Dead* indicate the universality of this encounter.

The adequate spiritual companion will be one who has some knowledge of all the methods that we have described and will go along with each individual using the methods that are most helpful to him or her. It is important that we know and are competent to use both apophatic and kataphatic methods and to have other guides available who can direct seekers when we are not competent to do so.

Storms and Anchorage on the Inner Way

The goal of the inner journey is to confront and relate to or even be at one with spiritual reality, not to be taken over by the contents of this realm of reality. There are autonomous psychoid contents that seem to delight in taking over human personalities. Sometimes in journal-keeping it is as if another personality takes over the human instrument. The material simply flows, with no effort on our part. This can result in automatic writing. Progoff fails to warn of this danger or its attendant consequences.

Often people with this capacity (like those using a ouija board) get inflated and come to view themselves as the final or only interpreter of the beyond. People who speak prophetically in some charismatic groups can fall into the same attitude. When discernment is not used on *all* such autonomous expressions, nonsense and mischief can result. Religious communities can be torn apart; hate and destructiveness can be expressed rather than love and creativity. Allowing unconscious contents to possess the personality can occur because a person knows no better, because the critical faculty is undeveloped, because of an unconscious desire to be important, or even as an escape from an unsatisfactory life situation. Hitler was certainly possessed by unconscious powers, but he nearly destroyed the civilized world. All spirits need to be discerned.

Even more serious is the situation in which some people are taken over by the negative and destructive elements of the psychoid realm. This can result in depression, despair, psychosis or even suicide. *The Diary of Vaslav Nijinsky* is the tragic record of a person slipping more and more deeply into depression and mental illness. Some of Nietzsche's later writings have the same quality. Some years ago a woman was sent to me by a psychiatrist. He feared that she was about to have a total mental breakdown. She was in a depression and felt that she had to tackle every dark mood that appeared. Instead, under my direction she learned to turn aside from them and use sacramental means of dealing with them. She has lived twenty creative and productive years since.

Whenever our journals or times of inward turning indulge in self-pity and self-recrimination or hopelessness, then the inner practice should be abandoned or help should be sought. When the journal glories in the hopelessness of our fate, then it is sickness that is recorded and not growth. I have noted this tendency in certain ethnic groups that have been brutalized and oppressed for generations; it is almost as if there is a social justification for inner oppression. Again, Progoff does not warn us of this danger. Before entering this inner way it is wise to find someone to whom we can turn if the going gets rough.

One real problem confronts us when we start the inner journey in earnest. Once started, it is very difficult to stop the process without real trouble. Again, when people feel impelled to go this way I would stress the importance of having available people who are caring and understanding with whom we can share all of what we have experienced and written. Keeping up the round of ordinary activities, remaining active in ordinary life is important in order to keep our balance. When Jung was passing through his most powerful confrontations with the unconscious, he wrote that living in a family and seeing patients and keeping up his professional contacts provided a healthy contact with outer reality that enabled him to pass through this experience without destructive results.

In addition, it is crucially important to maintain our critical and evaluative capacities. If we abandon our critical stance, we can be swept away into a mire of superstition, nonsense, and authoritarianism. For most of us it is necessary to have some sound, historical religious tradition against which we can assess the contents that emerge from the depth. The great religious leaders built on the foundations built by others; they did not start from scratch.

There are few practices that have been more helpful to me on the inner journey than keeping a religious journal. It has been my friend, my guide, my companion. It has helped me bring the strange and sometimes alarming contents of the unconscious into the light, where they can be examined and evaluated. It prodded me into seeking spiritual and psychological guidance. But this intensive inner journey is not for everyone, and we need to weigh carefully the consequences before we urge another upon that way. The inner journey should nearly always begin in a deep desire or need for this spiritual path, a desire and need that *rise from within that person.*

There is a sacramental way available for those who do not feel called upon or should not or cannot go upon this kind of inner journey. These people can arrive at the same destination as those who pursue the inner journey if they follow it with devotion and have competent guidance. For some of us, however, one form or another of this inner way is necessary for our religious growth or our survival.

The inner and sacramental paths are not mutually exclusive, any more than the way of encounter is totally different from the practice of imagelessness and union. These are simply different emphases. Indeed, I have discovered that the farther I go down the inner pathway, the more I need the sacramental life. One has led me to the other. Those whose emphasis is largely sacramental will also find experiences of ecstasy and union and the need for reflection and integration of their experiences into the pattern of their daily lives.

I want to make it perfectly clear that a complete dogmatic and sacramental system such as the Catholic Church provides is an excellent and perhaps the best pathway to God for some people. It provides many of the experiences and fruits of the inner journey that we have described in this chapter. For many people the inner way can be enhanced, enriched and fulfilled by sacramental participation. Churches and clergy need to be open and universal (catholic) enough to minister to both of these needs if we are to minister to people where they are. The tragedy is that some churches provide neither. Many churches either take advantage of insecure people, forcing them into a rigid belief pattern and skillfully extracting the mind at the same time, or they leave them floundering in the swamp of secular society with no anchorage points.

There is a way that avoids these hazards. It is the way of coming to know and experience the love of God by imagelessness, personal encounter, through images and sacrament. There are few things more needed in our society than people who have received the training and direction to lead people to the experience of God and who are ready to help others on their way, no matter where it may lead.

NOTES

1. C. G. Jung, *Memories, Dreams, Reflections,* recorded and edited by Aniela Jaffé (New York: Pantheon Books, 1963), pp. 48 and 56.
2. Gerald May describes this state very well in *Care of Mind Care of Spirit*, pp. 27–30, 68–92.
3. Ibid., pp. 29–30.

Chapter 8

PSYCHOLOGY AND
SPIRITUAL DIRECTION

The subject of the relationship between psychology and spiritual direction is a large one. There are wide differences of opinion as to how much training spiritual directors need in psychology. Many spiritual directors believe that spiritual development can be facilitated by those who have little knowledge of psychology. If the only psychology we know is one that has no place for the spiritual domain or even for a real psyche, then it is quite understandable why those interested in spiritual development believe that psychology has little to offer the art of spiritual companionship.

There are psychological theories that do have a place for spirituality, as I have shown at length in *Christo-Psychology*. Although some commentators like William McNamara and Martin Buber think that Jung pychologizes religion, this is not my understanding after thirty years of study. They fail to see that Jung has provided a very different theory of how we know and what we know.

The first need of those who would accompany others on the spiritual journey is to have a view of reality that is inclusive enough to have a place for body, psyche and spirit. If we do not possess such an integrated view of human nature and the world in which we live (both spiritual and physical), then we are likely to deny the claims that both of these aspects of reality have upon us. Unless we accept some variation of the gnostic idea that matter is evil and salvation is separating out from it, we are forced to believe that our deepest spiritual nature is involved with both psyche and body. Indeed, we human beings are a hybrid of spiritual and physical, and were so created by God, who apparently saw this as the best way by which we human beings could come to our divine potential. If this is true, then reflection upon the outer physical reality and the inner image can both be useful in leading us to the experience of God, who stamped his image upon us and who draws us through them to our fulfillment in the relationship with the divine.

Of course, we can no more describe this ultimate experience than we can fully describe any other experience, but we can develop symbols and images by which those of us who have experienced something of this reality can share our experiences with others and guide and accompany each other further on the journey. Whether God has a place for psychic images and matter in the ultimate nature of things I do not know. The early Church, in emphasizing the resurrection of the body, seemed to believe that these aspects of reality had ultimate significance.

Before we go further, let us take another look at the understanding that we diagramed earlier. In this diagram we have provided a real place for body, psyche, and human spirit. Psychosomatic theories provide a two-way street. We have real and significant bodies (contrary to the view of some Eastern religious thinking). These bodies can have a tremendous effect upon our psyches, and even upon our spirits, just as the human psyche and spirit can exert a profound infuence upon our physical bodies. Pavlov and Skinner have demonstrated how much of our physical environment and conditioning affect our personalities. Those who tell of near-death experiences or of experiences of the deceased after their deaths describe how the personalities they encounter seem to continue to bear the distinctive marks of the development that came from living within a physical world.

The human psyche has a structure and substantiality of its own, which is not reducible to anything else. Out of the depth of the unconscious psyche, consciousness and self-awareness slowly emerge, and then our rationality and capacity to think imaginatively and logically develop. The spirit is that part of the human psyche that is stamped with the divine image, with the hunger for God that cannot be satisfied by anything else. Each spirit-psyche is unique, and each of us will be fulfilled in somewhat different ways.

It is nearly impossible to separate these three elements out from one another. They are like three poles of a multidimensional, many-pointed scale. If we wish to be companions and guides for others on the inner journey, we will, of course, need to go along with others in their spiritual development, but we shall also need to accompany them in their psychological concerns and problems and in their attempts to live out their commitments to other human beings in this concrete and hard-fact physical world. Those who are not willing to provide such complete companionship to others on their journeys should probably not begin.

This diagram is essentially an adaptation of the insights of the analytical psychology of C. G. Jung. In spite of William McNamara's suggestion that Jung is confusing psychology and religion, he pays Jung one of the finest backhanded compliments I have encountered. He states, "The early Christian diagnosis of man makes Freud's comparable attempt seem like a very weak cup of tea indeed. The discoveries of analytical psychology do little else than repeat, in modern phraseology, and with detailed empirical evidence, the principle injunctions of the Christian way."[1] This is exactly what I discovered that Jung provided for me. He

PHILOSOPHICAL AND RELIGIOUS WORLD VIEW

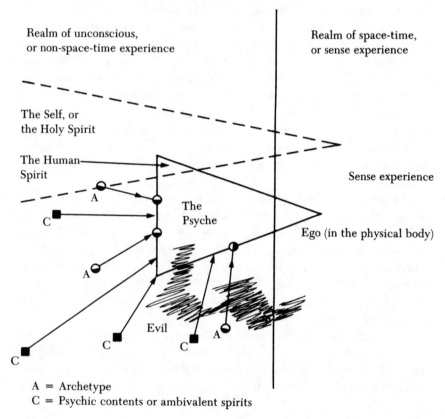

Realm of unconscious,
or non-space-time experience

Realm of space-time,
or sense experience

The Self, or
the Holy Spirit

The Human
Spirit

Sense experience

A

C

The
Psyche

Ego (in the physical body)

A

Evil

C

C

A

C

A = Archetype
C = Psychic contents or ambivalent spirits

verified from an objective, empirical point of view many of the insights of Christianity. He also introduced a new terminology, so that people who were turned off by the old language and its empty pious associations, might be able to view the evidence with an open mind and be led toward real religion. In my experience, many others besides me have the same need.

Reflecting upon this diagram, we can see that the psychological and religious goals are similar: to bring the total personality, conscious and unconscious, into integration under the self or Holy Spirit. We work at this goal and prepare for it, but this experience of integration is always in the end a gift. We human beings are psychologically and spiritually amphibious; we need both a physical life and a spiritual one.

If we deal with only the psychoid dimension of life and do not take the physical side seriously, or if we get these two aspects of reality confused, then we are called mentally ill. Psychosis is being unable to distinguish inner and outer reality. The autistic child and the psychotic do not accept and take seriously the common physical reality upon which society has agreed. Such people make those who are totally involved in the physical world very nervous, and so many conventional people like to have them put away. The reason that the Rorschach test is so helpful in revealing this problem is that psychotics and young children do not provide the common interpretations that most of us give for the ink blots.

Most of our psychological problems arise, however, from failing to deal with the personal and collective elements in our psyches. Neurosis is still a good general term for the different means by which we escape from dealing with the complex psychoid dimension of ourselves and of reality.

First of all, we can repress unpleasant aspects of our inner lives. We can try to live solely by conscious decisions, social regulations and rational considerations. This can result in anxiety, bursts of anger, depression and an infinite variety of tensions. These can exist when from the point of view of our outer lives in the world everything is just fine.

Or we can project these inner conflicts out upon other people. We can have phobias and be irrationally scared of perfectly stupid things; we can go to war with a glad heart, desiring to eliminate evil from the world; we can see beauty or horror in others that no one else is able to observe.

On the other hand, these contents can possess us, and then we have compulsive and objective acting-out behavior. One young man caught in socially unacceptable sexual behavior replied to my question of why he did it with the statement "I just don't know." Possession can take the form of the "prophet" who is really possessed by an archetype as were Hitler and Savonarola. Or the possession may be of the kind that often gets into the news when the scout leader or Sunday school teacher possessed by unconscious rage runs amok and kills ten people. There is also the rather rare phenomenon of multiple personalities.

Instead of the demonic possession of former times, or even the hysteria common one hundred years ago, we now have the problem of psychosomatic disease. Sometimes when we will not face our inner tension, stress and anxiety it comes out in the physical symptoms we described in an earlier chapter. Our psychic conflicts are converted into physical symptoms.

Believing that we live in a meaningless world can cause all sorts of physical and psychological disasters. Even a repression of the natural human desire for spiritual fulfillment, or a refusal to listen to the knocking of the Holy Spirit at the doors of our inner being, can make us very anxious and depressed. This is one kind of dark night of the soul. Whatever is repressed within us appears negative, even God. (There is the other kind of dark night in which we fall into the hands of the destructive downdrag of reality, the evil in the structure of the universe.)

The need for the transcendent can be projected upon the state. There is a subtle similarity between the emperor worship of ancient Rome and the state religions of China and Russia. In both examples it is heresy not to fall down and worship.

My own experience is that many of the people who came to me for spiritual direction discovered that their real interest was in solving psychological problems. And many of the people who came thinking that their problems were only psychological found that although they indeed had problems, their main need was for a method of dealing with the vast and frightening realm of spiritual reality. People who can work in both areas are much needed in the Church and in the psychological profession.

The rest of this book consists of a series of comments on the training and practice of those who wish to be experienced spiritual companions. We shall be approaching this subject from the religious-psychological-physiological frame of reference we have just elaborated. First of all, we shall point out the differences and distinctions between the various professions that deal with the restoration and integration of the psyche. We shal then point out the importance of spiritual directors being aware of psychological problems. Then we shall briefly sketch the various stages of psychic maturation as we move through life and describe how different stages require different guidance. We shall look at the implication of this growth process for education and conversion. We shall then examine, in a concluding chapter, the often neglected variable in psychological and religious transformation: the importance of the counselor's or director's genuine love and concern for the other person.

A Chart of Distinctions

I considered many different ways of presenting the differences among six of the principal professions dealing with some aspect of the human psyche. A chart seemed to be the easiest and most helpful way of showing the similarities and uniqueness of each. I am deeply indebted to Tilden Edwards for the idea of a chart of distinctions among the "helping" professions. A schema worked out by Dr. Gerald May stimulated my own thinking and resulted in the chart that appears here.[2]

Several things are apparent in this chart. Three of these professional territories overlap to a large degree: the word *psychiatry* in its Greek origin means the healing of the soul, *psychotherapy* in its root meaning is the attending or treating of the soul, the spiritual director B is the one who guides the individual through the healing process when religious factors are an essential aspect of the situation and then takes the individual from there on the inner journey. Practitioners in the first two categories will most likely cease when the pain and relationship difficulties have been largely resolved, unless the individual wishes the therapist to go further. Jung told me that the main reason that he became so deeply involved in religion and religious experience was that he could find no ministers trained to help people who needed guidance in these areas. My first three spiritual guides were two psychologists and a psychiatrist who realized that one of the essential roots of my difficulties lay in having a world view with no place for religion and my lack of any practice that could bring me experience of this dimension.

The psychiatrist is one who ideally will be aware of all levels of psychic disturbance and who then charts out whatever aspects of treatment he or she seems to be called to undertake. Psychiatry is a medical specialty and has unique legal responsibilities; it can be concerned with custodial or hospital care and use of drug therapy, but it also can be primarily involved in therapy, or even spiritual direction. Every therapist, pastoral counselor or spiritual director A or B should be on a consulting and referral basis with someone with psychiatric training.

There are few clear-cut differences among the psychotherapist, the

	Psychiatry	Pastoral Counseling / Psychotherapy / Social Case Work	Pastoral Care
Reason for Encounter	Person in pain, with inner conflicts, psychosomatic disease, or unable to fit in social group.	Person with same symptoms, but needing neither drugs nor a controlled environment. Can work with psychiatrist.	Reaching out to people in psychic pain, loneliness, grief. Initial contact may come from pastor.
Goal	To remove pain and enable person to function adequately within him- or herself and within the more intimate and larger social group. Except in case of disoriented persons, the patient decides termination of relationship.	Same goal as psychiatry, but limited to those who do not need drugs and custodial care. To provide insight and self-determination.	To bring comfort, renewal, relief of pain and sorrow and confusion, but without necessarily bringing insight.
Method	Any method necessary to bring healing, even understanding of world view and spiritual disciplines if necessary, but usually relying on custodial care and psychotherapy. Should be aware of existential roots of some problems and have a place for religion to avoid a limited point of view. Often uses chemical intervention. Sometimes utilizes dream analysis.	With the exception of use of drugs and custodial care, uses the same methods as psychiatrist. One works within a religious framework; the other has no necessary religious connection, but should be aware of religious and existential dimension of psychosomatic and psychic distress. Stops process at limits set by patient.	Concerned caring in one-to-one calling or in arranged social gatherings and fellowship, in study or prayer or sociality. Within Christian tradition usually connected with priesthood, but not necessarily with pastoral counseling or spiritual direction A or B. Takes seeker no further than he or she asks.
Personal Relationship to Seeker	Healing seldom occurs unless there is genuine care and humility. Not necessary for use of medical model, but still helpful.	The therapist's only scalpel is his or her personality. Caring, humility, and knowledge are all necessary.	Concerned caring with enough awareness not to encourage dependency.

	Priesthood	Spiritual Direction A: Apophatic–Nonmediational	Spiritual Direction B: Kataphatic–Mediational Shamanistic
Reason for Encounter	Providing sacrament, mental assistance towards God, or healing of body or mind. In most cases initiated by seeker.	A soul searching for God without any obvious disorder or acute need. Always initiated by seeker.	A psyche in pain seeking for integration of body, mind, and soul and release from pain. Usually initiated by seeker.
Goal	To achieve whatever goal is desired by individual.	Being and becoming in God without essential consideration of personal psychological problems. Particularly useful for once-born type as described by James. Never goes beyond individual's goals.	To alleviate the pain so person can function, to bring insight into how pain is related to inner journey, and to facilitate that journey. To continue with person as long as needed to bring individual to sustaining fellowship with God. Can offer goals.
Method	Providing individual and group sacraments, arranging worship, mediating of the Holy. Within Christian tradition this role is traditionally connected with pastoral care and even with spiritual directions A and B. Providing confession, absolution, Eucharist, anointing, etc.	Allowing self and relationship to be a vehicle of grace, of the will of God. Primary method: surrender, letting go whatever is in God's way. Abiding with the person making the journey. Referral of any significant problem to psychiatrist or therapist-counselor.	Whatever is needed to facilitate the individual through pains and on the way. Usually will not deal with psychotics and will be equipped with knowledge of pastoral care and pastoral counseling. Will be particularly equipped to deal with existential problems. Will use psychiatrists as consultants and will be so used by enlightened psychiatrists or therapists. Can use sacramental actions.
Personal Relationship to Seeker	Need be none, but in Christian framework it is a necessary ingredient if priest is a mediator of Christ.	Only God is responsible for whatever healing/growth occurs. *"Thy* will be done."	God gives transformation, but shaman/guide is mediator of experience, knowledge, critical understanding, and divine love.

social case worker and the pastoral counselor. Indeed, many pastoral counselors are no more experienced in dealing with spiritual or religious questions than good secular counselors. I have seen increasing numbers of pastoral counselors, social workers, family counselors and clinical psychologists seeking training and understanding in spiritual matters as more and more of their clients come to them with spiritual problems that pastors are not trained to handle. The spiritual director of the shamanistic variety is one who has experienced the confrontation with inner conflict and evil, found a way through it and *offers this expertise along with an understanding of human problems in which the nonmedical therapist is trained.* This person will probably refer to other professionals those whose primary interest is merely the removal of psychic pain and emotional and relationship difficulties. In my own experience, most seekers on the inner way are a jumble of religious and psychological problems, but, of course, with my own personal experience I would attract such people, both consciously and unconsciously. I would conclude that spiritual direction B is a branch of pastoral care in which the person has special training, inner experience and knowledge of the inner journey.[3]

Spiritual direction A need not involve a deep knowledge of psychological problems, as problems are usually dealt with in images, and this method, as described by Edwards and May and by Kenneth Leech, largely bypasses the use of the image. Their method could be used equally well for those with an orientation to Eastern world views. An excellent program of training for this point of view has been worked out by Edwards and May at Shalem. They are selective about those whom they accept for training. They provide a carefully planned several-year educational experience, which includes factual information, personal experience in being directed, and supervision of those whom the trainees are directing. Trainees become aware of the areas in which referrals should be made and of problems that occur in one-to-one relationships. I also believe that they need to be aware that there is a practice such as we have described as spiritual direction B, to recognize that there is a place for it, and to have available people who are trained in it when referral for this kind of companionship seems indicated.

Let me emphasize once again the importance of distinguishing between these two kinds of spiritual direction. One deals with the person who has been flung into the depth of the psyche and who must have more direct intervention than the gentler type of spiritual direction described by Edwards and May. This shamanistic type of direction is exemplified by Abbé Huvelin and some Jungian psychologists. William James describes the kind of person who needs this kind of help in his classic study. The Church is simply failing in its task if it does not provide for these people. There are also those who feel a gentler tug into the spiritual life. It is simply immoral to take these people into the depths that the other group *requires*. These two points of view are not opposed, but rather complementary.

Many ministries are focused primarily in the area of sacraments and pastoral care. The use of confession, penance and Eucharist can be incredibly sustaining and healing. Personal pastoral care may be enough for the individual. The ministers offering these need know only enough psychodynamics in order not to create problems in pastoral care or by the wrong use of the sacraments. They need to know the dangers of creating dependence. They also need to know when and where to make referrals as they meet problems of a purely psychological nature or of a psycho-religious origin; they need to know their limitations. Many people find that it is easier to accept help from a service connected with a church, and so it is helpful if pastoral counseling can be provided for those who desire something more than sustaining pastoral care and solace. The functions of preaching, teaching (education), and administration are quite different from those of pastoring and administering the sacraments. Again, it is important that those involved in these ministries have an understanding of the nature and development of human personality so that what they do is consistent with these other ministries and supports the full depth of life that is possible within a vital religious institution.

Although many ministers are given some training in pastoral care, very few are given any background or experience in either kind of spiritual direction that we have described. If the Christian Church, Catholic and Protestant, is to meet the challenge of agnostic secularism, militant atheism (which has captured much of the earth), or other quite different religious approaches to life, it needs to provide this kind of experiential grounding.

Awareness of Psychological Pitfalls

I have never known any human being who did not have some sexual problems and tensions and who did not have some kind of authority problem. One of the most comforting things about May's book is his humble self-assessment in one of the closing chapters of *Care of Mind*

Care of Spirit: "I, for example, tend to be compulsive. I sometimes experience ideas more than feelings, my self-image is strongly dependent upon my work performance, I am frequently anxious about spending money and would be a miser if I had my way, and it sometimes seems cosmically unfair to me that I should have to make any choices or decisions whatever."[4] It is a thin line sometimes between style of personality and spiritual and mental health.

If we would accompany others on their journeys and be able to accept all of them, we need to know about some of the sexual problems that are so common in our society, and we must know how to respond to them. No response can be the most horrible response of all. The same is true of problems with authority, sibling rivalries, family conflicts, childhood traumas, compulsive busyness. As we shall show in the next chapter, it is almost impossible to be open and accepting of others if we do not have this attitude toward ourselves, and this is nearly impossible until we realize that we are not much more peculiar than other human beings and have been able to share our strangeness with another person. We are part of a maimed human race. We share common human problems. This is the original meaning of original sin. (This is not the place to go into detail about these areas of our social heritage. A good background in pastoral counseling can give just what is needed.) It is for this reason that spiritual direction, particularly of the more intensive kind, should be firmly based in a knowledge of the counseling process and the findings of clinical psychology.

We need to have quite clear criteria for determining when people simply need reassurance and nonpsychologically oriented spiritual direction and when their inner conflicts, sexual difficulties, and authority problems have reached the stage of "disorders" or sickness that require pastoral counseling, psychotherapy, or spiritual direction. When our personality style causes those around us severe problems and keeps us from our maximum growth toward God it is no longer just a matter of our personality quirks. We often need objective evaluation by a qualified spiritual guide to decide which is the case and what our need really is.

Depression is a widespread and increasingly common human state. It is natural after some physical illnesses and during times of bereavement and personal tragedy. We need to know what is "normal" and when psychiatric intervention is indicated for the protection of the individual or the family involved. Any threat of suicide should be taken seriously, for one never knows when the window sill may be slippery.

Most ministers need to set careful priorities as to which areas of their work are to be given prime time. If the clergy do not believe that they are providing crucially important functions, mediating a spiritual world, they can easily spend all their time helping people with psychological problems. The needs are legion among us. When this happens the Church can become simply another social agency, and its primary function of mediating spiritual reality for people can be lost. Spiritual directors should also be careful not to become amateur psychotherapists, but to keep their focus on their primary function. In one kind of spiritual direction little attention will be paid to these problems; in the other they will be seen as roadblocks that need to be dealt with if spiritual growth is to be achieved.

This brings us to the perennial problem of transference, the psychological term for falling in love. Some of the wisest and most mature counselors and spiritual directors I have known have found themselves involved in powerful transferences. There is a deep need within all of us human beings to be loved. I doubt if I have even known any people who thought that they had all the love that they wanted in the way they desired it. I personally believe that our desire for love cannot be totally fulfilled through human sources, but only by God; there is a deep hunger that God has hidden in our inner abyss, which continues to draw us to the Divine Lover. Paradoxically, unless we have experienced the receiving and giving of genuine human love, we seldom understand this deep inner urge enough to realize where it is leading us. Once we have known the incredible love of God we are turned back into the world to give to others the kind of love that the Divine Lover has given us, and this involves us again in human entanglements, emotions and desires. I have argued at length with the Divine Lover that these things are difficult for one of my fragile nature, but God has not changed the way things are for me. In addition to all this, genuine falling in love and genuine loving care are both ecstatic experiences that open us beyond ourselves and need to be assimilated if they are to be of real value.

Human love involves us in the same sort of paradox as the development of an ego. Unless we have a center of I-ness and self-concern, we cannot assimilate experiences of the divine. Unless we give it away and are given a new center of wholeness, we cannot grow. This process of dissolving old attitudes and developing new ones goes on forever. Those who value the changing perspective and those who value the permanence are often at odds with one another. Both are complementary and necessary. They are related to the poles of detachment and attachment described by von Hügel.

Gerald May has written profoundly on transference in his chapter "Relationship" in *Care of Mind Care of Spirit*. If we need to be careful of transference in the kind of spiritual direction he is describing, we must be many times more aware and careful in the more total human involvement that is required in the more shamanistic direction we have described. I have several guidelines to add to those he suggests.

1. Recognize the incredible power of this experience of transference-love-sexuality.

2. Those who think that they are not vulnerable to this experience are sitting ducks for it. Pride goeth before the fall.

3. Do not enter into deep one-to-one counseling or pastoral relationships unless willing to deal with transference.

4. Recognize that within each of us is the desire to be the "divine" giver of love, and also the deep need to be satisfied by having another provide this love for us.

5. Although touch is at times very healing, important and necessary, it can be very dangerous in the private, continuous, one-to-one relationship and can turn into something quite different than was intended. It is so easy for people to want to give us what we have not consciously recognized that we desired.

6. It is essential that any of us who are in a relationship that involves transference keep a running reflection in our journals of our own honest reactions and feelings.

7. Counselors need to be quite clear that they come into the counseling situation to give rather than to receive, and when this is not true there is a great need for careful reflection. We need to be as aware as possible of both our conscious and unconscious expectations in regard to those with whom we relate in depth.

8. Every person (seldom do I use the word every) involved in depth counseling or in continuous one-to-one relationships needs to have peers with whom he or she can discuss *all* aspects of these relationships and seek objective guidance. The director requires direction if the blind are not to lead the blind.

9. Once relationships have been established in depth, particularly when the transference is directed toward the counselor-director, it is simply immoral to break these relationships without a full discussion of the situation with the individual concerned and if possible a totally mutual agreement as to its resolution.[5]

10. Whenever possible, those who are going to be involved in close pastoral relationships need to be provided supervised pastoral experience. Few programs that now exist are really adequate to fulfill this need. The kind of training provided by Shalem might well be instituted as a regular part of seminary training for all who wish to be involved in the pastoral or spiritual direction ministries. It is within this setting that the problems unique to each of us can be handled most creatively. I am grateful that God does not need perfect instruments to further his kingdom, for then only the unconscious and psychotics would be able to apply.

Spiritual Direction and the Stages of Life

If we are to direct human beings along the spiritual path, it is almost necessary to have some understanding of the pattern of psychological growth that has been much before the public in recent years in the work of Erik Erikson and Gail Sheehy's popular book *Passages*. This, of course, requries an integrated psycho-religious point of view such as we have sketched out at the beginning of this chapter. Not only is this important for spiritual direction, but also for Christian education.

Real religious education should be an attempt (within the schema we have presented) to guide each of us to an experience of God through loving concern guided by a knowledge of a religious tradition and sifted through a critical understanding and knowledge of the religious experiences of others. Real spiritual companionship is one element in an adequate Christian education, and real religious education will initiate a process of religious experience and knowledge that will make use of sacraments, pastoral care and spiritual direction of whichever type the individuals require. Christian education has to be individually oriented if it is to be Christian.

The various stages of psycho-spiritual growth require very different kinds of spiritual teaching, support and companionship. As I have reflected on the subject over the years I have come to perceive seven quite different stages of human development relevant to our *spiritual* growth. On the next page I have sketched out the seven stages in spiritual development. It is necessary to recognize that each stage has quite variable "normal" or customary age limits, and what I suggest is only an average. Unfortunately, some people persist in one stage or another, or a part of them is still caught in one stage or another. If we are to grow to our spiritual potential we need to be able to move from stage to stage. One rea-

SEVEN STAGES OF SPIRITUAL DEVELOPMENT

Stage	1 *Infancy and early childhood*	2 *Childhood*	3 *Adolescence*
Age:	0–4 to 7	Infancy through 11 to 15	Childhood through 21–26
Special Character:	Development of ego and individual personality Emerging from unconsciousness	Avid desire to learn about environment Acceptance of parental value	Establishment of unique values, goals Sexual differentiation Career planning
Special Needs:	Continuous love to establish value of dealing with outer world and provide an experience of a loving God	Learning about the world and how to deal with it	Becoming a separate and unique person, often in rebellion Adult spiritual companion
Dangers:	Without love world becomes a fearful place	Without open teaching, child can become rigid	Without guidance revolt may be chronic and self-destructive

son for spiritual direction is to enable us, through spiritual companionship, to pass through some of the stages that are particularly difficult to
go through alone.[6]

One of the tasks of spiritual directors will be for them to pass from one
stage to the other themselves and so be able to assist others in the rites of
spiritual passage. If we are to do this it is necessary to be clearly aware of
the various stages of the trip we call life. What is adequate and appropriate behavior at one time in life is quite inappropriate and immature at
another. The most striking example of this was given me by a psychiatrist
who was treating a young man I had referred to him. This boy had held
off the police force with his twenty-two rifle in a suburb of Los Angeles
and had threatened to shoot his mother. I considered this an indication of
severe disturbance. The doctor, however, said that although it was a lit-

4	5	6	7
Adulthood	*Midlife Crisis*	*Golden Age*	*Old Age*
Adolescence through 30–45	21–45 but can occur anytime to end of life	After midlife crisis to old age	possible from 30 on
Establishment in outer life with business, family, and children	Recognition that outer life is not enough Confusion	Period of productivity, creativity, and resolution of conflicts	Turning inward to step into other dimension, detachment, introversion
Development of confidence in ability to cope with life	A world view that can give meaning to crisis A companion who has been through this way	Companions on the way	Time alone, Spiritual companionship World view that can make time valuable Coming to terms with what life has been
Caught into total occupation with outer world	Crisis with drugs or alcohol Depression	Trying to push people to this point	Lack of view of continuing life leads to bitterness and atrophy

tle extreme, the attitude of this young man of eighteen was extreme but not abnormal for adolescence. However, if such behavior occurred in a child or in an adult over thirty, it would indicate severe psychological trouble.

As we have already stated, every parent and every good teacher is a spiritual director whether he or she likes it or not. Each church needs someone competent in both kinds of spiritual direction who can work with the church planning process so that we may help people to spirttual maturity. Those who are spiritual directors need to have a clear understanding of the stages of development and be able to discern the individual's stage and make the proper response to it.

Stage 1. In the first stage we can observe the seed of human personality beginning to unfold, just as a redwood or mustard seed germinates and then slowly becomes what it was intended to be. We can watch the emergence of a person out of the unconscious psychic potential. New-born children have almost no sense of their own individuality. Two-year-olds who are beginning to talk refer to themselves as "the baby." It is difficult for children before five to distinguish between the inner and outer worlds, between material and nonphysical experiences. Many children have imaginary playmates, who seem as real to them as actual people. Most adults are just a little nervous when children talk about this world unless they have a clear view of the two aspects of reality. This openness to the inner world is not something to be totally outgrown, but rather to take its place alongside the physical world.

It is essential that these young children learn that there are two kinds of experience. It is difficult in our materialistic age not to play down the reality of the spiritual dimension. Christian education that does not have a place for spiritual reality cannot educate children to creative and proper growth in regard to this dimension. They are like tender, sensitive plants. They can be educated, allowed to unfold so that they are open to relating to a loving God who can give confidence in the ultimate nature of the universe (known as *faith* in theological language), or they can be closed to that idea and live in deep-rooted fear because of what they have been taught and how other human beings have treated them. The most essential element in early Christian nurture is consistent human warmth and understanding, kindness and love. Unless people receive these things as children, they find it very difficult to believe in them as adults. In *Religion and Agnosticism*, von Hügel studied the life of the famous agnostic geologist Sir Alfred Lyall and pointed out that the coldness of his parents practically slammed the door on any possiblity of faith for him.

This brings us to a crucial fact of growth. We can grow at any time. The human being is far more plastic than most of us ordinarily believe. However, the task that we need to learn, the development we need to achieve, can only be accomplished earlier or later at a much higher cost than at its proper time. Much of psychotherapy consists of providing the environment in which people can live through a stage that they missed before. Spiritual direction of the shamanistic type will involve this kind of direction and counseling and companionship for the simple reason that *the various stages each provide essential elements in a full and mature religious life.* We cannot skip grades in spiritual development. This principle usually applies to each of the following stages.

As small children grow they can learn to distinguish between different aspects of reality rather than being taught to deny one part of it entirely. This is only possible where those who teach children believe in and live in the reality of this spiritual dimension. People who would teach children religiously should be in some kind of spiritual growth pattern, either the sacramental way or one of the two kinds of spiritual direction we have described.

There is no better understanding of the spiritual implications of this stage of growth than Frances Wickes' classic *The Inner World of Childhood*. This book presents the depth and complexity of this stage of life with clarity and sympathy. It gives us a basis for understanding the next stage as well. It also provides us adults an understanding of our own childhoods, which enables us to work at our unfinished business. Alice Miller has shown adults how important it is for us to deal with our own hurt inner children in her recent book *Prisoners of Childhood*. Unless we are aware of the child within us we will seldom be able to help children grow spiritually to maturity. It is helpful for teachers to continue in a learning process, with spiritual direction available for those who desire it. This also applies to teachers who would guide us through each of the following stages.

Stage 2. As soon as children have developed a center of personality so that they can distinguish between inner and outer reality, and have begun to take the outer own seriously, they are said to have begun to develop an ego. They are then ready for the next stage of development. *Ego* has no negative moral or spiritual connotations; it is simply my stable "I-ness." There can be no mature religious life until I have the capacity to distinguish between inner and outer from an established standpoint. There may come a time for some people when they have to let loose of confining ego categories, but we cannot give up what we have not already achieved.

This stage of development continues the learning process that begins within the womb. But here the emphasis is on learning, drinking in knowledge. In any society children must learn the lore, the techniques, the morals, and the values of their culture. We must learn a language and learn those incredible memory and thinking aids—reading, writing and manipulation of numbers. This process is most fully activated when at the same time children continue to express their inner reality through music, painting and story. What is given to animals in instincts human children must learn during these years.

This brings us to the subject of psychological types. Children come into the world with a potential structure in their ways of perceiving or looking at the world. Early training reinforces this pattern so that children develop very different interests and therefore different abilities. Just as the right number of males and females are mysteriously born to reproduce the race, so also (thank heavens) not all of us become mathematicians or atomic physicists or carpenters or artists. If we are going to be able to help people in their own unique development, intellectually and socially and *religiously,* we need to recognize that people grow in different ways to achieve different objectives. Jung has suggested that there are four essentially different types: those whose primary interest is in sensation, a capacity to perceive and deal adequately with outer, physical reality; those who are interested in "feeling," which essentially is the capacity to perceive and deal with human values; those who direct their interest to thinking, which is perceiving and dealing with purely logical implications and connections; and, finally, those whose interest is intuitive, and who have a capacity to perceive and to deal with meanings and connections that relate to the unconscious dimension of reality. Unfortunately, our society, our school system and our religious institutions have in recent years given almost exclusive priority and value to the intuitive and thinking types of people, and they are but a small portion of the total population. Interesting studies have shown that children who are primarily oriented to using and developing sensation are the first to drop out of school. But after all, reading, writing and arithmetic are all thinking-intuitive functions, and those who do not develop skill in these areas are seldom given a chance to mature in their own functions.

It is believed that children are most likely born with a tendency toward a definite type-structure and should be helped to develop what they already are. It is like right- and left-handedness. We seldom develop as much skill in other functions as we do in those with which we are naturally endowed.

People who are not encouraged to develop their own unique type-structure can seldom develop the religious pattern that is most adequate for them. My wife, Barbara Kelsey, has spent much of the last fifteen years in the study of types and particularly in the implications of type for spiritual direction and religious education. We cannot do full justice to the subject here. I have published her findings on typology and spiritual formation and spiritual guidance in *Christo-Psychology.*

If children are to be given the opportunity to grow in knowledge and general development, they need to appreciate who they are. Nearly every objective educational research study that has investigated these questions has come up with the same data and the same conclusions: children learn more easily and more deeply and grow in maturity when they are treated with understanding, love, compassion and human warmth. This kind of caring stimulates growth in every way—morally, intellectually and spiritually. Studies show that children who have been treated with this kind of love interiorize the values of their models and develop conscience. Children treated with physical punishment tend to use violence towards others. One of the most unusual programs that was developed at St. Luke's under the direction of Ollie Backus was the program of listening to children, in which we provided supervised listening sessions for children who wished it; we never were able to fill the demand. This time of growth and development is the time in which the disciplines of life are most easily structured; without some discipline there can be little later full maturity.

Except under the most unusual circumstances, children up through this stage should never be encouraged to dig deeply into the unconscious. Dreams and other examples of unconscious expression should be treated in a matter-of-fact way, but should not be interpreted. Some Pentecostal sects encourage childhood preaching and commitment. This is close to moral evil, as children who are close to the spiritual world become mouthpieces of it rather than learning to encounter it. There is then a resistance to going on to adolescence and adulthood. Many priests in the Catholic Church who started religious training in late childhood and early adolescence developed the "little adult" fixation and never became genuine self-determined adults.

Stage 3. Somewhere between eleven and fifteen another quite different attitude develops. It is the time of puberty, and this attitude is undoubtedly influenced by hormonal stimuli. Young men and women become more interested in their peer groups than in their family units. They stay away from their homes as much as possible; they revolt against parental discipline and values; they form intimate and sexual bonds unrelated to the family and sometimes in defiance of it. In nearly all conventional societies (and I use that term rather than the pejorative *primitive*) there are initiation rites to help young men and young women step into full adulthood. Young men have an even greater problem at this time than women, for they have been reared in their earlier years by women, and now they must identify with the masculine role. We in the

West have lost so much of the sense of ritual and ceremony that we provide almost no ways of helping young people through this stage. For this reason many young men, in particular, come to a time of crisis during this period.

It is impossible to deal creatively with this age group educationally or religiously unless we treat each young person as an individual growing toward autonomy and independence. Doubts and questions should be encouraged. Young people who have revolted against the materialism of their parents can at this time understand and appreciate the ideas presented in the chapter on agnosticism. All young people need someone with whom they can talk over their fears and doubts as they come to a mature religious commitment. This creates a problem for the religious or spiritual guide or director, as they will hear much from adolescents that will be at great variance with their parents' values. And children in most countries are still legally subject to parental control through their seventeenth or twentieth year.

During the years of childhood most children accept their parents' religion and other values with enthusiasm; they will fight for them with their friends, even when relations with parents are strained. Now a real change takes place. The religious practices of parents are rejected, parental values are questioned and sometimes diametrically opposed values are espoused.

This period is very difficult for parents and requires real religious maturity on their part. However, this rebellion is almost necessary if adolescents are to come to a firm establishment of their independence and autonomy. The Church had a good idea (which at present is seldom actualized) in providing godparents. Children and adolescents need someone who is close to them and yet outside the family to whom they can relate during this time of confusion, struggle and rebellion.

There are three stages at which individuals are most open to religious counsel from outside the family and have the greatest need for it. In early childhood, if we are presented with genuine, consistent understanding and love, we develop a loyalty to the religious group that has provided it that is seldom broken. The same is true of those who are rescued from adolescent turmoil by wise support and befriending. The third stage is in the time of midlife crisis, when the Church needs to be available with intellectual, psychological and religious openness, and expertise, as well as with caring concern. If the Church were to spend money and energy wisely in religious education it would provide nursery schools, kindergartens, and high schools staffed with the best trained personnel possible, and have adult education and spiritual direction available for the midlife crisis.

Young people in revolt put parents and teachers in a double bind. The authority figures are wrong if they resist this movement toward self-determination, and they are also wrong if they go along with it and cooperate too enthusiastically. Some wise parents build some rules into the family discipline that can be broken without catastrophic damage to the rebellers, for these young people need to have limits, and an absence of them can be viewed as lack of caring.

Sometimes young people do very foolish things just to show that they are free and independent. They are probably still tied to their parental values when they pursue a course in opposition to their mothers and fathers. They cannot really "own" a value system as their own unless they have first questioned the old one and worked out a new one. Sometimes the new one will not be essentially different from the old; the struggle through to acceptance, however, makes it their own.

One of the wisest actions on the part of my wife and me was to allow the rebellion of our daughter. She had been very close to us and to religion and church. At fifteen she decided that she was an agnostic and said that of course we would not want her to be hypocritical and go to church. My wife and I had an immediate conference, and we decided that if we had not made our impact by this time, force would not create it now, and so we went along with her. After some years of rebellion she fell in love with a young man raised as an agnostic, who was rebelling from that way, and converted him to the Church. They were married and are as mature in their religious commitment as any adults I know.

During this period of psychological, social, and physical turmoil and growth young people are open to the unconscious and to religious influences. Robert Johnson has sketched this religious development in his remarkable study of the Parsifal myth entitled *He*. It is very dangerous at this period to push young people into a religious decision that cannot be changed, for they often have not established their own point of view, and they may rebel violently later. Many convents and monasteries suffered from this reaction once the Catholic Church loosened its authoritarian stance.

Stage 4. Late adolescence merges almost imperceptibly into young adulthood. In adolescence the foundations are laid for sexual intimacy, for choice of profession, for autonomy and responsibility. Young men and women come to the point where they are no longer led by their peer groups, but by their own values. They find a way of making a living and move out on their own. Someone has remarked that one of the greatest values of going away to college is to get children out of their homes and keep them in a relatively safe environment until they grow up. In our society adolescence is often extended beyond its natural limits into the middle twenties, and even later, because of the time required to prepare for a profession.

Young adulthood is a time for establishing ourselves in the world. It is a time for forming permanent relationships, developing intimacy and coming to sexual maturity. It is the time for achieving competence and success in our jobs or professions, for taking a place in the community, the church and a circle of friends. A home is usually established, and often there are children. In many instances this is not a time for deep inner search, nor should that be encouraged unless individuals are seeking on their own without outside encouragement. Like the later part of childhood, adulthood is the time for assimilation and growth, for laying solid foundations for life, for development of potential. It can be a time of outer challenge. In adulthood the assimilation is according to *our own pattern* and not just according to that of parents and teachers.

Many young adults find it difficult to settle down in one profession. As I have said before, I like to point out to them that a full life may contain several professions. What they decide to do need not keep them in chains forever. Many creative people develop one profession after another. Seldom is this possible, however, until we have first selected one area of work and become successful in that.

There was a time, not many years ago, when few young adults found this period of late twenties and thirties a time of doubt, uncertainty, and questioning. Jung, in his chapter "The Stages of Life," in *Modern Man in Search of a Soul*, suggests that few people turn inward and find themselves struggling with the meaning until after thirty-five. However, times have changed, and our culture is different from that of Switzerland fifty years ago. I do not know all the causes, but undoubtedly the drug culture, the more objective and informed view of the world and its questionable politics available in our free culture, an intuitive grasp of the physicists' doubts about the certainty of scientific laws, and the development of depth psychology are some of the significant reasons for the change.

It is most important to realize that any person past childhood can be faced with a crisis of meaning and a confrontation with inner darkness and evil. One gifted college student who found himself in this crisis in his senior year in college found Jung's writing on this period of inner crisis extremely alienating. Jung offered him no suggestion that such an experience could happen to one as young as twenty-one, though he was experiencing exactly what Jung was describing. He wondered what was wrong with him. I was once asked by the parents of a precocious thirteen-year-old to counsel their son who was deeply depressed; he was facing a crisis of meaning at that age and passed through it with support and understanding. Jung and many Jungians do not face this reality, and this lack of acknowledgement can impede those who at an earlier age need this kind of help. Usually this kind of crisis occurs at an early age only to the most gifted young people.

I discovered that many college-age adolescents and young adults are forced into dealing with the depths of themselves, searching for meaning, reaching out to relate to spiritual reality. It is difficult enough to deal with this problem when we already have a family and have attained a position in the world, but for young people who are also struggling with the problems of intimacy and sexuality and selection of a way of making a living, this added burden is almost intolerable. They have the added difficulty of dealing with this crisis without the wisdom and balance that experience can provide. Often they are thrown into *spiritual confusion and despair*. For them secular counseling is not the answer, nor is spiritual direction that does not take cognizance of their problems and deal with them. For them only a shamanistic kind of spiritual direction and companionship fills the bill. The church and society need to wake up to this reality and train people capable of dealing with this common modern problem.

Stage 5. Sometime after childhood, usually between thirty-five and fifty (or earlier, as we have indicated), many people enter a fifth stage of development. Most people by this time have achieved some status in the world, and what we have attained seldom gives us the satisfaction we had hoped for. Crossing the midpoint in life, we realize that our physical capacities are on the decline. Death begins to rear its ugly head, and the problem of meaning or purpose becomes more intense. Or else children have left the nest or no longer need us as they did. This creates a particularly serious problem for women who had focused their energies mainly on the home.

The classic statement of this midlife crisis is given by Dante in the opening pages of the *Inferno*. He found himself lost in a dark wood, "savage and rough and strong." It was like the valley of death, a place from which no mortal escaped alive. Then in "twisted helplessness" he sees a place of escape, but is set upon by three beasts. Dante writes that this happened in the middle of life's pathway. It was the year 1300; he was thirty-five, an acclaimed poet and had been elected one of the priors of Florence. Yet he was lost and "so bitter is it that death is hardly more." Then he writes, "I came to myself again." Sam Keen has written a modern version of what Dante endured in an account of his own midlife crisis in his book *Beginnings Without End.*[7]

There can be the more gentle search for meaning that May and Edwards have dealt with so well in their writings. People who experience this have probably had a more adequate religious experience as growing children and teenagers. But there are others upon whom chaos suddenly descends. Writing *Encounter with God* was my attempt to give expression to the results of my struggle to find meaning in a materialistic world and to share the insights that had been given me at that time. Unless we are able to find meaning and purpose, either in some social or religious group or within ourselves, the years of middle adulthood can become barren and bitter. Alcohol and escapist busyness can fill the gap. Underneath these we often find deadly boredom. Life has turned to dust and ashes in our mouths. Many men and women try all sorts of devices to avoid any serious encounter with themselves. Mr. Smith looks into the mirror one morning and wonders if his life has any meaning after all, and then he concludes that it doesn't even matter and that nothing matters.

Even if we have been closed off from genuine religion since early childhood, or if we have never had any religious background, we may be open to the spirit at this time of crisis. Agnostics, as I have already pointed out, are not morally evil; they are spiritually starved and need nourishment. Loss of meaning can result in a host of emotional, physical and social problems. Behind much of the midlife crisis lies the problem of meaning, for which our secular society on the whole simply has no answer. If we do not have a coherent view of an essentially meaningful or purposeful universe, in spite of all the evil around us, *and* a way of experiencing that meaning or purpose, we are left with two unsatisfactory alternatives. Either we remain in our chaos or we accept some sectarian religion that requires giving up our independence and our critical capacities.

It is difficult to put too much stress on the importance of listening to people concerned with the meaning of their lives and of the universe; those who wish to talk may be adolescents, young adults, or middle-aged people, right up to people on their death-beds. If we dismiss these questionings, or give pat answers to them, the great steel doors clang shut, and significant relationship is likely to be over. It was difficult for me to realize that many college students at twenty-one were where I was in my early thirties. Life is full of surprises, and we never know when people are going to seek us out to talk about the meaning or purpose of this world in which we live. There is a gnawing hunger in many people in our society, a hunger which has been fed only with materialism, which neither satisfies nor nourishes. Few people except religious geniuses are able to pass through this stage of crisis in our society without spiritual guidance or companionship. John Welch shows the struggles of two religious giants, Jung and Teresa of Avila, in his recent book *Spiritual Pilgrims*. Many of those who write on the subject of spiritual direction do not deal with the crisis of confronting our inner depth.[8]

Stage 6. For some who pass through this midlife crisis and find meaning there may dawn a golden age. Life has ultimate purpose, and we can try to integrate that meaning into the texture of our days and hours. Often at this stage we are no longer struggling with raising and educating a family. Often financial concerns are not as pressing as they have once been. We have come to see that most things pass and have achieved some detachment from the things of this world. It is easier to simplify our style of living. Our wants become fewer. We can allow the creative and religious desires within us to emerge, blossom and come to fruition.

During this period we can reflect on and try to accomplish those things that will be most fulfilling to us and of greatest help to others. We can reach out to those close to us and rebuild relationships; we can take up some project of social action as our particular bundle. We can keep a journal, even when we have never done it before. Often writing our own autobiographies makes even more clear the purpose that has been moving throughout our lives. And how important it is to have spiritual companionship at this time as we are trying to discern what new venture will be most creative for us. It can be a joy to share with others who have come to the same stage, what they have experienced and how they see life before them. The golden age does not mean that there are no problems, but that we have found some means of coping with them and that we see the journey stretching out indefinitely before us.

One of the most creative classes we developed in our program of adult education at St. Luke's Church was a class for people over sixty. How seldom in our society do we turn our attention to the needs, interests and concerns of those who have passed through the crisis of meaning and who are trying to find the most fruitful way of rounding out their interests, their relationships and their spiritual strivings. To our surprise, people who had never had any leaning toward our educational program welcomed this class enthusiastically.

The center of gravity of the populations of many Western countries is moving into an older age bracket. If, indeed, there is something beyond death, this is a time for bringing the tag ends of our multifaceted beings together. The importance of spiritual direction and guidance at this period can hardly be overestimated. In order to deal with this group and with the next we must have a clear vision of the boundless extension of life, or we cannot be the hopeful companions that these people need.

Stage 7. Whether we pass through a golden age or not, whether we come to a midlife crisis or not, all of us face death, and many of us face old age. As rector of a parish, I once thought of having a canvass mailing piece that pictured a casket being carried by six pallbearers down the front steps of the church with a caption beneath it: *This might be you.* It is amazing how successfully we can shut off consideration of death and what it means. When I am asked to speak on the subject of the afterlife to church groups I find that there are usually present only half the number that I can count on when I speak on almost any other subject! It is almost as if Christians have been so imbued with the materialism of our era that they cannot conceive that one can have anything of value or hope to offer on the topic, and so heads are resolutely thrust deep into the sand.

How little our society or churches do to reach out to the aged and dying. Indeed, secular groups interested in aging and dying seem more concerned with this subject than the Church. If, indeed, we see old age as the end of a meaningless journey, with no future, there is nothing to be done but to grin and bear it. And for those of us who are still troubled by doubts about any life beyond this one, dealing with the aged, the senile and the dying rubs our noses into our mortality and fragile humanness. There are few greater social evils in our society than the way we treat our aged and dying. Nursing homes and rest homes (as they are euphemistically called) are often places where we put people away so that we need not face our mortality and responsibility.

A meaningful dealing with old age and death *necessitates* a picture of and hope in life beyond death. If life leads in the last analysis only to the grave, to extinction and dissolution back into the clay, there isn't much we can offer except stoic fellowship. There can be little joy. I have presented the evidence for such a life and a picture of the Christian vision in my book *Afterlife. All those who would be spiritual directors need to be equipped to deal with the subject of death and life after it, for we never know when those whom we are companioning are going to face death.* This is certainly no time for referral.

One of the most helpful discussions of this subject was written by psychiatrist Franz Riklin of Zurich. He was working with a woman who developed terminal cancer. He reflected that there was no reason to stop the analysis because she was going to die, for he believed that the soul with which he was working would continue on. It was an important aspect of analysis to prepare her for this step. As a matter of fact, our dreams take very little notice of physical death, almost looking at it as a matter of little consequence, taking for granted that our psyches persist, continue on. Dr. Riklin's patient had amazing dreams pointing to life beyond death.

Some people feel that the aged do not seek relationship or understanding. Nothing could be further from the truth. Often their contemporaries have died, and they are alone. How grateful these people are for interest, empathy, the listening ear, spiritual companionship, sensitivity and love. Of course, they need to be given what they need in the way they need it, not what we think will meet their needs. Reaching out to the aged in this way is a ministry in which many of us could be creatively involved. There are many forgotten lonely and aged people around us.

Browning once wrote, "Grow old along with me, the best is yet to be." For those who see old age as a time of stepping into another dimension of life, this can be a most creative time, a preparation for a major rebirth. It can be a time of withdrawal, introversion, establishing ourselves in ultimate meaning, a time for deepening and enriching our psyches, getting ready for the next mutation. If there is any stage at which people are likely to be open to and need spiritual companionship, it is as they face age and death.

In *Man and His Symbols*, Jung gave an account of a series of dreams that were written down and given to her parents by a ten-year-old girl as a Christmas present. She died about a year later. In them the unconscious of this child was struggling with the problems of death and rebirth, as one would expect from an aged person. It was as if the unconscious was taking this young child through all the stages of life and preparing for rebirth into a new life. Again, we need to remember that we never know when the subject of death will occur and when we will need to deal with it.

I have sketched out seven different stages on the long journey. In all but the first two there is a real place for one-to-one spiritual companionship, guidance and direction. For some who find themselves dropped into the abyss of meaninglessness or attacking negativity, spiritual companionship is not just helpful, it is a necessity if they are to survive. If we are to minister to those around us and bear one another's burdens, there are few undertakings more important than preparing men and women, clergy and lay, who are capable of this work of fellowship and love. There are many ways of being a spiritual companion. We need to find our ways of walking with others on the great journey.

A Word on Conversion

There are basically two quite different kinds of conversion. In one kind the rejected aspects of our inner being emerge and are integrated into what we are and have been. In the other, which Jung calls *enantiodromia*, there is simply a turning upside down of the personality, with the former life being buried securely in the unconscious and the unconscious coming to the surface. People who experience this second kind are then likely to become as rigidly "righteous" as they were thoroughly dissipated and angry and destructive before.

There is a lot of talk about being born again. And certainly all of us need to be born again and again. When I am asked if I have been born again, I like to reply, "Which time?" The idea that with one conversion all of our confusion and chaos can be wiped away and we are pure and sinless would be humorous were it not so tragic. Most people with this frame of reference bury their former evil impulses and actions and then project them out onto others. They become standard-bearers for law and order and righteousness. But they want nothing to do with spiritual direction, nor do they wish to share all of their inner being with another person, for then they may have to face the suffering and pain that are involved in every genuinely integrated life. And churches that suggest that one conversion solves everything usually treat spiritual guidance, direction and companionship as the plague.

Genuine conversion brings us to the realization that there is a part of us that is open and seeking God and that there is before us the long and arduous struggle to become whole and integrated. Genuine conversion results in that kind of life that Paul describes in I Corinthians 13. The truly converted person is patient, kind, envies no one; such a one is never boastful, conceited, nor rude; never selfish, not quick to take offence; keeps no score of wrongs, does not gloat over others' sins, but delights in goodness and truth.

Nearly all the saints have stated that they were the worst of sinners. Nearly all the saints sought out someone to help them along the way to wholeness and holiness. When we are aware of the complexity of our nature and the necessity of integrating the shadow and standing against evil, we realize that we must have some objective, outside point of view so that we are not deceived by ourselves. Real conversion presents us with the blackness of our own evil, with the love of God, which is simply incomprehensible to most of us, and with the task of becoming like the one who has saved and loved us. This is a task that continues throughout life and probably into the life beyond. If there is one thing that those on this path desire and require, it is spiritual companionship and guidance.

Some conversions are violent and dramatic, and some are so gradual that they are hardly noticed. In the latter, people add one insight after another. They are often those whom James calls the once born. For them the kind of direction offered by Edwards and May is usually most satisfactory.

Educational Psychology and Spiritual Direction

Over the last fifty years a body of knowledge has accumulated on how we human beings are best helped to learn. I was immersed in the whole subject of educational expertise while teaching in the Department of Graduate Studies in Education at the University of Notre Dame. The head of the department, James Michael Lee, was one of the most knowledgeable people in educational theory and practice in the country.

People learn best when they are treated as Jesus taught them: when there is interaction between pupil and teacher, where questioning is encouraged, and where an atmosphere of warm, concerned caring prevails. Classes of more than fifteen students seldom stimulate the best learning, and the lecture is without a doubt the poorest means of educational communication yet devised if students are able to read. Students who have read a prescribed body of material and come to discuss it and seek help in understanding it from one who knows the field learn most and retain the learning best.

When I entered the department at Notre Dame I was not aware of the amount of solid educational research findings extant. Ollie Backus had already introduced the same basic idea of education in our educational program at St. Luke's. Now I was given the data, and I taught classes using these principles. I was forcibly struck by how well they worked. Dr. Backus had often remarked that lecturing is not treating people as equals, but demeaning them. Except for a few professors at Notre Dame, a half-dozen out of six hundred, who had a dramatic flair, students felt exactly this way. I have described the results of this teaching experience in my book *Can Christians Be Educated?*

When I first met Dr. Backus she asked me, "Has it ever occurred to you that Christians need to be educated according to Christian principles if a vital Christianity is to be conveyed?" The medium of communication must be consonant with the message, or the message will be garbled or not taken seriously.

If there is any place where education should follow these principles it is in the training of men and women preparing for the Christian ministry. If there is any place where this educational knowledge is almost totally ignored or unknown it is within the seminaries of our churches. And then ministers go out with this inadequate model of education and try to use it in parishes. It is a scandal. There is a large body of well-established facts about the best methods of educating adults. These are largely ignored within our seminaries, which continue lecturing to large groups of people and using antedeluvian grading and testing systems. Leaders protest that they do not have enough money to provide the right kind of education. That is nonsense. Where vital Christianity is being communicated, the support will be forthcoming. When ministerial students are not given the tools of modern education it is no wonder that the growth of informed, vital Christianity is so meager.

If there is any aspect of training for ministry that must use Christian methods if it is to succeed, it is that of facilitating the growth and development of spiritual companions and guides. Those who desire to grow in their capacities to be companions to others on the Christian inner journey need to be treated in formal classes and in private as we would have them treat others. The best educational methods will use small-group discussion techniques, and provide one-to-one meetings with each student as well. They cannot become spiritual companions unless their leaders are spiritual companions to them. The educational theory of Zen is quite different from that of Christianity.

If spiritual companions and guides are to be provided for the Church they need to have psychological knowledge about the educational process as well as about the depth of the human psyche. They can only be adequately prepared if they are trained in an open and caring atmosphere. Only thus will they be able to provide Christian spiritual companionship to groups and individuals wherever they are sent.

NOTES

1. William McNamara, "Psychology and the Christian Mystical Tradition," in *Transpersonal Psychologies,* edited by Charles Tart (New York: Harper and Row, 1975), pp. 410–411.

2. Tilden Edwards, *Spiritual Friend,* p. 130.

3. I have explored this very problem in chapters 6 and 7 of my book *Prophetic Ministry.*

4. Gerald May, *Care of Mind Care of Spirit,* p. 147.

5. I have presented a more complete discussion of this difficult subject in chapter 7 of *Caring,* "Love, Sex and Christianity."

6. I have discussed the stages of psychological development from a similar perspective in chapter V, "Psychology, Religion and Discernment," of *Discernment, A Study in Ecstasy and Evil.*

7. Sam Keen, *Beginnings Without Ends* (New York: Harper and Row, 1977).

8. In addition to May and Edwards, several others have written on the subject of spiritual direction. Carolyn Gratton, in *Guidelines for Spiritual Direction,* offers many helpful insights using the basic framework of Adrian van Kaam. Katherine Marie Dyckman and L. Patrick Carroll, in *Inviting the Mystic Supporting the Prophet,* do the same from the point of view of Matthew Fox. Neither of these deals with the overlap that so often is occasioned by the midlife crisis. William A. Barry, S.J., and William J. Connolly, S.J., have written an excellent book on spiritual direction based on their experiences in the Center for Religious Development at Weston School of Theology in Cambridge, Massachusetts; it is titled *The Practice of Spiritual Direction.* Little attention is given, however, to the crisis experiences that William James describes. John Jungblut, who has directed the program at Wainwright House in Rye, New York, is working on a manuscript based upon his experience there. It is called *The Gentle Art of Spiritual Guidance.*

Chapter 9

THE MYSTERY OF LOVE

L ove is a mystery in which the human and divine sometimes touch in a unique way. M. Scott Peck, in his magnificent study of love, *The Road Less Traveled*, writes of the mysterious nature of love. In his reflections at the end of his autobiography Jung writes that the human capacity to love is as important in understanding the universe as our rational reflection. He then states, "I have again and again been faced with the mystery of love, and have never been able to explain what it is." Like Job, he says, we must simply come to reverent silence before this mystery and place our hands over our mouths. If we possess a grain of wisdom we will name the unknown by the more unknown; we will name love with the name of God. Jung concludes, "This is a confession of our subjection, our imperfection and our dependence; but at the same time a testimony to our freedom to choose between truth and error."[1]

There is no need at this point to say anything more about the centrality of love within the Christian vision of the universe. We are told that God *is* love and that we are the disciples and followers of Jesus of Nazareth when we love one another as he has loved us. Wherever the embers of vital Christianity have blazed forth into flame and kindled and enlightened the hearts and minds of those around them, there we will find someone who has embodied, incarnated, this kind of love; we often call these people saints: Francis of Assisi, Catherine of Genoa, Catherine of Siena, William Law, John and Charles Wesley, Philip Neri, Mother Teresa of Calcutta and all those secret saints who have made life better for us, "those who have led hidden lives and rest in unvisited tombs." Karen Armstrong concludes the story of her life as a nun with these words: "Religious life is about love and love is about risk. Perhaps none of us risked enough."[2]

William McNamara writes from within the monastic life, "The mystic is not one who engages in unusual prayer or ascetic practices but a person whose life is ruled by the primacy of charity. Our prayer or ascetic practice is valuable only insofar as it causes, fosters, or preserves charity: love of God first, then of our neighbor, for the ultimate test of our love of God is its overflowing love of neighbor. . . . Our own lives must therefore reflect the continuum of a contemplatively active life 'for the others' and an actively contemplative life 'from the Other.' "[3] He also maintains that this kind of spiritual life and growth is practically impossible without spiritual guidance, even though he recognizes that adequate guidance is difficult to find.

When all is said and done, the heart of all the helping professions is providing an atmosphere of love in which people may be healed and then continue to grow. I have no hard data, but I am convinced that behind almost all successful psychotherapy lies the hidden variable of concerned caring, of love. This probably as much as any other factor facilitates healing of mind, soul, emotions, body and society. However, as James Lynch points out so clearly in his book *The Broken Heart*, love is difficult to define and does not fall into simple, objectively verifiable categories. And so love becomes the hidden and neglected variable. Bruno Klopfer, the psychologist who established the use of the Rorschach test, once said to me that fifty percent of all psychotherapy is warm, accepting listening. This, he said, did not have to be confined to psychological professionals.

Those of us who are making inner journeys of our own and feel called to walk with others who seek our companionship and guidance on the adventure inward will find that the kind of fellowship we offer will depend upon how we envision the goal of the journey. This, in turn, will be shaped by our deepest experience of God.

If we are to lead people *only* to a state of egoless abandonment in the presence of indescribable divine light, or to absorption into the ineffable divine presence, then love will play a much less central role than in the other way of companionship I have been describing, and spiritual direction will be more passive and objective. I am sure that for some people this is the proper kind of spiritual companionship. However, I have a nagging and persistent belief that even in this kind of direction human love is still a very significant variable, whether acknowledged or not.

Few people will reveal and share the depth of their souls unless the other person sees the soul as holy. Peck defines love well in these words: "The will to extend one's self for the purpose of nurturing one's own or another's spiritual growth."[4] This means seeing the soul as holy.

If, on the other hand, we perceive the goal of spiritual direction as an encounter with a healing, saving, restoring Divine Lover, then we almost inevitably see ourselves as instruments of that love. Seldom can we lead others to Love except by love. This loving God makes only one demand upon us; he sends us out into the world to share with others the love we have received. Then we can return to Love and slake our insatiable thirst for love once again. Then we go out again to help slake the thirst of others. Spiritual direction within this frame of reference is sharing love with others that they may come to know Love. As we have stated so many times before, this love is only Christian love as it is informed by Christian tradition, undergirded by personal experience, and guided and directed by our critical capacities and by a knowledge of the nature and depth of the human psyche.

Both of these ways of companionship are probably necessary, and both are true, as difficult as this is for our limited human minds to understand. The best spiritual friends are comfortable with both ways, although most of what they do will probably be one or the other. Others have written wisely, deeply, and well on the first of these ways, and there is no need to repeat them. In this closing chapter I confine myself to the second way of looking at the goal of the Christian spiritual adventure and the emphasis that it places on love in the fellowship that companions and guides offer to those they accompany on their way.

For nearly thirty years I have been trying to love others as I have been loved by God, to offer to others the same kind of forgiveness, compassion, understanding, mercy and love that I have experienced in my deepest communion with God. I often have these experiences of mercy and compassion when I have fallen on my face and feel utterly useless and valueless, or when I have been attacked by the very darkness itself. I experience being saved from the devouring void, picked up and loved as a weaned child, then set on my feet and told to go and do likewise.

For thirty years I have been trying to obey, and I find the task impossible. I am not up to it. As I said in the beginning of this book, I find that I usually give too much or too little or the wrong kind, or I misunderstand where others are, or I avoid the person who appears impossible to me. *And yet* I find that when I try my best to embody this kind of love, mysterious changes often take place in the people around me; doors open for them, and sometimes they themselves come to feel the touch of the Divine Lover. I find that it is better to love badly and faultily than not to try to love at all. God does not have to have perfect instruments, and the Holy One can use our feeble and faltering attempts at love and transform them. My task is to keep on trying to love, to be faithful in my continuing attempt, not necessarily to be successful. The quality of my love may well be the most important element of my spiritual guidance.

The kind of love that the Divine Lover would have me give is not an instinctive drive. We have flashes of desire and moments of desiring to embody it, and at those moments we are carried as on eagle's wings, but our task is to walk in this way without tiring of this love, even when we feel little inspiration in our loving. Genuine Christian love is forged against the anvil of our selfishness and possessiveness, of our anger and our fear, and this involves suffering. No one needs to wear hair shirts or chains, cultivate lice, or live on cabbage leaves in order to pick up crosses and follow Jesus. All we have to do is come to God and ask that we be forged into adequate instruments of divine love.

It is important to remember that love is more than a feeling. It is active and transitive. The real test of my loving is not that I feel loving, but that the other person feels loved by me. Love is what I do to create this sense of feeling cared for. It is independent of my personal feelings.

Thirteen Pieces of a Puzzle

The subject of love is so central to an understanding of Christian life and practice that I wrote a book called *Caring* several years ago to examine some of the ways in which we can learn to love each other more adequately. I have learned a good bit more in these last two years. As I look at love from the perspective of the spiritual companion and guide, some more pieces of this mysterious and overwhelmingly enticing puzzle have fallen into place. I am not entirely sure how all these pieces fit together, and I know that there are pieces I have not yet found. And so I will make thirteen personal reflections on the mystery of love and then conclude by relating an old story with a new ending. The following pages are a very brief summary of an essential part of spiritual direction.

It is difficult to love. I can always find a million lousy excuses for not loving. I can excuse myself from the wedding feast by saying that to love does not mean to like. There is always a good reason not to love. If I am to start on the arduous process of being shaped according to the pattern of love, it is essential that first of all I place a *conscious* priority on being a loving person. This means that I make a *conscious* commitment to Love.

Of course I fail, but if my commitment is to Love, I pick myself up and try again. One reason I believe in an afterlife is that none of us can be shaped into a worthwhile instrument of love in one lifetime. Whenever I find myself turning away from love as my goal I must stop, reflect and return to the presence of the Divine Lover. Then I realize that people who appear unlovable are not much more so than I am at times. I then remind myself of von Hügel's statement: the goal of real love is to reach out to the unlovable so that they can become lovable.

I have come to see more and more that I cannot love until I am disciplined. To discipline does not mean to punish, but to help another person gain control of his or her actions. A disciple must be disciplined. These words have the same derivation. The word *discipline* has had a bad press. Within a genuine discipline, however, there is freedom. Disciplined people are not subject to every whim, are not run by every unconscious motive and desire. They are not pushed around by other people. We need to have some control of our lives if we are to follow any pathway with consistency. M. Scott Peck stresses the fact that we simply cannot begin to love in any depth until we have developed some modicum of discipline.

It is painful and difficult to be conscious. In order to follow the best path, we have to choose not to take other paths, and we often want to take the others. The results in our actual actions are not too different whether our goal is to lose all our desire or to center all our desires in one reality—Love. God, whose service is perfect freedom, can only give us that freedom (and the joy that goes with it) as we begin to pick up the fragments of our lives and offer them one by one as gifts to be transformed. Once this choice is made, discipline—the second piece of the puzzle—is necessary to continue the effort needed to shape our lives by our best light.

And then it is necessary that we learn to accept and love ourselves, as God constantly accepts and loves us, no matter what we are or do. This is even more painful than discipline, for we must face all of ourselves: the idiot and the murderer, the inner Judas, the inner Pilate, the inner Hitler, the inner Caiaphas, all of ourselves. I, myself, am the enemy who must be loved, for when I do not try to love myself I am rejecting Jesus' death and resurrection, which show his love for me.

And what happens if I don't face and accept all of me? Then I usually project these hidden and unaccepted elements within me onto others, and then there is gossip and backbiting, violence, murder, war and strife. Or I internalize this self-hatred, and I am dragged down by psychosomatic disease or depression or anxiety. Or I let this inner ugliness possess me, and I become the leader of a pogrom or a lynching party.

And how can I possibly accept and love all of me? It is impossible for me to do alone. I don't have the power. Again it is only possible as I call out to the Christ who has conquered all evil with love and in prayer-meditation invite him to come and love me and so enable me to accept and love myself. When I have experienced this, then it is easier for me to put up with the faults of others. Love and prayer cannot in any way be separated from each other. They are different aspects of the same divine whole.

This brings us to the fourth piece of our puzzle. We simply can't love in any depth unless we learn to pray. All other love eventually wears out. Only the person whose love is constantly being infused and renewed by the love of God can keep on loving. The ministerial training of many clergy has given us no belief that God is personally interested in us and ready to touch our lives. Most of us were given no experience in how to practice a restoring prayer life. We may believe in a loving God, but have been given no ways by which we can live in that sustained relationship, where we can be picked up out of depression and darkness and hopelessness. The result is often clergy burnout.[5]

Most of us need some companionship and guidance if we are to find the Divine Lover and be infused with love. The pathway is circular. If we are to be spiritual companions we need to be loving. If we are to be loving we need to learn to pray and come into the presence of the Divine Lover, and this requires that we be instructed and guided and companioned. But perhaps it is a spiral staircase. The fifth piece of our puzzle is that we need to have the humility to seek help in coming to know the saving God and to seek until we find. Without this kind of intimate spiritual fellowship we can seldom grow in knowledge and love of God or of human beings. Those who would love need to be loved; those who would pray need to be prayed with. Humble, human fellowship in prayer is part of the mystery of love. But if I can't find anyone? God has many hidden friends who are ready to go along with us when we are ready. It is nearly

impossible to go on this journey with others unless we have found someone to walk with us.

The Place of Knowing

There are few people who would set out to bring help to a country suffering from starvation without first learning something about modern
productive agriculture. There are few who would try to assuage and heal
the diseases that afflict so many people without learning about the amazing successes of modern medicine. And how can we deal with the depth
and complexity of the human psyche unless we have some knowledge of
its depth and nature, which has been revealed by psychology? Here we
need to sift truth from error. We need to use our critical capacity as
much when we look at the findings of psychology as when we examine
the religious traditions in which we have been raised.

One of the most certain findings of modern psychology is that the
therapist is seldom presented with the real agony within a human soul
until that person trusts the therapist. It is usually only within the environment of caring and love that we are trusted. Then healing of anxiety, depression and alienation can begin to take place. It is also interesting and significant that I have learned more about the importance of love
from modern psychologists than I have from modern theologians or my
religious teachers. Except for those who believe that we can best be
changed through the kind of conditioning with which we train dogs or
pigeons, psychologists repeatedly emphasize the nature and quality of
love as a part of the therapeutic process. We modern Western Christians
are more likely to take love seriously once we realize that most clinical
psychologists find it a necessary ingredient in the healing process.

Love as Listening to Different Kinds of People

Carl Rogers has built an entire theory of psychotherapy around listening. Listening is an art, and it is also a science. We can learn to listen. We
simply can't pretend to love anyone to whom we do not listen. Listening
gives the first sign to a person that he or she has worth and is valuable
enough to be attended to. We shall never be able to go far with others on
their spiritual adventure unless we can learn to listen with warmth,
openness and nonjudging attentiveness. We simply can't direct the soul
of anyone we haven't listened to. We will not be spiritual companions,

but rather spiritual dictators, if we do not listen to people. We would be like a doctor prescribing drugs without listening for symptons or without performing an examination.

One of the problems of spiritual direction in seminaries is that it is almost impossible for one to have authority over another and also be his or her spiritual companion. If I have the final decision as to whether a person is presented for the ministry, students are either naive or embedded within a mother complex if they tell me everything about themselves. Likewise, people are not going to talk to me unless they know that I will never use what I know against them and will never repeat what I have heard. Spiritual companionship needs the same seal of secrecy as the confessional.

The seventh piece of our puzzle is learning to listen intelligently and warmly, and to keep our tongues bridled. Every spiritual companion needs training in the art of listening. Unless we have known and accepted ourselves it is very difficult to listen to the full details of human iniquity without some reaction. And when we react we are not usually listening in love.

People are very different. We have mentioned a little about how differently we perceive and relate to our world. Perfectly decent people have very different values. Understanding how different we are takes some study. One of the tools that my wife and I have found useful in helping people recognize differences is the Myers-Briggs Type Indicator. It presents our differences in a graphic and easily understood manner. (It is often difficult for us to see how those of a totally opposite type from ourselves can be Christian!) We have spoken earlier about the importance of learning, appreciating, and understanding our differences. This is vital for every teacher (or else they assume everyone will learn as they do), for every parent, for every group of people working together in the world, and especially in churches. It is also crucial for those who would accompany other people on their spiritual pilgrimages. Different people have different roads to follow, and we must go with others on the best road for them, not the one upon which we are most comfortable.[6]

And then we have different values, as the discipline of value clarification has shown us. It is difficult for us to accept values very different from ours. Our task as spiritual companions is to encourage people in the development of their own values, not in accepting ours. We are only loving when we perceive differences and encourage others on their own unique ways.

These two clues to the mystery of love—love as listening and love as recognizing and appreciating and encouraging individual differences—lead us to an eighth piece of the puzzle. We need to learn how to deal with our hostilities without either giving explosive vent to them or repressing them, and this is a neat trick. There has been a tendency among many Christians to deny any feelings of aggression, hostility, anger, or hurt. We simply swallow everything. Acting in this way often results in two serious problems. First, we become so bland and such "nice guys" that we relate to no one. There is nothing that separates us more from others than the perpetual sickening smile, as David Augsburger points out in his book *Anger and Assertiveness in Pastoral Counseling*. Second, swallowed hostilities may build up and then explode in most destructive ways, usually upon the defenseless or those closest to us.

Another piece of the puzzle of love is the need to deal with our hostilities. We need to examine them, to see which are justified and which have no basis. Then we can turn to those who have misused us and stirred up our natural aggressive reactions and speak to them of our feelings of hurt. Someone has pointed out that love is not avoiding conflicts or pretending they are not there; rather, love is sharing hurt feelings.

All spiritual companions should avail themselves of this body of knowledge about hostility. And this includes any of us who would share on a deep religious level with others, as well as those who have a special vocation in walking with others on the spiritual journey. But this again involves self-knowledge, which can be painful. How difficult it is for us to make progress and to see how often we have failed. But this natural suffering can be very creative. Abbé de Tourville writes, "Rejoice to think that after having recovered yourself in the midst of interior pain and difficulty, you will be able to help others in their turn. No one can help except the one who has suffered."[7] We cannot deal adequately with our hostilities without suffering.

Loving the Family and the Acquaintance

I can love anyone for an hour or two a week in a counseling session; it is quite different living with people twenty-four hours a day. It is easy to give love to people who appreciate us and give us adulation, but people who live with us know all our faults, and often do not appreciate them. Children rebel. Families and religious communities are probably the best schools for growth in love available. Until we can continue to give love to those with whom we live, even when we get very little in return, we have not come to understand what love is all about. Loving the family or those with whom we live is a ninth piece of the puzzle of love.

Unless my love extends in a natural and healing way to those with whom I live, I am missing a central piece of the puzzle. Jesus simply assumes that we would love our families and those who love us. We see how little real understanding and practice of love there is among us when we look at the dreary record of domestic misery in our country and the lack of genuine caring in religious communities. My family members have taught me more about the mystery of love than any other group of people.

A good friend, Jack Smith, was president of a manufacturing company. It was given to him, and he felt that he had to run it. The company was having many problems, and in a moment of desperation he went into his office, closed the door, and said to himself that he didn't know what to do with the company. He thought for a moment and told himself that he had two options. He could either get drunk or he could pray. He reflected that if he prayed and nothing happened (which he expected would be the case) he could get drunk later on. He threw his head down on his hands and prayed, "Lord, I can't run this business anymore. It's beyond me. What shall I do?" There was a deep and strained silence, and then these words shot through his head: "Create the conditions whereby the individuals may develop to the maximum of their capacity within the opportunities at hand." He was so stunned at this answer that he asked again, and the words came again.

One of the aspects of real love is just this: it tries to create the conditions in which other people may grow to the maximum of their potential within the opportunities at hand. This is still another part of the puzzle. It is a perfect description of a loving attitude in regard to those with whom I work. It is a perfect description of the task of the teacher, of the minister, and of *the spiritual director.*

My friend was so impressed that he went back to the New Testament and read it with great care over and over again. Out of this came a list of eleven suggestions that helped him put this general principle into practice.

Reaching Out to Strangers

For years as a parish priest in the mobile atmosphere of southern California I tried to induce the congregation to reach out to the newcomers who came trooping in and by. After twenty years of urging it was still the clergy who made most of the contacts with strangers, who welcomed them, and followed them up. The main reason for our refusal to reach out to strangers is that most of us are so caught up in ourselves that we do not even see them. We are so insecure that we seldom think that the other person would want to speak to *us*. Hospitality and welcoming is another part of the complex picture of love.

We can create tragedy when we don't reach out to the stranger. Notre Dame has one of the best systems of reaching students of any university I know, yet a tragedy occurred there. A young man took his life. The priest in charge of student affairs was determined to find the cause of this suicide. He interviewed all the students who lived along the corridor of the dormitory where the student had lived. He also invited students who had been in the smaller classes with this young man to come and visit him one by one. When all the data was in the priest had the reason for the suicide. No one had known him! If love does not reach out to strangers, to welcome them, it lacks an essential element, and we are the greatest losers.

My travels have made me realize how many suffering strangers there are in the world: the beggars in Chittagong, the lepers in Belawan, the hungry in so many places, the orphans at St. Scholastica's convent. It is so easy for those of us who live in a prosperous part of the world, an extravagantly luxurious part of the world, to forget who our neighbors are. I do not know the answer to the hunger, the war, the overpopulation, the sickness, the political torture, the crushing out of religion that I have observed. But unless I do something about this crushing burden of agony and pain in the world I am not living in the kind of love of which Jesus speaks.

What can I do so that this element of the total reality of love may not be missing in my life? Tragically, I can meet a stranger in my own church and not even be aware that this person is a stranger. There is no offering of love to those who are strangers until we perceive them and their loneliness and alienation. I can read about some of the misery in the world, but reading about it and seeing it are quite different. We don't have to go halfway around the world to see poverty. We can go to El Paso, Texas and see the work of Our Lady's Youth Center and other groups there, as they reach out to those living and dying in cardboard shacks on the city dumps of Juarez.

I cannot take responsibility for all this pain and suffering, but I can select one aspect of this work, find one group of neighbors, near or far, and minister to them or help those who are doing so. If I ignore the misery of the world, in our own country and beyond it, then an essential element is lacking in my love.

Loving the Enemy

Jesus said some ridiculous things, and one of the most ridiculous was that if we are to be perfect like our Abba in heaven we need to love our enemies, just as God loves those who ignore, hate, and despise the Divine Lover. How can I love those who persecute me and say all manner of evil against me? How can I love those who belittle me, cheat me, and hurt me and those I love? It is very difficult, but the secret of the success of the Christian Church in its many times of persecution was that people actually were able to bless those who threw them to the wild animals and crucified them and murdered them.

St. Perpetua was asked why she didn't rail and curse against those who had informed against her by revealing the names of those who had attended a secret Eucharist, against the judge who condemned her, and against the soldiers and guards who were about to put her out into the arena to die. She replied that they were already so attacked by evil that they needed no condemnation from her. This kind of love is not easy to achieve, but unless this thirteenth piece of our picture puzzle is there, we do not see all of the essential nature of love.

How can I love my enemies? First of all, I must recognize that I have them, and I must realize that my enemies are not only those whom I do not like, but those who do not like me. Then I simply have to cease unkind actions toward them; I must bridle my action. Then I need to cease talking about those who are my enemies, even though sometimes my tongue seems to have a life all of its own; I must learn to bridle my tongue. There is almost no reason for ever saying anything unkind about others.

And then I can pray for my enemies. I change, and sometimes others change as I pray for them. It certainly makes me a hypocrite when I continue to do them ill or gossip about them after I have asked that God bless them. And then I must look long and hard at my enemies until I can find some qualities of their lives that are attractive, and then I can speak of these things, particularly when others are criticizing them. And last, I can do some kindness for my enemy and see the joy rise in his or her eyes. It is almost impossible as a human being to continue to despise someone whom we have made happy. So often it is our children, for whom we have done the most, that we love the most.

As I continue to work on loving the enemy and the stranger I pray over and over to myself these words: "Oh Divine Master, grant that I may not so much seek to be consoled as to console, to be understood as to understand, to be loved as to love." The attitude of this prayer puts me in the frame of mind in which love can grow in and through me.

A New Conclusion to an Old Story

In *Caring* I told the story of my eleven-year-old son who had not done well in school. We finally sent him to a remedial school, where he was interviewed and tested, and I was called in to discuss the problems that had been discovered. I was confronted with a very competent psychologist who informed me that one of this child's basic problems was that he didn't believe that I really loved him.

Although I thought that this was pure nonsense, I followed his suggestions. This son and I went horseback riding together. Even though I have the manual dexterity of a palsied hippopotamus I tried to do cabinetwork with him. The great breakthrough came in Laguna Beach, where we often spent our days off. I came into the motel room in which he was sitting watching television. I asked him if he wanted to go swimming with me. He said to me, "Naw, I'd rather watch television." This time, instead of reacting like a hurt child, I listened quietly, and then playfully (and that attitude is so important) I turned off the TV, and we tussled about the room, then out the door, and finally onto the beach and into the ocean. When we came up out of the first wave he blew the water out of his nose and said, "Father, I wondered how long it would take you to do this."

All was not easy sledding from then on, but he was able to express the fact that he had never been very fond of me, and I didn't explode. On another occasion the deep hurt he had received as a small child was revealed; it went back to a time when he was seven, and I had not listened to his repeated requests to read to him when his brother was gone. But now John and I had eliminated our hidden barriers, and we could really begin to relate.

But it was during the last few years that the relationship was really restored. My wife and I had been away, and she had been very severely injured. We brought her back to Los Angeles for many weeks in the hospital. We did not know if she would recover or if she would walk again. I wanted to be close enough to the hospital so that I could go in daily to spend time with her and have Eucharist with her and the laying on of hands for healing. My son John was living not far from the hospital, in a one-bedroom apartment. He invited me to live with him. He worked nights, and I was up during the day, and so we kept the bed warm most of the time. I was there when he came home from working nights at the Hyatt Regency. I was there when he awoke, and we talked about all sorts of things. I did most of the shopping, did the washing, and kept the place clean and neat. These were new activities for me. We became good friends.

My wife was finally released from the hospital months later, and she and I went out to a friend's house to continue her convalescence. When I moved out of his apartment John handed me a card. On the front of it were two iguanas facing each other; one of them was weeping iguana tears. On the inside of the card were printed these words: "Iguana miss you." And then he wrote, "It seems strange how we were forced together. You have become truly my best friend. I love you more than I ever imagined. I can truly see why all of those kids have always looked up to you. I only hope that we can continue to spend time together. I hope all goes well with Mother's recovery, and if you need my help, you know that I am here."

The years that the locust had eaten were restored. It is difficult to assess or predict the transforming and mysterious power of love. The Apostle Paul wrote that love never fails. When authentic love is added to the other prerequisites for the spiritual guide, the companion on the inner way may become the instrument of God's miraculous transforming spirit.

NOTES

1. C. G. Jung, *Memories, Dreams, Reflections*, recorded and edited by Aniela Jaffé (New York: Pantheon Books, 1963), pp. 353 f. (Paraphrased).

2. Karen Armstrong, *Through the Narrow Gate* (New York: St. Martin's Press, 1981).

3. William McNamara, "Psychology and the Christian Mystical Tradition," in *Transpersonal Psychologies*, edited by Charles Tart, p. 430.

4. M. Scott Peck, *The Road Less Traveled: A New Psychology of Love, Traditional Values, and Spiritual Growth* (New York: Simon & Schuster, 1978), p. 81.

5. John Sanford has written a clear and penetrating book on this subject, *Ministry Burnout* (New York: Paulist Press, 1982).

6. Those who wish to learn more about type differences can read Isabel Briggs Myers' *Gifts Differing* (the best on the subject), David Keirsey and Marilyn Bates' *Please Understand Me*, or Gordon Lawrence's *People Types and Tiger Stripes*. The Center for Application of Psychological Types, Inc., in Gainsville, Florida also offers training sessions in understanding and using type material.

7. *Letters of Direction: Thoughts on the Spiritual Life from the Letters of Abbé de Tourville*, with an introduction by Evelyn Underhill (New York: Thomas Y. Crowell, Co., 1959), p. 100.

BIBLIOGRAPHY

Abbé de Tourville, *Letters of Direction: Thoughts on the Spiritual Life from the Letters of Abbé de Tourville*. New York: Thomas Y. Crowell Co., 1959.

American Psychiatric Association. *Diagnostic and Statistical Manual of Mental Disorders: Third Edition*. Washington, D.C.: American Psychiatric Association, 1980. (DSM-III) The full volume is rather extensive, but an abbreviated version is also available from the A.P.A.

Aristotle. *Metaphysics*. Many editions.

Augsburger, David. *Anger and Assertiveness in Pastoral Care*. Philadelphia: Fortress Press, 1979.

St. Augustine. *Confessions*. Many different editions.

Bailey, Kenneth. *The Cross and the Prodigal*. St. Louis: Concordia Publishing House, 1973.

Baldwin, Christina. *One to One: Self-Understanding Through Journal Writing*. New York: M. Evans, 1979.

Barry, W. A. "Spiritual Direction and Pastoral Counseling." *Pastoral Psychology* 26 (Fall 1977).

Barry, William A. and Connolly, William J., *The Practice of Spiritual Direction*. New York: Seabury Press, 1982.

Bergson, Henri. *The Two Sources of Morality and Religion*. New York: Doubleday & Company, Inc., 1954.

Bornkamm, Günther. *Jesus of Nazareth*. New York: Harper and Row, 1960.

Buber, M. *Eclipse of God*. New York: Harper Torch Books, 1952.

Bunyan, John. *Pilgrim's Progress*. Many different editions.

Came To Believe . . . Alcoholics Anonymous World Services, Inc., Box 459, Grand Central Station, New York, N.Y. 10017.

Campbell, Joseph. *Myths to Live By*. New York: Bantam Books, 1973.

Carroll, L. Patrick and Dyckman, Katharine Marie., S.N.J.M. *Inviting the Mystic, Supporting the Prophet: An Introduction to Spiritual Direction*. New York: Paulist Press, 1981.

Clift, Wallace, *Jung and Christianity*. New York: Crossroad, 1982.

The Cloud of Unknowing. Edited with an introduction by James Walsh, S.J. New York: Paulist Press, 1981.

Dante. *Comedia* or *Divine Comedy*. Translated by Dorothy L. Sayers and Barbara Reynolds. Baltimore: Penguin Books. Vol. I: *Hell*, 1949; Vol. II: *Purgatory*, 1955; Vol. III: *Paradise*, 1962.

Descartes, René. *Discourse on Method*. Many different editions.

Doran, R. "Jungian Psychology and Christian Spirituality." *Review for Religious*, July, August, and September 1979.

Edwards, Tilden. *Spiritual Friend.* New York: Paulist Press, 1980.

Eliade, Mircea. *Shamanism: Archaic Techniques of Ecstasy.* Princeton, NJ: Princeton University Press, 1970.

Eliot, T. S. *The Cocktail Party.* New York: Harcourt, Brace and World, 1950.

———. *Four Quartets.* New York: Harcourt, Brace and World, 1943.

Erikson, E. *Childhood and Society.* 2nd Ed. New York: W. W. Norton, 1964.

Fairchild, R. *Finding Hope Again.* San Francisco: Harper & Row, 1980.

Fletcher, Joseph. *Moral Responsibility: Situation Ethics at Work.* Philadelphia: Westminister, 1967.

Foster, Richard. *The Celebration of Discipline.* San Francisco: Harper & Row, 1978.

Frank, Jerome. *Persuasion and Healing.* New York: Schocken Books, 1969.

Freud, Sigmund. *The Future of an Illusion.* Translated by W. D. Robson-Scott. New York: Doubleday & Company, Inc., 1964.

———. *Psychopathology of Everyday Life.* Translated by A. A. Britt. New York: Mentor Books, 1960.

Goethe, *Faust/Part Two.* Translated by Philip Wayne. New York: Penguin Books, 1977.

Gratton, C. *Guidelines for Spiritual Direction.* Denville, NJ: Dimension Books, 1980.

Greeley, Andrew. *The Sociology of the Paranormal: A Reconnaissance.* Beverly Hills, CA: Sage Publications, 1975.

Harding, Esther. *Journey Into Self.* New York: David McKay Co., 1956.

Heisenberg, Werner. *Physics and Philosophy: The Revolution in Modern Science.* New York: Harper and Row, 1958.

Holmes, Urban. *A History of Christian Spirituality: An Analytical Introduction.* New York: Seabury Press, 1980.

Huizinga, Johan. *Homo Ludens.* Boston: Beacon Press, 1955.

Huxley, Aldous. *Doors of Perception.* New York: Harper and Row, 1970.

———. *Tomorrow and Tomorrow and Tomorrow, and Other Essays.* New York: Harper and Row, 1956.

I Ching or *Book of Changes.* (The Richard Wilhelm translation). Princeton, NJ: Princeton University Press, 1978.

Ignatius Loyola. *The Spiritual Exercises.* Translated by Anthony Mottola. New York: Image Books, 1958.

Imitation of Christ. Many different editions.

James, William. *The Varieties of Religious Experience.* New York: Longmans, Green and Co., 1920.

Jones, Alan. *Journey Into Christ.* New York: Seabury Press, 1977.

St. John of the Cross. *Dark Night of the Soul.* Translated by E. Allison Peers. Garden City, NY: Doubleday & Company, Inc., 1959.

Johnson, Robert. *He.* King of Prussia, PA: Religious Publishing Company, 1974.

Jung, C. G. *Analytical Psychology in Theory and Practice.* New York: Vintage Books, 1978.

———. *Collected Works.* New York: Pantheon Books for the Bollingen Foundation.
　　Vol. 6 : *Psychological Types,* 1971.
　　Vol. 10: *Civilization in Transition,* 1964.
　　Vol. 11: *Psychology and Religion: West and East,* 1958.

———. *Man and His Symbols.* Garden City, NY: Doubleday and Company, Inc., 1964.

———. *Memories, Dreams, Reflections.* Recorded and edited by Aniela Jaffé. New York: Pantheon Books, 1963.

———. *Modern Man in Search of a Soul.* New York: Harcourt, Brace and World, Inc., 1933.

Jung, C. G. and Wilhelm, Richard. *The Secret of the Golden Flower.* Translated and explained by Richard Wilhelm. London: Routledge & Kegan Paul Ltd., 1950.

C. G. Jung Letters. Selected and edited by Gerhard Adler, in collaboration with Aniela Jaffé. Translated from the German by R. F. D. Hull. Vol. I. Princeton, NJ: Princeton University Press, 1973.

Kant, Immanuel. *Critique of Pure Reason.* Translated by Norman Kemp Smith. London:

Macmillan and Company, Ltd., 1929.

———. *The Dreams of a Ghost-seer, Illustrated by the Dreams of Metaphysics.* 1766. Many translations.

Keen, Sam. *Beginnings Without End.* New York: Harper and Row, 1977.

Kelsey, Morton. *Adventure Inward.* Minneapolis, MN: Augsburg Publishing House, 1980.

———. *Afterlife: The Other Side of Dying.* New York: Paulist Press, 1979. Paperback: New York: Crossroad, 1982.

———. *Can Christians Be Educated?* Mishawaka, IN: Religious Education Press, Inc., 1977.

———. *Caring, How Can We Love One Another?* New York: Paulist Press, 1981.

———. *The Christian and the Supernatural.* Minneapolis, MN: Augsburg Publishing House, 1976.

———. *Christo-Psychology.* New York: Paulist Press, 1982.

———. *Discernment: A Study in Ecstasy and Evil.* New York: Paulist Press, 1978.

———. *Dreams, A Way to Listen to God.* New York: Paulist Press, 1978.

———. *Encounter with God.* Minneapolis, MN: Bethany Fellowship, 1972.

———. *God, Dreams, and Revelation: A Christian Interpretation of Dreams.* Minneapolis, MN: Augsburg Publishing House, 1974.

———. *Healing and Christianity.* New York: Harper and Row, 1973.

———. *Myth, History and Faith.* New York: Paulist Press, 1974.

———. *The Other Side of Silence: A Guide to Christian Meditation.* New York: Paulist Press, 1976.

———. *Prophetic Ministry.* New York: Crossroad, 1982.

———. *Tongue Speaking: An Experiment in Spiritual Experience.* New York: Crossroad, 1982.

———. *Transcend.* New York: Crossroad, 1981.

Krieger, Dolores. *The Therapeutic Touch.* Englewood Cliffs, NJ: Prentice-Hall, 1979.

Kuhn, T. S. *The Structure of Scientific Revolutions.* 2nd Ed. Chicago: University of Chicago Press, 1970.

Leech, Kenneth. *Soul Friend: The Practice of Christian Spirituality.* San Francisco: Harper and Row, 1980.

LeShan, Lawrence. *The Medium, the Mystic and Physicist: Toward a General Theory of the Paranormal.* New York: Viking Press, 1974.

Lonergan, Bernard. *Insight.* London: Longmans, Green and Company Ltd., 1964.

Lorenz, Konrad. *On Aggression.* New York: Bantam Books, 1970.

Lovejoy, A. O. *The Revolt Against Dualism.* La Salle, Illinois: Open Court, 1960.

Luke, Helen. *Dark Wood to White Rose.* Pecos, NM: Dove Publications, 1975.

Lynch, James. *The Broken Heart: The Medical Consequences of Loneliness.* New York: Basic Books, 1977.

May, Gerald. *Care of Mind Care of Spirit.* San Francisco: Harper and Row, 1982.

McDonaugh, John M. *Christian Psychology.* New York: Paulist Press, 1982.

McGlashan, Alan. *Gravity and Levity.* Boston: Houghton Mifflin Co., 1976.

McNamara, W. "Psychology and the Christian Mystical Tradition." In *Transpersonal Psychologies,* edited by Charles Tart. New York: Harper and Row, 1975.

Mehl, Duane. *No More for the Road: One Man's Journey from Chemical Dependency to Freedom.* Minneapolis, MN: Augsburg Publishing House, 1976.

Miller, Arthur. *After the Fall.* New York: The Viking Press, 1964.

Moody, Raymond. *Life After Life.* Atlanta: Mockingbird Books, 1975.

Myers-Briggs Type Indicator. Available through Consulting Psychologists Press, 577 College Avenue, Palo Alto, CA 94306.

Nagel, Ernest and Newman, James R. *Gödel's Proof.* New York: New York University Press, 1964.

Nijinsky, Romula, ed. *The Diary of Vaslav Nijinsky.* Berkeley: University of California Press, 1971.

Osis, Karlis and Haraldsson, Erlendur. *At the Hour of Death*. New York: Avon Books, 1977.

Otto, Rudolf. *The Idea of the Holy*. New York: Oxford University Press, 1950.

Panati, Charles. *Supersenses: Our Potential for Parasensory Experience*. New York: Quadrangle/New York Times Book Co., 1974.

Peck, M. Scott. *The Road Less Traveled*. New York: Simon & Schuster, 1979.

Pennington, Basil. *The Centering Prayer*. Garden City, NY: Doubleday & Co., 1980.

Plato, *Laws*. Many editions.

———. *Phaedrus*. Many editions.

———. *The Symposium*. Many editions.

Portier, Lucienne. *Un precurseur, L'abbé Huvelin*. Paris: Les Editions du Cerf, 1979.

Progoff, Ira. *At a Journal Workshop: The Basic Text and Guide for Using the Intensive Journal*. New York: Dialogue House, 1975.

Pseudo-Dionysius or *Dionysius the Areopagite*. Many different translations.

Renault, Mary. *The Mask of Apollo*. New York: Paulist Press, no date.

Ring, Kenneth. *Life at Death*. New York: Coward, McCann and Geoghegan, 1980.

Russell, Bertrand and Whitehead, Alfred North. *Principia Mathematica*. (3 vols.) Cambridge: Cambridge University Press, 1925–27.

Sabom, Michael. *Recollections of Death: A Medical Investigation*. New York: Harper and Row, 1981.

Sanford, John. *The Kingdom Within*. Philadelphia and New York: Lippincott Co., 1970.

———. *Ministry Burnout*. New York: Paulist Press, 1982.

Sargant, William. *Battle for the Mind*. Baltimore: Penguin Books, 1961.

Schaer, Hans. *Religion and the Cure of Souls in Jung's Psychology*. London: Routledge & Kegan Paul Ltd., 1951.

Shakespeare, William. *Cymbeline. The Tempest. The Winter's Tale*. Many editions.

Sheehy, Gail. *Passages*. New York: Bantam Books, 1980.

Simons, George. *Keeping Your Personal Journal*. New York: Paulist Press, 1978.

Simonton, Carl, et al. *Getting Well Again*. New York: J. P. Tarcher, 1978.

Smith, Huston. *Beyond the Post-Modern Mind*. New York: Crossroad, 1982.

Tart, Charles. *Altered States of Consciousness*. New York: John Wiley & Sons, Inc., 1969.

Thomas, D. M. *The White Hotel*. New York: Viking Press, 1981.

The Tibetan Book of the Dead. Edited by W. Y. Evans-Wentz. New York: Oxford University Press, 1957.

The Tibetan Book of the Great Liberation. Edited by W. Y. Evans-Wentz. Commentary by C. G. Jung. New York: Oxford University Press, 1974.

Toben, Bob. *Space-Time and Beyond*. New York: E. P. Dutton & Co., Inc., 1975.

von Hügel, Baron Friedrich. *Eternal Life*. Edinburgh: T. & T. Clark, 1929.

———. *The Mystical Element of Religion as Studied in Saint Catherine of Genoa and her Friends*. London: J. M. Dent and Sons Ltd., 1927.

———. *The Reality of God and Religions and Agnosticism*. London: J. M. Dent and Sons Ltd., 1931.

Watts, Alan. *Behold the Spirit*. New York: Pantheon Books, 1947.

Weil, Andrew. *The Natural Mind*. Boston: Houghton Mifflin, 1972.

Welch, John L., O. Carm. *Spiritual Pilgrims, Carl Jung and Teresa of Avila*. New York: Paulist Press, 1982.

Wickes, Frances. *The Inner World of Childhood*. New York: Appleton Century, rev. 1966.

Williams, Charles. *The Figure of Beatrice, A Study of Dante*. New York: Octagon Books, 1980.

Wink, Walter. *Transforming Bible Study*. Nashville: Abingdon, 1980.

Woolman, John. *Journal*. Many different editions.

Youcenar, Marguerite. *The Abyss*. Translated from the French by Grace Frick, in collaboration with the author. New York: Farrar, Straus and Giroux, 1976.

INDEX

DATE DUE

4 30 87	
APR 0 7 2001	